macmillan education

CB126779

3

InstaEnglish

Patrick Howarth   Patricia Reilly   Olivia Johnston

#InstaEnglish Walkthrough

STUDENT'S BOOK

Your book is made up of a Starter unit, 8 regular units, plus Review and Life Skills activities. Each unit is divided into the sections introduced here. Check out how your book is structured so you can make the most of it!

Starter

This two-page unit provides strategic language for you to kick off your studies!

Opening

All units open with a visual treat that will trigger your first thoughts on the main subject. What pops into your head as soon as you look at it?

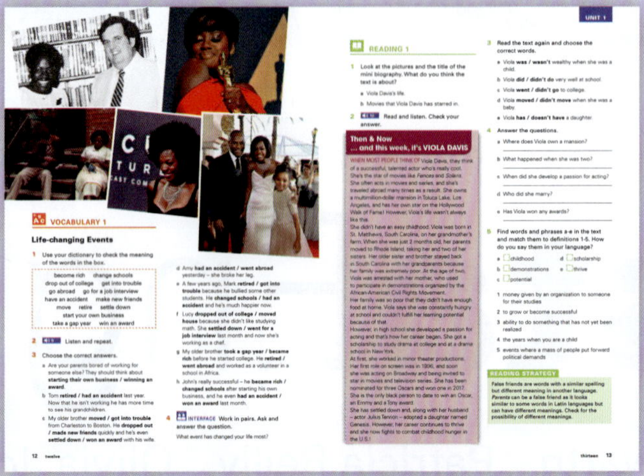

Vocabulary 1

Here you will read, listen to and look at pictures of words or phrases to begin exploring the unit topic.

Reading 1

Different text genres provide interesting content to practice your reading skills and introduce relevant language to be explored throughout the unit. The **Reading Strategy** box gives you tips on how to improve your reading.

Grammar 1

Grammar topics that were introduced in the reading text are systematically explored so you can easily work out all the rules and patterns.
Tip boxes give you some advice to help make your learning easier.

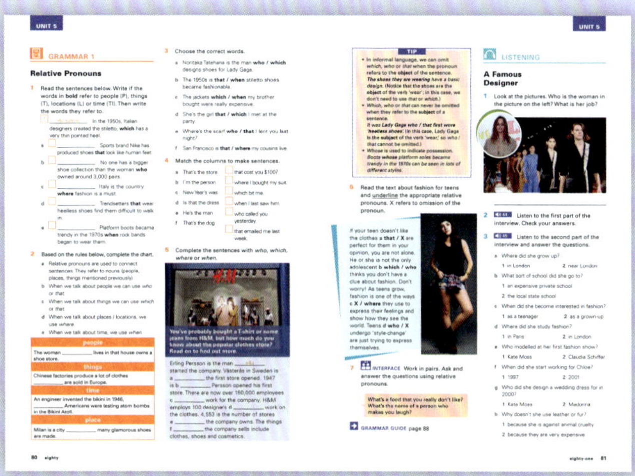

Listening

Learn and practice oral comprehension through engaging and contextualized oral texts.

Speaking

A clearly guided activity will help you practice your speaking skills using functional language in everyday situations.

Culture

Discover cultural aspects of everyday life in countries around the world!

Vocabulary 2

The second vocabulary set provides more words and phrases to allow you to go further into the unit topic.
Pronunciation boxes help you master the tongue to speak more naturally.

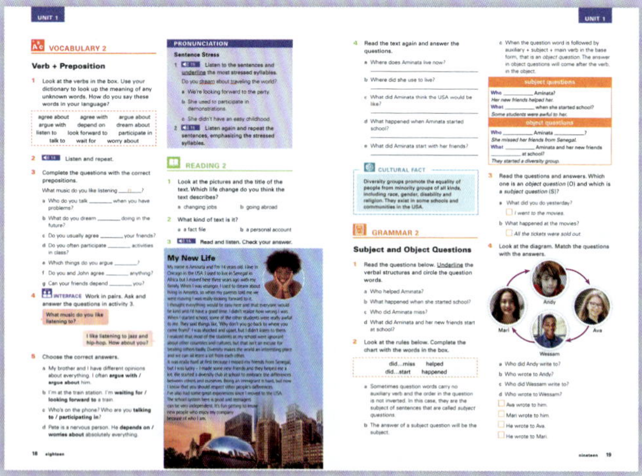

Grammar 2

This section introduces a new grammar topic in the same contextualized and systematized way that Grammar 1 does.

Reading 2

The second reading text digs further into the main topic and provides more language to be explored.
Cultural Fact boxes add little bits of cultural info to expand the topic.

CLIL

Integrate your learning of the English language with other school subjects through fun texts and activities in every odd-numbered unit.

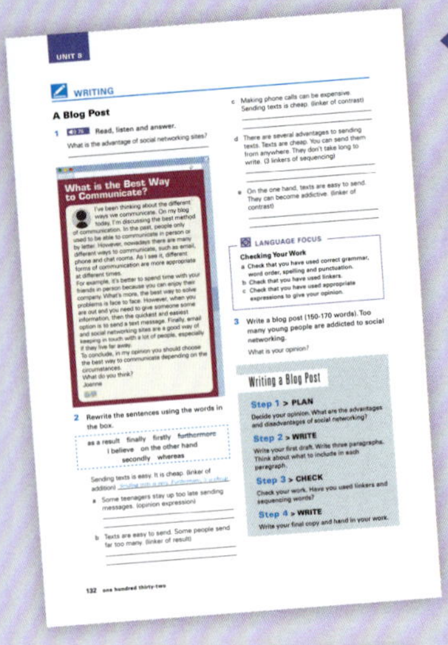

Writing

This section provides a model for the different text types you will get to practice in even-numbered units. The **Language Focus** box highlights useful language for written communication.

Vocabulary in Pictures

Have fun reviewing all the words and phrases learned in the **Vocabulary** sections, all richly illustrated!

Grammar Guide

This is a reference section for all the grammar topics explored in the unit.

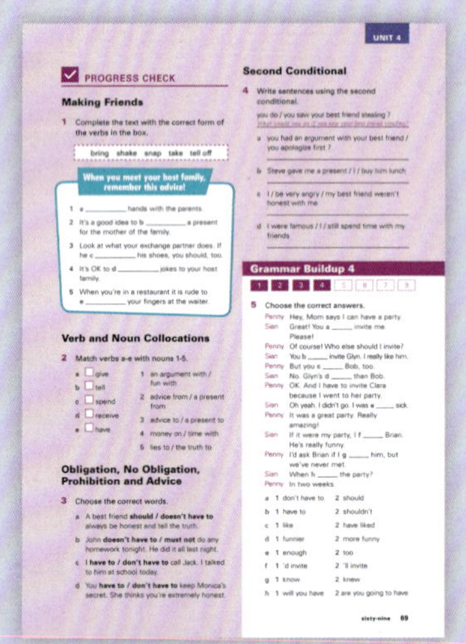

Progress Check

These activities help you revise core language and check your overall progress.

Reviews

Review the vocabulary and grammar from the previous two units starting with a game!

Life Skills

Learn skills to boost your talents, be a world citizen and deal effectively with the challenges of everyday life.

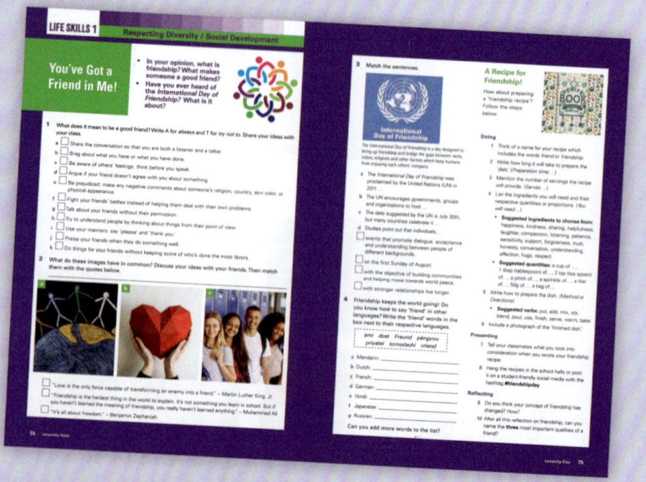

Irregular Verbs

A list with the most commonly used irregular verbs in their *base*, *past* and *participle* forms for you to check whenever you need them!

WORKBOOK

The workbook offers target-language practice and additional study material (consolidation and extension). It can be used as homework, independent study or extra classroom practice. Some of the sections correspond to sections in the Student's book:

Vocabulary 1

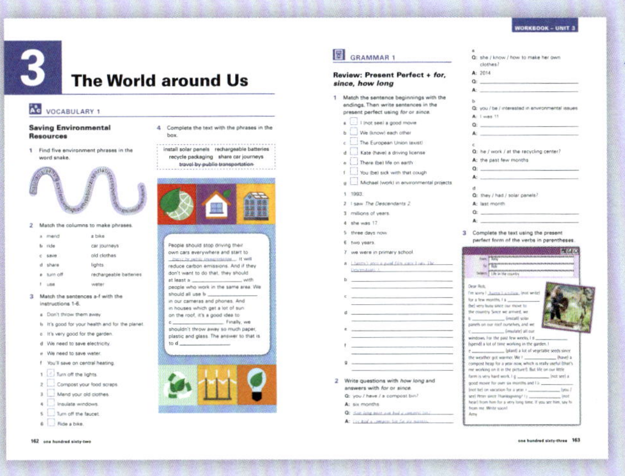

Grammar 1

Vocabulary 2

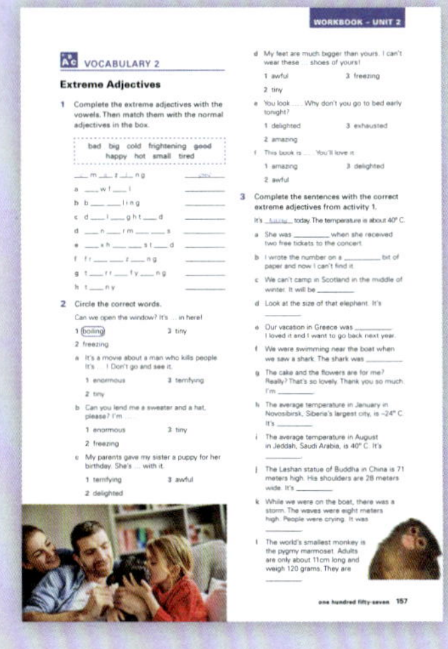

Grammar 2

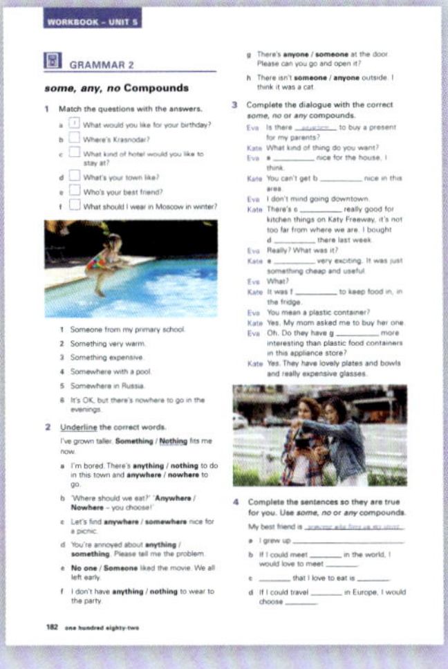

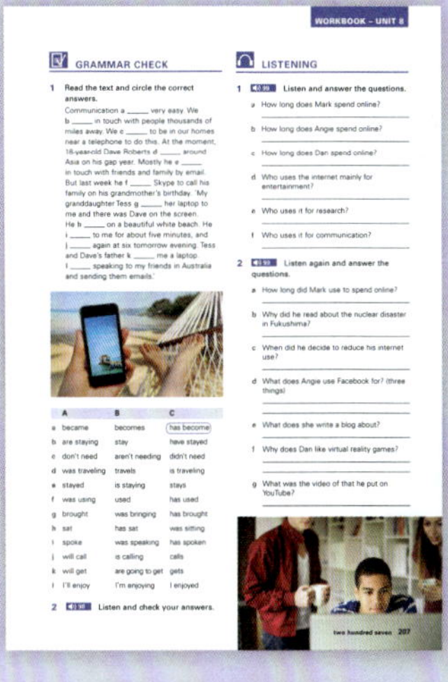

Grammar Check

A text with interesting, curious facts helps you check your reading and language skills.

Listening

Extension

This engaging section offers an extra challenge on grammar and vocabulary items.

Vocabulary Plus

Learn more words related to the unit topic in a fun way! All words are illustrated.

Wordlist

An alphabetical list of the key vocabulary in the **Student's Book** and from the **Vocabulary Plus** sections. It includes phonetic transcriptions and audio recordings.

DIGITAL STUDENT'S BOOK

This is the digital version of your **Student's Book** and **Workbook**, and you can easily access them everywhere! You will be able to read all the texts while having easy access to embedded audio tracks. Beside that, we also offer extra activities that can be monitored by your teacher so you can get the most out of your course!

CONTENTS

Starter

Jobs and Life Events

1 What are Gavin's and his friends' plans for the future? Complete their sentences with the words in the box.

actor architect engineer get a job get married go to college have children learn to drive leave home nurse police officer teacher work

a Hi, I'm Gavin. I really like to interact with people. I want to help people who are ill or injured, so my dream is to become a ______________.

b Hello. I'm Monica. I feel passionate about design and I want to be an ______________ so that I can design houses and buildings.

c I'm Hunter. I want to be a ______________ to serve my community and help people feel safe. I also dream about having a family, so I want to ______________ and ______________.

d My name is Siena. I love cars and I can't wait to ______________. I'm also interested in everything related to machines and electronics, so I want to be an ______________.

e I'm Owen. When I finish school, I want to become financially independent, so my plan is to ______________ and start to ______________. I also love studying, so I want to ______________ and become a ______________.

f Hi, I'm Sadie. I want to become an ______________ so that I can perform in plays and movies. I also plan to ______________ and travel the world.

2 02 Listen and check your answers.

Clothes and Accessories

3 Unscramble and write the name of clothes and accessories.

a k n s a e r s e ______________

b f s r a c ______________

c e d s r s ______________

d t a o c ______________

e k t i r s ______________

f t a s n p ______________

4 03 Listen and check your answers.

Prepositions

5 Number the pictures according to the prepositions they represent.

1 around 2 into 3 over 4 toward

a ☐

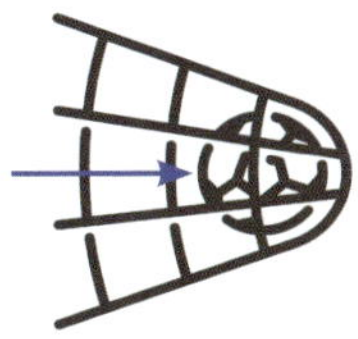

c ☐

b ☐

d ☐

6 04 Listen and check your answers.

make and *do*

7 Choose the correct words.

a Think twice before you **do / make** a decision that can change your life forever.

b The best way to **do / make** friends is just to be yourself.

c People who **do / make** exercise regularly have better memory retention.

d It doesn't matter if you win or lose, just **do / make** your best.

8 05 Listen and check your answers.

should / shouldn't

9 Complete the advice sentences using *should* or *shouldn't*.

a You ____________ post private information on social media.

b You ____________ save money in an emergency fund.

c You ____________ always act according to your beliefs.

d You ____________ care so much about what people think about you.

10 06 Listen and check your answers.

will and *be going to*

11 Complete the sentences with the most appropriate future tense.

a I loved your products. I ____________ buy from you again for sure!

b It's very likely that I ____________ be home within two or three hours.

c I ____________ have my first spin class today.

d I ____________ fall asleep pretty soon.

12 07 Listen and check your answers.

First Conditional

13 Order the words to make sentences.

a you'll / If / keep / an open mind, / you / more opportunities / see

____

____

b without / listen / if / a better friend / You'll / judging / be / you

____

____

c plants / water / if / Your / don't / won't / you / them / grow

____

____

d that topic / some more research / If / have time, / on / I / I'll / do

____

____

14 08 Listen and check your answers.

1 Changing Lives

VOCABULARY 1

Life-changing Events

1 Use your dictionary to check the meaning of the words in the box.

become rich	change schools
drop out of college	get into trouble
go abroad	go for a job interview
have an accident	make new friends
move retire	settle down
start your own business	
take a gap year	win an award

2 9 Listen and repeat.

3 Choose the correct answers.

a Are your parents bored of working for someone else? They should think about **starting their own business / winning an award**.

b Tom **retired / had an accident** last year. Now that he isn't working he has more time to see his grandchildren.

c My older brother **moved / got into trouble** from Charleston to Boston. He **dropped out / made new friends** quickly and he's even **settled down / won an award** with his wife.

d Amy **had an accident / went abroad** yesterday – she broke her leg.

e A few years ago, Mark **retired / got into trouble** because he bullied some other students. He **changed schools / had an accident** and he's much happier now.

f Lucy **dropped out of college / moved house** because she didn't like studying math. She **settled down / went for a job interview** last month and now she's working as a chef.

g My older brother **took a gap year / became rich** before he started college. He **retired / went abroad** and worked as a volunteer in a school in Africa.

h John's really successful – he **became rich / changed schools** after starting his own business, and he even **had an accident / won an award** last month.

4 INTERFACE Work in pairs. Ask and answer the question.

What event has changed your life most?

READING 1

1 Look at the pictures and the title of the mini biography. What do you think the text is about?

a Viola Davis's life.

b Movies that Viola Davis has starred in.

2 🔊 10 Read and listen. Check your answer.

Then & Now
... and this week, it's VIOLA DAVIS

WHEN MOST PEOPLE THINK OF Viola Davis, they think of a successful, talented actor who's really cool. She's the star of movies like *Fences* and *Solaris*. She often acts in movies and series, and she's traveled abroad many times as a result. She owns a multimillion-dollar mansion in Toluca Lake, Los Angeles, and has her own star on the Hollywood Walk of Fame! However, Viola's life wasn't always like this.

She didn't have an easy childhood. Viola was born in St. Matthews, South Carolina, on her grandmother's farm. When she was just 2 months old, her parents moved to Rhode Island, taking her and two of her sisters. Her older sister and brother stayed back in South Carolina with her grandparents because her family was extremely poor. At the age of two, Viola was arrested with her mother, who used to participate in demonstrations organized by the African-American Civil Rights Movement.

Her family was so poor that they didn't have enough food at home. Viola says she was constantly hungry at school and couldn't fulfill her learning potential because of that.

However, in high school she developed a passion for acting and that's how her career began. She got a scholarship to study drama at college and at a drama school in New York.

At first, she worked in minor theater productions. Her first role on screen was in 1996, and soon she was acting on Broadway and being invited to star in movies and television series. She has been nominated for three Oscars and won one in 2017. She is the only black person to date to win an Oscar, an Emmy and a Tony award.

She has settled down and, along with her husband – actor Julius Tennon – adopted a daughter named Genesis. However, her career continues to thrive and she now fights to combat childhood hunger in the U.S.!

3 Read the text again and choose the correct words.

a Viola **was / wasn't** wealthy when she was a child.

b Viola **did / didn't do** very well at school.

c Viola **went / didn't go** to college.

d Viola **moved / didn't move** when she was a baby.

e Viola **has / doesn't have** a daughter.

4 Answer the questions.

a Where does Viola own a mansion?

____

b What happened when she was two?

____

c When did she develop a passion for acting?

____

d Who did she marry?

____

e Has Viola won any awards?

____

5 Find words and phrases a-e in the text and match them to definitions 1-5. How do you say them in your language?

a ☐ childhood

b ☐ demonstrations

c ☐ potential

d ☐ scholarship

e ☐ thrive

1 money given by an organization to someone for their studies

2 to grow or become successful

3 ability to do something that has not yet been realized

4 the years when you are a child

5 events where a mass of people put forward political demands

READING STRATEGY

False friends are words with a similar spelling but different meaning in another language. *Parents* can be a false friend as it looks similar to some words in Latin languages but can have different meanings. Check for the possibility of different meanings.

GRAMMAR 1

Review: Simple Past

1 Look at the chart. Then underline the words to complete the sentences about the simple past.

simple past	regular verbs	irregular verbs
+	She developed a passion for acting.	She got a scholarship.
–	They didn't move with the family.	She didn't have an easy childhood.
?	Did she star in many movies?	Did she win several awards?
short answers	Yes, she did. No, she didn't.	Yes, she did. No, she didn't.

a The simple past tense is used to express **finished** / **unfinished** actions in the past.

b To form the simple past affirmative of **regular** / **irregular** verbs, *-ed* or *-d* are usually added to the base form of the verb.

c **Regular** / **Irregular** verbs usually have a different form in affirmative sentences.

d In negative sentences, the auxiliary *didn't* is used to form the simple past tense. It comes **before** / **after** the main verb.

e In questions, the auxiliary *did* is used **before** / **after** the subject. The main verb keeps its base form.

f In short answers, the auxiliaries *did* (affirmative) / *didn't* (negative) **are** / **aren't** used.

2 Complete the mini bio with the simple past form of the verbs in parentheses.

Penélope Cruz **a** ___*was born*___ (be born) in Spain in 1974. When she was younger she **b** ____________ (want) to be a ballet dancer, and she **c** ____________ (study) ballet for nine years. Then she **d** ____________ (decide) to become an actress. She **e** ____________ (appear) in a music video for the group Mecano when she **f** ____________ (be) only 15. She **g** ____________ (make) her first movie in 1992 at the age of 17 and **h** ____________ (become) famous as a result. She **i** ____________ (win) an Oscar for Best Supporting Actress in 2008. She **j** ____________ (start) going out with actor Javier Bardem in 2007 and they **k** ____________ (get) married in 2010 and had two babies.

3 Complete the statements and questions about Penélope Cruz in the simple past tense.

a ____________________ any Academy Awards?
Yes, she won the Academy Award for Best Supporting Actress in the 2008 film *Vicky Cristina Barcelona.*

b Did she marry Tom Cruise?
No, ____________________. She ____________________ Javier Bardem.

c Who ____________________ with in *Loving Pablo?*
She starred in this movie with Javier Bardem!

d When ____________________ that?
That was in 2017.

4 Do these sentences express single finished actions in the past? Mark (✓) or (✗).

a ☐ Jennifer Lawrence dropped out of school at the age of 14.

b ☐ Viola's mom used to participate in civil rights demonstrations.

c ☐ Viola got a scholarship to study drama.

d ☐ Penélope Cruz used to study classical ballet.

e ☐ At the age of 25, Penélope Cruz moved to Hollywood.

used to

5 Look at the chart and choose the correct information in the sentences below.

	used to
+	She **used to** participate in demonstrations.
–	She **didn't use to** have lunch at home.
?	**Did** she use to walk to school? Yes, she **did**. No, she **didn't**.

a We use *used to* to talk about

☐ past habits and states that no longer happen now.

☐ single finished actions in the past.

b The sentence structure is:

☐ used to / didn't use to / did + subject + use to + main verb in the simple past.

☐ used to / didn't use to / did + subject + use to + main verb in the infinitive.

6 Complete the text using the correct form of the verbs in parentheses. Use *used to*.

Our lifestyles have changed a lot thanks to computers, the internet and cell phones. People **a** *used to look up* (look up) information in reference books such as encyclopedias, but now they **b** ______ (use) the internet. They **c** ______ (write) letters, and communication **d** ______ (take) days or weeks, but now they **e** ______ (send) emails or text messages and communication **f** ______ (be) instant. Thirty years ago, people **g** ______ (not have) cell phones, they **h** ______ (use) landlines or use phone booths. It's true that communication **i** ______ (be) easier and faster now, but people **j** ______ (spend) more time talking face-to-face.

7 Read the text again. Write questions with *used to*. Then answer the questions.

a people / use the internet / 30 years ago?

______

b communication / be instant?

______

c people / send emails?

______

d people / make phone calls from phone booths?

______

8 INTERFACE Work in pairs. Ask and answer questions with *used to*.

What did you use to do when you were 10?

I used to play soccer every Saturday.

GRAMMAR GUIDE page 22

LISTENING

Lifestyle Changes

1 Look at the pictures and talk to a classmate. How do you think people's lifestyles change at these ages?

2 11 Listen to the radio show. Do they mention any of your ideas?

3 11 Listen again and match the people to the activities.

a Emma
b Frank
c Gary
d Helen
e Ivan

☐ usually bikes twice a week
☐ retired 8 months ago
☐ used to go out a lot but doesn't go out much now
☐ used to go on vacation with her parents
☐ started his own business last year

4 11 Listen again and complete the sentences with the correct number.

2 2.5 3 4 ~~5~~
~~10~~ 9 26 40

Emma went to Cancun with *5* friends for *10* days.

a Frank is in his ______s and he bought a bike ______ years ago.

b Gary is ______ years old and he finished college ______ years ago.

c Helen had a baby ______ years ago. The last time she did any art was ______ years ago.

d Ivan has ______ grandchildren.

SPEAKING

Moving Abroad

12 Liz is telling Jane what it was like when her family moved to the U.S. Listen and complete the dialogue.

So, tell me, Liz, how **a** __________ you __________ when your mom and dad told you you were moving here?

Well, I was 14 at the time and **b** __________ it at all. Leaving my family (grandma and grandpa especially) and friends behind **c** __________ tough!

I can imagine! How about school?

I **d** __________ to a very small school in Melbourne and here... oh gosh! So many students in a massive building... I felt completely lost at first!

So it was good when I **e** __________ to you and started a conversation...

Yeah, that was great! You **f** __________ me feel at home...

When I first saw you, I thought "she looks nice..." Well, the language **g** __________, too, as you are from Australia...

It surely **h** __________! Change can be quite scary for people who speak other languages or have a very different culture, lifestyle...

I bet! But if we see the positive side, **i** __________ can make you more adaptable, stronger and **j** __________.

Quite true!

FUNCTIONAL LANGUAGE

Talking about Life Experiences

How did you feel when...?
It was... at first...
I didn't like it.
I used to...

Speaking Task

Write a dialogue between you and a person who has moved to a foreign country.

Step 1

Choose a home country to describe: what life was like there, what was left behind, how the person / family probably felt about moving.

Step 2

Think about characteristics of the new country; positive and negative aspects about this change in life.

Step 3

Work with your partner. Write your dialogue. Follow the conversation above as a guide.

Step 4

Take turns practicing your dialogue.

CULTURE

Namasté, America

People from many corners of the world have always wanted to live the 'American dream' in the land of prosperity, and for the Asian Indian population it was no different.
The first wave of immigration, between 1900 / 1920, consisted of young male Sikhs who married Mexican women and created the so-called "Mexican Hindu" culture.
The second wave happened between 1965 and 1990. At that time, those immigrants owned small businesses such as restaurants, travel agencies and motels.
The third wave came in the early twenty-first century: those who had technology-based skills, degrees and professional talents were allowed in 'Uncle Sam's land.'
At some point around 2000, the size of the Asian Indian population in the U.S. exceeded one million. Nowadays, they are a diverse group: they come from different parts of India and other countries as well, such as England, Tanzania, Guyana and Trinidad. They follow different religions, including Hinduism, Sikhism and Christianity. Many of them are skilled professionals working in science, technology, engineering and math fields, are fluent in English and used to Western culture. In fact, they are wealthy people and the most highly educated immigrants in the U.S.

1 🔊 13 **Read and listen to the information about Asian Indian immigration in the U.S. and answer the questions below.**

a When did the first Asian Indians arrive in the U.S.? Who were they?

b What did the immigrants who arrived between 1965 and 1990 do in America?

c Who was allowed into the U.S. during the early twenty-first century?

2 **Check (✓) the information provided in the text about Asian Indians in the U.S. today.**

- ☐ Most of them come from small cities in India.
- ☐ They follow different religions.
- ☐ They speak English very well.
- ☐ They are poor people and do not come from a highly educated background.
- ☐ Many of them work in science, technology, engineering and math fields.

3 **Is immigration a reality in your country? Where do most immigrants come from?**

4 **What is it like to be an immigrant in your country? Share your answers with your friends.**

VOCABULARY 2

Verb + Preposition

1 Look at the verbs in the box. Use your dictionary to look up the meaning of any unknown words. How do you say these words in your language?

agree about	agree with	argue about
argue with	depend on	dream about
listen to	look forward to	participate in
talk to	wait for	worry about

2 14 Listen and repeat.

3 Complete the questions with the correct prepositions.

What music do you like listening ___*to*___?

a Who do you talk ________ when you have problems?

b What do you dream ________ doing in the future?

c Do you usually agree ________ your friends?

d Do you often participate ________ activities in class?

e Which things do you argue ________?

f Do you and John agree ________ anything?

g Can your friends depend ________ you?

4 INTERFACE Work in pairs. Ask and answer the questions in activity 3.

What music do you like listening to?

I like listening to jazz and hip-hop. How about you?

5 Choose the correct answers.

a My brother and I have different opinions about everything. I often **argue with / argue about** him.

b I'm at the train station. I'm **waiting for / looking forward to** a train.

c Who's on the phone? Who are you **talking to / participating in**?

d Pete is a nervous person. He **depends on / worries about** absolutely everything.

PRONUNCIATION

Sentence Stress

1 15 Listen to the sentences and underline the most stressed syllables.

Do you <u>dream</u> about <u>tra</u>veling the world?

a We're looking forward to the party.

b She used to participate in demonstrations.

c She didn't have an easy childhood.

2 15 Listen again and repeat the sentences, emphasizing the stressed syllables.

READING 2

1 Look at the pictures and the title of the text. Which life change do you think the text describes?

a changing jobs b going abroad

2 What kind of text is it?

a a fact file b a personal account

3 16 Read and listen. Check your answer.

My New Life

My name is Aminata and I'm 14 years old. I live in Chicago in the USA. I used to live in Senegal in Africa but I moved here three years ago with my family. When I was younger, I used to dream about living in America, so when my parents told me we were moving I was really looking forward to it.

I thought everything would be easy here and that everyone would be kind and I'd have a good time. I didn't realize how wrong I was. When I started school, some of the other students were really awful to me. They said things like, 'Why don't you go back to where you came from?' I was shocked and upset, but I didn't listen to them.

I realized that most of the students at my school were ignorant about other countries and cultures, but that isn't an excuse for treating others badly. Diversity makes the world an interesting place and we can all learn a lot from each other.

It was really hard at first because I missed my friends from Senegal, but I was lucky – I made some new friends and they helped me a lot. We started a diversity club at school to embrace the differences between others and ourselves. Being an immigrant is hard, but now I know that you should respect other people's differences.

I've also had some great experiences since I moved to the USA. The school system here is good and teenagers can be very independent. It's fun getting to know new people who enjoy my company because of who I am.

4 Read the text again and answer the questions.

a Where does Aminata live now?

____

b Where did she use to live?

____

c What did Aminata think the USA would be like?

____

d What happened when Aminata started school?

____

e What did Aminata start with her friends?

____

CULTURAL FACT

Diversity groups promote the equality of people from minority groups of all kinds, including race, gender, disability and religion. They exist in some schools and communities in the USA.

GRAMMAR 2

Subject and Object Questions

1 Read the questions below. Underline the verbal structures and circle the question words.

a Who helped Aminata?

b What happened when she started school?

c Who did Aminata miss?

d What did Aminata and her new friends start at school?

2 Look at the rules below. Complete the chart with the words in the box.

did...miss helped
did...start happened

a Sometimes question words carry no auxiliary verb and the order in the question is not inverted. In this case, they are the subject of sentences that are called *subject questions*.

b The answer of a subject question will be the subject.

c When the question word is followed by auxiliary + subject + main verb in the base form, that is an *object question*. The answer in object questions will come after the verb, in the object.

subject questions
Who __________ Aminata?
Her new friends helped her.
What __________ when she started school?
Some students were awful to her.
object questions
Who __________ Aminata __________?
She missed her friends from Senegal.
What __________ Aminata and her new friends __________ at school?
They started a diversity group.

3 Read the questions and answers. Which one is an *object question* (O) and which is a *subject question* (S)?

a What did you do yesterday?

☐ *I went to the movies.*

b What happened at the movies?

☐ *All the tickets were sold out.*

4 Look at the diagram. Match the questions with the answers.

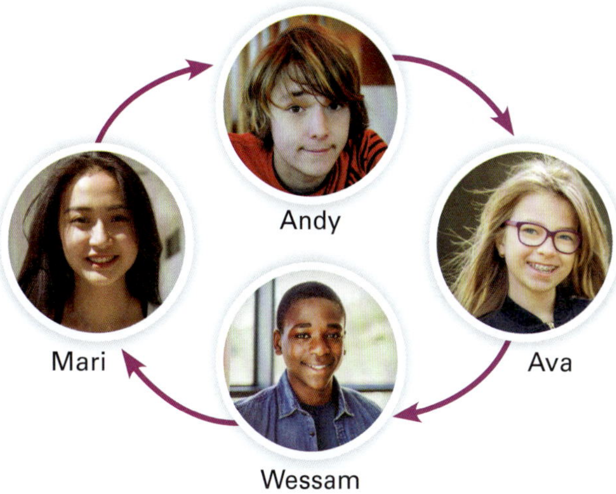

a Who did Andy write to?

b Who wrote to Andy?

c Who did Wessam write to?

d Who wrote to Wessam?

☐ Ava wrote to him.

☐ Mari wrote to him.

☐ He wrote to Ava.

☐ He wrote to Mari.

CLIL

SCIENCE

Animal Migration

Many species in the animal kingdom migrate, including birds, fish, mammals and reptiles. They often travel great distances to reach another part of the world. Humpback whales swim more than 5,000 miles in one direction, while one species of bird flies 7,000 miles non-stop in just eight days. Animals migrate because they need to find food (some plants or animals may only be available in a certain area at particular times of the year), a better climate (the winter may be very cold) or the best place to reproduce.

The migration cycle may happen every time the seasons change, once a year, or perhaps just once in the animal's lifetime. For example, Scottish salmon are born in freshwater rivers. Then they swim thousands of miles north to find food in the Atlantic Ocean. When it's time for the salmon to reproduce, it swims back to the river where it was born. After it lays its eggs there, it dies.

1 🔊 17 Read and listen. Answer the question.

Why do Scottish salmon migrate?

____

____

2 Find and circle four types of animals that migrate.

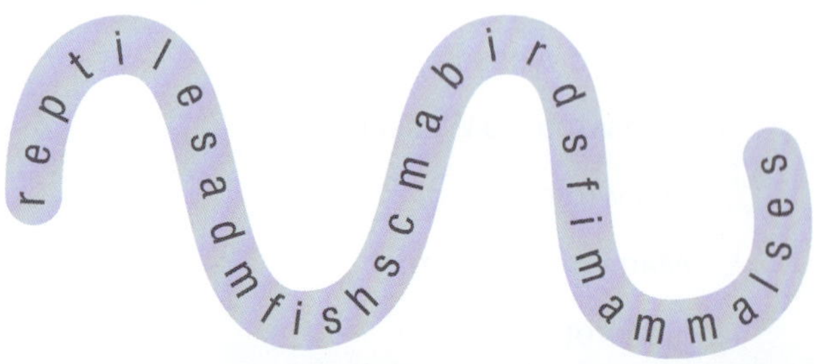

3 Complete the sentences with the words in the box.

climate distances food lifetime miles reasons year

a When animals migrate they often travel great __________.

b Humpback whales swim more than 5,000 __________ in one direction.

c Animals migrate for many different __________.

d They often migrate at a particular time of the __________.

e Some animals migrate in order to find __________.

f When they migrate, some animals are looking for a better __________ or a place to reproduce.

g Some animals migrate every year and some only once in a __________.

VOCABULARY IN PICTURES

Life-changing Events

become rich

change schools

drop out of college

have an accident

get into trouble

go abroad

go for a job interview

make new friends

move

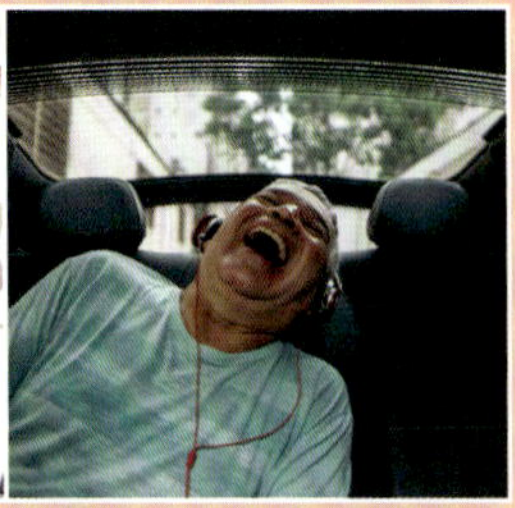
retire

settle down

start your own business

take a gap year

win an award

Verb + Preposition

agree about/ agree with

argue about/ argue with

depend on

dream about

listen to

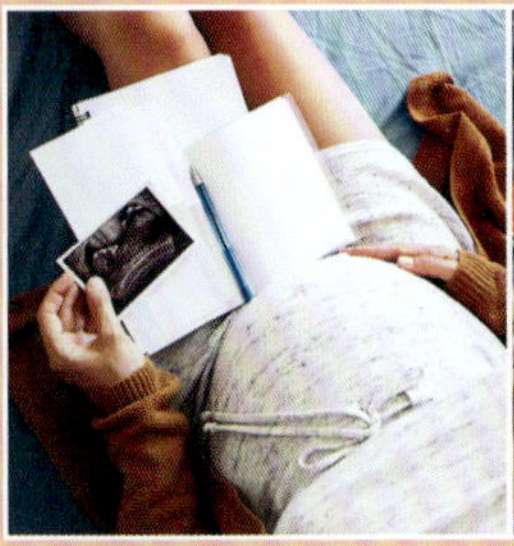
look forward to

participate in

talk to

wait for

worry about

GRAMMAR GUIDE

Simple Past

+	I / You	**moved.**
	He / She / It	**moved.**
	We / You / They	**moved.**
–	I / You	**didn't move.**
	He / She / It	**didn't move.**
	We / You / They	**didn't move.**
?	**Did** you **move**? Yes, I **did**. No, I **didn't**.	

- we use the simple past to talk about events in the past, especially if we express a definite point in past
  I **played** tennis yesterday.
- we form negative sentences with *didn't* + the base form of the verb
  They **didn't walk** to school.
- we form questions in the past with *did* + base form of the verb. In short answers, we don't repeat the main verb
  Did he **buy** a car? Yes, he **did**.

used to

+	She **used to** participate in demonstrations.
–	She **didn't use** to have food at home.
?	**Did** she **use to** travel abroad? Yes, she **did**. No, she **didn't**.

- we use *used to* + base form of the verb to talk about past habits and situations. We use it to talk about things that people did regularly in the past but that they don't do now
  They **used to** live in Chicago, but now they live in Boston.
  He **used to** ride his bike to work, but now he takes the bus.

Subject and Object Questions

subject questions
Who went to the movies yesterday? Joe went to the movies yesterday.
object questions
What did Joe **do** yesterday? He went to the movies.

- question words can be either the subject or the object of the verb.
- if the question word is the subject of the question, we don't use an auxiliary verb
  Who made the cake? **Jenny** made the cake.
- if the question word is the object of the question, we use an auxiliary verb (*do*, *does* or *did*)
  What did Jenny make? She made a **cake**.

PROGRESS CHECK

Life-changing Events

1 Match a-d with 1-4 to make sentences.

a ☐ Dan and Mandy moved
b ☐ They decided to start
c ☐ Mike made
d ☐ Kathy said that she wanted to take

1 their own business.
2 a gap year before college.
3 last year.
4 new friends after he changed schools.

Verb + Preposition

2 Complete the expressions with the correct prepositions.

a agree ________ someone
b talk ________ something
c look forward ________ something
d depend ________ someone
e participate ________ something

Simple Past and *used to*

3 Choose the correct answers.

a I **used to move / moved** to France three years ago.
b I **used to go / went** hiking twice a month when I was younger.
c Last weekend I **used to go / went** shopping but I **didn't use to buy / didn't buy** anything.
d What **did you use to do / did you do** on weekends when you were 10?
e Peter **used to get / got** married last week.

4 Complete the questions and answers with the correct form of the verbs in parentheses.

a Did you ________ to ________ (live) in a different town or city?
Yes, I __________ (live) in Albuquerque, but I ________ (live) in Miami now. I ________ (move) here two months ago.

b ________________ (Sue / like) vegetables?
No, she ____________ (not like) them, but now she ________ (be) a vegetarian. She ________ (stop) eating meat last year.

c What ________________ (Tony / do) every Saturday?
He ________ (go) swimming, but last year he ________ (start) playing football. He __________ (not go) swimming now.

Subject and Object Questions

5 Write subject or object questions with *who* or *what* for the information in bold. Then answer the questions.

Sally went shopping **with her friends**.
Who did Sally go shopping with?
She went shopping with her friends.

a **Sally** went shopping with her friends.
____
____

b Mike visited **the new museum**.
____
____

c **Mike** visited the new museum.
____
____

Grammar Buildup 1

1 2 3 4 5 6 7 8

6 Choose the correct answers.

Nick **a used to win / won** the lottery ten years ago and he **b used to change / changed** his life. Before, he **c got up / used to get up** early, but then he **d used to start getting up / started getting up** very late, like 12 o'clock! In his old life, he **e was working / used to work** very hard, but he **f stopped working / didn't use to stop working** after the lottery. To get to work he **g was catching / used to catch** the bus, but he **h used to buy / bought** a new car and he **i traveled / used to travel** everywhere in his car for about three years. Nick **j didn't use to go / didn't go** to dinner parties or travel abroad, but since winning the lottery he's done that many times!

2 Incredible Journeys

VOCABULARY 1

Travel

1 Match pictures 1-4 with activities in the box.

arrive ☐ buy a guidebook ☐
buy souvenirs ☐ come back home ☐
get off a bus ☐ get on a train ☐
have adventures ☐ meet people ☐
pack a suitcase ☐ plan a journey ☐
send postcards ☐ set off ☐

2 🔊 18 Listen and repeat.

3 Choose the correct words.

To: Sarah
From: Kate
Subject:

Hi Sarah,
Well, we **a** **set off** / **arrived** in Rome four days ago. We **b** **set off** / **got on** last Sunday morning at 6am. Mom didn't **c** **pack** / **get on** her suitcase until 5:30am, so she forgot lots of things, like the guidebook. We had to **d** **buy** / **get off** one at the airport. Suzy and I have **e** **met** / **had** lots of adventures. On the first day we **f** **met** / **bought** a Spanish family at the hotel. We went to the Colosseum with them today. Tomorrow we're **g** **getting off** / **planning** to go on a trip to the Vatican. I've taken lots of pictures to show you when we **h** **get off** / **come back** next week. I've **i** **bought** / **had** you a great souvenir – a Roma soccer shirt!
Kate

READING 1

1 Skim the magazine feature beside. In what ways do you think Albert is a typical young man? In what ways is he not typical?

____

____

____

____

____

____

2 19 Read and listen. Check your answers.

3 Read the text again and answer the questions.

a What are *The World on Wheels* and *Without Frontiers*?

____

b How many countries has Albert visited?

____

c Does he usually travel with someone else?

____

d How does he make money when he's traveling?

____

e What advantages are there to traveling in a wheelchair, according to Albert?

____

4 Find words and phrases 1-5 in the text and match them with definitions a-e.

a	☐ disease	1	alone
b	☐ on his own	2	being frightened
c	☐ fear	3	illness
d	☐ pick someone up	4	hurt someone
e	☐ harm	5	stop and offer someone a lift in your car

5 INTERFACE Work in pairs. Have you ever been on a long journey? Where did you go?

Yes, I have. I traveled from New York to Los Angeles with my parents.

The World on Wheels

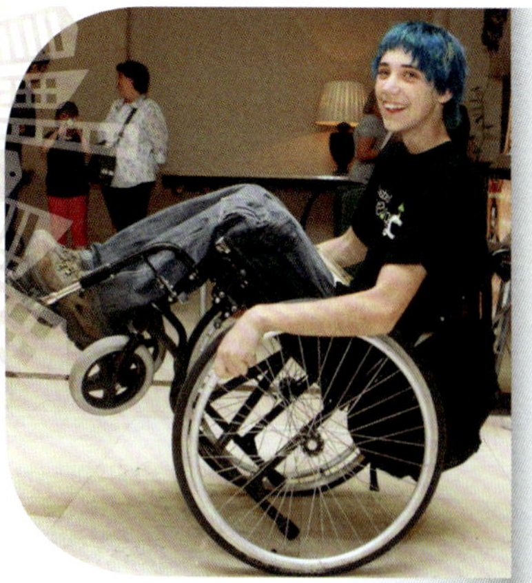

Albert Casals is a typical young man in many ways. He likes reading science fiction books, he enjoys playing Dragon Ball and he's interested in science. But in other ways Albert is very different. He has visited more than 80 countries alone and he has written two books, *The World on Wheels* and *Without Frontiers*. And one more thing makes him different: Albert has been in a wheelchair since he was eight years old.

Albert was born in 1990 and lives in the town of Esparreguera, Barcelona, Spain. He became ill with leukemia when he was five, but the disease hasn't stopped him from having fun.

Albert has traveled around Europe and in 2007 he set off for South America. He always travels on his own, he often hitchhikes and he never takes much money. In fact, Albert took €20 with him to South America and came back six months later with the same amount! He gets money by working and doing tricks with his wheelchair. Albert has had lots of adventures. He has slept on boats and desert islands.

He has learned how to repair his wheelchair himself. He has taught himself how to get on and get off buses and trains without help.

Albert wants to encourage more people in wheelchairs to copy him. 'The chair helps you to travel because it eliminates fear,' Albert explains. 'When you hitchhike, drivers pick you up because you are not considered dangerous. And another advantage is that people talk to me because they want to meet a boy who travels the world alone in a chair. And so I make new friends who help me.' He says that he has learned that the world is mostly full of kind, friendly people who want to help him, not harm him.

So, what's next for Albert? More and more travel. And maybe his next book, of course.

GRAMMAR 1

Review: Present Perfect and Simple Past

1 Look at the following sentences. Underline the verb forms.

a He has visited more than 80 countries alone.

b He has written two books.

c He became ill with leukemia when he was five.

d The disease hasn't stopped him from having fun.

2 Read the rules below and complete the chart with the verb forms in the box.

a The present perfect is formed from the verb *have* (*have*, *has*) + the past participle of the main verb.

b Negative sentences in the present perfect need *haven't* or *hasn't*.

c Questions follow the structure: *have* / *has* + subject + main verb in the past participle.

d The past participle of regular verbs usually take *-d* / *-ed*.

e Irregular verbs have different past participle forms.

f The present perfect is used to talk about past actions or experiences without saying when they happened.

g The simple past is used to talk about completed actions at a definite time in the past.

has had   has traveled   have ... helped
have ... helped   hasn't felt
made   set off

present perfect	simple past
Albert __________ around Europe. He __________ lots of adventures. __________ people __________ Albert get on / off trains? He __________ lonely.	In 2007 he __________ for South America. Albert __________ lots of friends on his journey that year.

3 Write sentences using the present perfect.

a J.K. Rowling / have / an influence / all over the world.

____

____

b Many people / read / books / written by her.

____

____

c She / give / some of her wealth / to charity. Because of that, she / fall / from the publication's list of the world's wealthiest people.

____

____

4 Fill in the blanks in the sentences with the verb forms in the box below.

has happened   has taken
have adopted   have you got
haven't been

a __________ more time than money?

b Backpackers in South Africa __________ a 'kikoi' (sarong-like piece of clothing). It's usually boiling hot all year long and kikois are comfortable for long walks.

c Quite a lot __________ in South Africa in the past 20 years. The country __________ lots of good steps.

d Race relations __________ so hard.

5 Read this testimonial of a backpacker in India and fill in the blanks with the present perfect or simple past of the verbs in parentheses.

"The first time I **a** __________ (be) in India, I **b** __________ (not have) a good experience. I **c** __________ (try) to see the whole country in just one month – I **d** __________ (travel) quickly and I **e** __________ (get) sick because I **f** __________ (eat) lots of spicy food. The good thing was that I **g** __________ (travel) with a friend so I **h** __________ (feel) much better. After that trip, I **i** __________ (be) back 5 more times. I **j** __________ (travel) with friends, on tours and, sometimes, alone. I **k** __________ (also meet) people from all over the world!"

6 Circle the correct verb forms to complete the dialogue below.

Jed What are you reading?
Beth I'm reading *Around the World in 80 Days*. **a Have you read / Do you read** it?
Jed No. Is it good?
Beth Yeah. I **b did read / have read** it before, I really liked it.
Jed Who's it by?
Beth Jules Verne. He **c has written / wrote** it in 1873.
Jed Oh, I know him. I **d have read / read** *Journey to the Center of the Earth* a few years ago.
Beth I **e have saw / have seen** the movie of that one. **f Did you like / Have you liked** the book?
Jed Yes, it **g was / were** great. You should read it. You know, I **h have seen / saw** a TV show called *Around the World in 80 Days* last year.
Beth With Michael Palin? Yes, I remember it. He **i has made / has make** lots of travel shows. They're really good.
Jed He's really lucky. I **j haven't been / have been** to any foreign country.
Beth Haven't you? I **k have been / has been** to lots. Last year I **l have gone / went** to Greece with my family.
Jed Lucky you!

GRAMMAR GUIDE page 36

LISTENING

Dream Vacations

1 Look at the pictures. What type of vacations do they show?

____

2 20 Listen to the advertisements and number the journeys.

a ☐ A family adventure vacation
b ☐ The Trans-Mongolian Express
c ☐ A Mediterranean cruise

3 20 Listen again. Then write T for *true* or F for *false*.

a ☐ On a cruise you travel by ship.
b ☐ The cruise takes you to France.
c ☐ The Trans-Mongolian is a train journey.
d ☐ The Trans-Mongolian goes from Moscow to Beijing.
e ☐ On the family adventure you travel by plane.
f ☐ The family adventure vacation is in India.

4 20 Listen again and underline the correct answers.

a How many countries does the cruise visit?
1 ten 2 three 3 six

b How can you get information about the cruise?
1 online 2 by phone 3 both

c Which other country does the train go through?
1 Thailand 2 Mongolia 3 Kazakhstan

d What can you ride in India?
1 a camel 2 a horse 3 a tiger

e Where can you stay for two nights in India?
1 a hotel 2 a palace 3 the Taj Mahal

5 INTERFACE Work in pairs.

Which journey do you think is the most interesting?

The Trans-Mongolian because I love traveling by train.

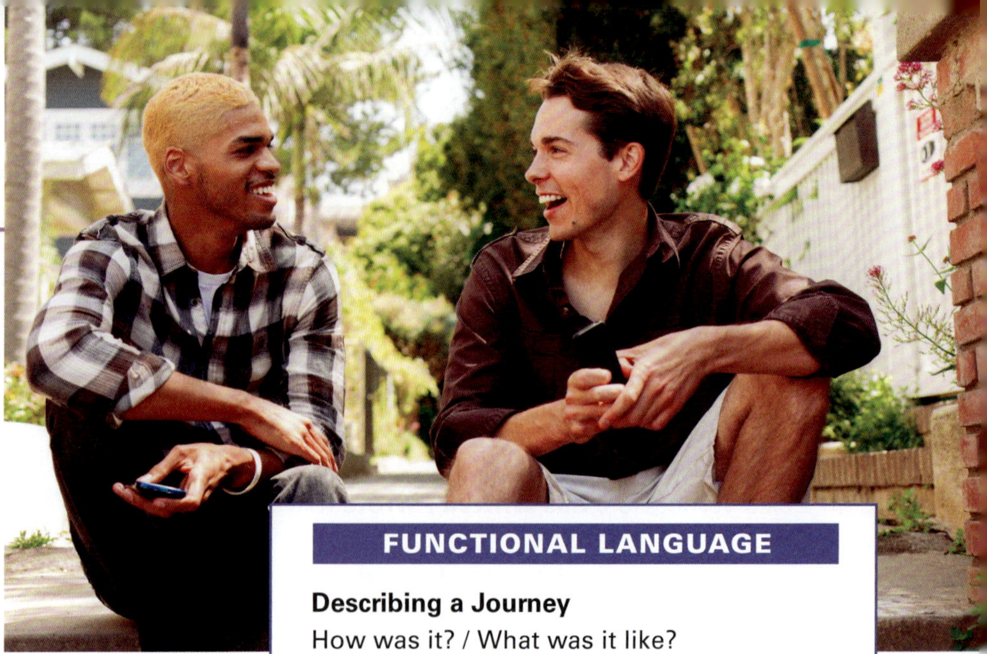

SPEAKING

The Trip of a Lifetime!

21 Jack and Ron are talking about Ron's adventure in New Zealand. Listen and complete the dialogue.

How **a** ____________ your trip to New Zealand, Ron?

It **b** ____________ such an adventure. New Zealand is an incredible country! Anyone who loves being active and the outdoors will feel at home there.

So, tell me, what **c** ____________?

So many things... I **d** ____________ to Wai-O-Tapu Thermal Wonderland. The geothermal pools and volcanic acidic lakes are awesome! This natural attraction **e** ____________ called one of the twenty most surreal areas in the world!

Cool! How about Zorbing? **f** ____________ it?

You bet! Rolling down a hill on a plastic ball was so much fun! High adrenaline!

What **g** ____________ best there?

Actually, I **h** ____________ the Tamaki Maori Village. I was welcomed by the Powhiri – It's a formal welcoming ceremony; the Maori **i** ____________ war dances and **j** ____________ ... a real blast!

Yeah, an excellent way to learn about local culture.

Absolutely! A must-see.

FUNCTIONAL LANGUAGE

Describing a Journey

How was it? / What was it like?
Where did you go?
Have you tried ...?
What did you like best?

Speaking Task

Write a dialogue between you and a friend about an incredible journey.

Step 1

Choose an incredible journey you've recently taken abroad or in your own country.

Step 2

Think about the places you've visited / things you've seen and how you liked it.

Step 3

Work with your partner. Write your dialogue. Follow the conversation above as a guide.

Step 4

Take turns practicing your dialogue.

CULTURE

David Livingstone and his Journey in Africa

"DR. LIVINGSTONE, I PRESUME."

DR. LIVINGSTONE READING THE BIBLE TO HIS MEN

David Livingstone was a Scottish doctor, famous missionary and abolitionist who crossed Africa in the mid-19th century. During his travels, he witnessed the horrors of the African slave trade. He believed in the dignity of Africans and he spoke out in favor of commercial enterprises for the continent. He was devastated when, in the village of Nyangwe, he saw Arabic slave traders killing hundreds of people.

Livingstone wrote and published *Narrative of an Expedition to the Zambesi and Its Tributaries* in 1854 and *Missionary Travels and Researches in South Africa* in 1857. In the first book, he described his use of quinine for malaria and the connection between malaria and mosquitoes.

Livingstone took many journeys in Africa and came across a wonderful waterfall on the Zambesi River on the border between Zambia and Zimbabwe. He named it Victoria Falls. In the local language, it is called Mosi-oa-Tunya – "The Smoke that Thunders."

Livingstone married Mary Moffat, had several children and died from dysentery and malaria in 1873, at the age of 60, in a small village in Zambia (called North Rhodesia at the time).

1 🔊 22 **Read and listen to the information about David Livingstone. Then write T for *true* or F for *false*.**

a ☐ David Livingstone was born and lived all his life in Africa.

b ☐ He was a doctor, missionary and abolitionist.

c ☐ In his book *Missionary Travels and Researches in South Africa*, he described his use of quinine for malaria and the connection between malaria and mosquitoes.

d ☐ Livingstone took many journeys in Africa and came across a wonderful waterfall on the Zambesi River which he named Niagara Falls.

2 **Write about a famous historical journey in your country. Share it with your friends.**

____

____

____

VOCABULARY 2

Extreme Adjectives

1 Match the extreme adjectives with the adjectives on the right.

a	amazing	☐ frightening
b	awful	☐ good
c	boiling	☐ big
d	delighted	☐ tired
e	enormous	☐ happy
f	exhausted	☐ small
g	freezing	☐ bad
h	terrifying	☐ cold
i	tiny	☐ hot

2 🔊 23 Listen, check and repeat.

3 Write the extreme adjective for each sentence.

I don't like flying. It's frightening. *terrifying*

a The journey was really bad. ____________

b I love Greek food. It's good. ____________

c My sister was tired when she came back home from New York. ____________

d Mark was happy when he saw his hotel room. ____________

e It's hot on this bus. Can I open a window? ____________

f There were 300 people on our flight. The plane was big. ____________

4 Choose the correct words.

a I really enjoyed my vacation. Athens was **amazing / delighted / enormous**.

b I'm **tiny / exhausted / freezing**. I'm going to bed early.

c Oh no, I haven't drunk my coffee and now it's **boiling / freezing / terrifying**.

d Julie was **delighted / tiny / exhausted** with the souvenir I gave her.

READING 2

1 Look at the picture and the title of the text. What do you think the biography is about?

____

2 🔊 24 Read and listen. Check your answer.

Solo Sailor

Mike Perham didn't have much time to celebrate his 17th birthday. Not because he had exams or was working, but because he was in the middle of the Indian Ocean. Mike has just become the youngest person to sail around the world solo. His amazing journey took him nine months and he sailed over 30,000 miles on his 50ft yacht, called totallymoney.com.

Mike had a lot of adventures on his trip. Sailing conditions in the Indian Ocean were wonderful, but he had to sail through enormous 50ft waves in the South Pacific after leaving New Zealand. He didn't have many problems with his boat. However, he had to stop in the Canary Islands, Portugal and Cape Town to repair his auto-pilot, the machine that sailed the boat while Mike slept. Fortunately, he didn't meet any whales or sharks!

Mike returned home to the UK exhausted, but ecstatic to be a world record holder. What was the first thing he wanted? Some steak and chips! Mike didn't have any fresh food on the boat, so he didn't eat a lot of fruit or vegetables while he was sailing. What an amazing and terrifying journey!

3 Read the text again. Answer the questions.

a Where did Mike celebrate his 17th birthday?

____

b What world record did Mike set?

____

c How big were the waves in the South Pacific?

____

d Why did Mike stop in the Canary Islands?

____

4 CLASS VOTE Do you think Mike was too young to sail around the world alone?

GRAMMAR 2

Review: Quantity and Uncountable Nouns

1 Look at the chart. Circle the quantifiers and underline the countable and uncountable nouns.

countable nouns how many...?	uncountable nouns how much...?
a He saw a lot of whales.	b He had a lot of fresh food.

c He saw some / a few whales.	d He had some / a little fresh food.

e He didn't see many whales.	f He didn't have much fresh food.

g He didn't see any whales.	h He didn't have any fresh food.

2 Look at the sentences in activity 1 again and complete the rules of countable and uncountable nouns with the words and phrases in the box.

a lot of (2x) can't be *many* *much* one by one plural (2x) *some* or *any* (2x)

a Countable nouns can be counted ____________ and can be made ____________. To indicate large quantities, countable nouns can be preceded by ____________ or ____________. To refer to an indefinite quantity, they can be preceded by ____________.

b Uncountable nouns ____________ counted one by one, nor can they be made ____________. To indicate large amounts, uncountable nouns can be preceded by ____________ or ____________. To refer to an indefinite amount, they can be preceded by ____________.

TIP

How many and *How much* are used to ask about quantities and amounts.
How many + countable noun in the plural
How much + uncountable noun

How much is also used to ask about prices:
How much did that trip cost?

3 Complete the questions with *How much* or *How many*.

a ____________ is a trip to Australia?

b ____________ countries would you like to visit?

c ____________ free time do you have for a visit to the museum?

d ____________ people are traveling with you?

4 Choose the correct words.

Dear Parents,

Next week is the annual school adventure camp for 9th Grade students.

All students will need to bring a **some / much** warm clothes, but they don't need b **many / much** because the camp only lasts for three days. Please pack c **a few / a little** extra socks because the camp is cold at night. Students do not need to bring d **any / many** food. The camp provides all meals with e **a lot of / much** fresh fruit and vegetables.

They can bring f **a little / a few** money, but not too g **much / many**. Students cannot bring h **a little / any** gadgets like mp3 players or cell phones. The teachers have cell phones for emergencies. See you next week!

The Teachers

GRAMMAR GUIDE page 36

WRITING

A Description of a Journey

1 🔊 25 Read and listen. Where is Kate?

____

From: Kate
To: Nick
Subject: Plane Journey!

Hi Nick,
Well, we've arrived – at last! What a journey! It was a nightmare! 😱😱😱
The plane left London on time. The food was OK and the in-flight movies were excellent. I watched *Avengers: Infinity War*. Have you seen it? It's great. But when we were only 30 minutes from New York there was a disaster! We couldn't land because of bad weather. First, we had to fly to Washington, DC. Then we had to wait for three and a half hours to get off the plane. Then we waited for an hour in line at the immigration desk. Next, we lined up for another two hours for a hotel. After that we waited 45 minutes for the shuttle bus to the hotel. We finally arrived at the hotel at midnight – eight hours after landing! And the restaurant was closed, so there was no food!
We're going to New York this morning, I hope.
I'll send you an email when we get there.
Kate

2 Read the email again and order the events.

- **a** ☐ had to fly to Washington
- **b** ☐ arrived at the hotel
- **c** ☐ waited at the immigration desk
- **d** ☐ the plane left London
- **e** ☐ lined up for a shuttle bus
- **f** ☐ lined up for a hotel

LANGUAGE FOCUS

Linkers

First, we had to fly to Washington, DC.
Then we had to wait for three and a half hours.
Next, we lined up for another two hours for a hotel.
After that we waited 45 minutes for the bus.
We **finally** arrived at the hotel at midnight.

3 Look at the Language Focus and complete the rules below with the words in bold.

- **a** We use ________ to indicate the beginning of an event.
- **b** We use ________, ________ and ________ to indicate the order of events.
- **c** We use ________ to indicate the end of an event.

4 Choose the correct words.

Have you ever been on a sightseeing bus tour? We went on one in New York last year. We set off from Broadway and **a next** / **first** we went to Times Square, in the center of Manhattan. **b Then** / **Finally**, we drove up one side of Central Park and saw the Museum of Natural History. **c After** / **Next**, we went to Harlem and saw the Apollo Theater. Michael Jackson sang there when he was young. **d After that** / **First**, we drove down Park Avenue. Lots of famous people live there. The buildings are really beautiful. **e Then** / **Finally**, we got off the bus by the Guggenheim Museum. It was wonderful!

5 Write a short email (120-150 words) to a friend describing a journey.

Writing a Description

Step 1 > PLAN

Think about the journey and make notes. Where were you going? Was it a good or bad journey? What happened?

Step 2 > WRITE

Write your first draft. Include an introduction, a description of where you were going, what happened and a closing phrase. Remember to use linkers to show the order of events.

Step 3 > CHECK

Check your work for errors. Have you used linkers?

Step 4 > WRITE

Write your final copy and hand in your work.

VOCABULARY IN PICTURES

Travel

arrive

buy a guidebook

buy souvenirs

come back home

get off a bus

get on a train

have adventures

meet people

pack a suitcase

plan a journey

send postcards

set off

Extreme Adjectives

big / enormous

small / tiny

good / amazing

bad / awful

frightening / terrifying

tired / exhausted

happy / delighted

cold / freezing

hot / boiling

GRAMMAR GUIDE

Present Perfect and Simple Past

- we use the present perfect to talk about experiences in the past when we don't know or don't mention the exact time
  They **have been** to the USA.
- we never use the present perfect for something that happened at a specific time in the past, we use the simple past in this case
  We **went** to the movies **last Saturday**.
- we use the simple past to talk about completed actions at a definite time in the past
  They **went** to the USA in 2009.
- we use the present perfect to ask questions about experiences in the past
  Have you ever **been** to the USA?
- we use simple past questions to ask for more information about the experience
  When **did** you **go** to the USA?

time expressions	
present perfect	**simple past**
this week	yesterday
in the last week	last year
never	when I was young
recently	in 2009

Quantity and Uncountable Nouns

	countable nouns	uncountable nouns
+	He had **a lot of** apples. He had **some / a few** apples.	He had **a lot of** money. He had **some / a little** money.
–	He didn't have **many** apples. He didn't have **any** apples.	He didn't have **much** money. He didn't have **any** money.
?	How **many** apples did he have? Did he have **any** apples? Yes, he did. / No, he didn't.	How **much** money did he have? Did he have **any** money? Yes, he did. / No, he didn't.

uncountable nouns	
food	music
fruit	rice
information	space
milk	tea
money	water

- we use *some, any, a lot of, a few, a little, much* and *many* to talk about quantities of things
- we use *a lot of* with plural countable nouns and uncountable nouns to talk about a large quantity
  They eat **a lot of** fruit and vegetables.
- we use *some* in affirmative sentences with plural countable nouns and uncountable nouns to talk about a medium quantity
  All students will need to bring **some** warm clothes.
- we use *a few* in affirmative sentences with plural countable nouns to talk about a small quantity
  Please pack **a few** extra socks as the camp is cold at night.
- we use *a little* in affirmative sentences with uncountable nouns to talk about a small quantity
  You can bring **a little** money.
- we use *many* in negative sentences with plural countable nouns to talk about a small quantity
  I don't have **many** friends.
- we use *much* in negative sentences with uncountable nouns to talk about a small quantity
  She doesn't have **much** time.
- we use *any* in negative sentences with plural countable nouns and uncountable nouns to talk about zero quantity
  Students don't need to bring **any** food.
- we use *How many ...?* with plural countable nouns and *How much ...?* with uncountable nouns to ask questions about quantity
  How many friends do you have?
  How much fruit have you eaten today?

PROGRESS CHECK

Travel

1 Complete the sentences with the words in the box.

adventures	home	journey
postcard	souvenir	suitcase

a You haven't packed your __________. You're going to be late!

b My mom bought me a __________ T-shirt in Venice.

c Paul sent me a __________ from Australia.

d I planned a __________ with my guidebook.

e Lucy had lots of __________ when she went to Japan.

f I had such a great vacation that I didn't want to come back __________!

Extreme Adjectives

2 Match adjectives a-f with extreme adjectives 1-6.

a	☐ big	1	awful
b	☐ small	2	enormous
c	☐ cold	3	exhausted
d	☐ tired	4	amazing
e	☐ good	5	tiny
f	☐ bad	6	freezing

Review: Present Perfect and Simple Past

3 Complete the sentences with the present perfect or simple past form of the verbs in parentheses.

a __________ you __________ (be) to Tunisia?

Yes, I have. I __________ (go) there in 2012. It was great.

b __________ you ever __________ (read) a Harry Potter book?

Yes, I have. I __________ (not like) it.

c __________ you __________ (send) your dad a postcard?

Yes. I __________ (send) it yesterday.

d __________ your brother __________ (go) to Australia?

Yes, he has. He __________ (set off) two days ago.

Review: Quantity and Uncountable Nouns

4 Choose the correct words.

a I haven't packed **any / much** socks.

b Nick's bought **much / a lot of** souvenirs.

c I don't have **many / much** time.

d Did you meet **many / much** people while you were traveling?

e I only spent **a little / a few** money on vacation.

Grammar Buildup 2

1 2 3 4 5 6 7 8

5 Choose the correct answers.

Alice **a** _____ to France, Mark?
Mark Yes, I have. It's **b** _____ country I've ever been to.
Alice When **c** _____?
Mark Two years ago.
Alice Did you eat **d** _____ snails?
Mark Yes, I did. They were awful. I **e** _____ them.
Alice And did you buy **f** _____ souvenirs?
Mark No, they were **g** _____ expensive. So, have you ever visited Paris?
Alice No, I've never been abroad.

a **1** Do you go **2** Did you go **3** Have you ever been

b **1** better **2** the best **3** best

c **1** did you go **2** have you gone **3** were you going

d **1** much **2** any **3** a little

e **1** didn't like **2** haven't liked **3** am not liking

f **1** any **2** much **3** a little

g **1** enough **2** too **3** not enough

Review 1

VOCABULARY GRAMMAR

Start

1

No way I'm going out!
It's __________ out there.

2

It didn't take long for me to
______________ when I moved to France.

8

Last night I ____________
flying tied to balloons.

7

If you go to the Andes, don't forget to visit the
local shops to ____________.

9

We had breakfast and ________ very early
in the morning to ride the forest trail.

10

Will had to ____________ because his family
moved to the other side of the city.

15

Alexis has just heard she was admitted
to college. She's __________!

Finish

3

_________ that train now, because it leaves in five minutes!

4

She has gotten married, moved to a new house and finally ___________.

6

My cousins took a ___________ to study cooking and hike the Italian Alps.

5

This *Little Prince* miniature is so cute! The pieces are very delicate and _________.

11

My aunt always rolls her clothes when she _________ her suitcase.

12

My friend _____________ her team's performance in the championship.

14

Lots of students _____________ the protest against the closing of public schools.

13

Laura is ___________. She's studied for hours with no break.

Review 1

VOCABULARY

GRAMMAR

Simple Past and *used to*

1 Complete the sentences using the verbs in parentheses. Use the simple past affirmative and negative.

Sammy *didn't make* (not make) friends at school.

a Jayden ___________ (get) into trouble with his teacher again.

b We ___________ (not win) first prize in the competition.

c My mom ___________ (take) a gap year before she went to college.

d My cousin ___________ (study) math at college.

e She ___________ out of college when she failed all her exams.

2 Complete the sentences using the simple past or *used to*.

I *used to sit* next to my cousin in class but now I sit next to Harry.

a Now my uncle works in Philadelphia, but he ___________ in Georgetown before that.

b I usually have milk for breakfast but yesterday I ___________ hot chocolate.

c My mom never watches TV, but when she was younger she ___________ TV every day.

d You never ___________ angry but now you often get angry.

3 Write questions using the simple past or *used to*.

Justin Bieber / get in trouble / when he was younger ?
Did Justin Bieber use to get in trouble when he was younger?

a Kirsten / buy a guidebook / when she was in France ?
____

b your parents / buy souvenirs / when traveling ?
____

c Viola Davis / drop out of / college ?
____

d Tom / get off the bus / in Boynton or Delrey beach ?
____

Subject and Object Questions

4 Are these questions subject or object questions?

Where did you go for vacation? *object*

a Who cooked dinner yesterday? ___________

b Who did you see last night? ___________

c Why did he drop out of college? ___________

d Who ate all the chocolate? ___________

e What did Jeremy say? ___________

5 Match the questions with the answers.

a ☐ Who called you?

b ☐ Who did you call?

c ☐ Who wrote Romeo and Juliet?

d ☐ What did William Shakespeare write?

1 William Shakespeare wrote Romeo and Juliet.

2 I called my friend.

3 He wrote about 38 plays, including Romeo and Juliet.

4 My friend called me.

VOCABULARY

GRAMMAR

Present Perfect and Simple Past

6 Underline the correct words.

My parents love having adventures, so every year we go traveling. We **'ve seen / saw** some amazing places so far. We **a 've been / went** to Africa, Australia and South America, and last summer we **b 've stayed / stayed** in the Arctic for three weeks! We **c haven't stayed / didn't stay** in a hotel; we went camping!

7 Complete the sentences with the present perfect or the simple past form of the verbs in parentheses.

We ___bought___ (buy) a guidebook when we were in the museum.

a That man ____________ (get) on the train ten minutes ago.

b We____________ (be) on the bus for six hours now.

c 'How ____________ you ____________ (feel) when you were at the top of the mountain?'

'Exhausted!'

d I ____________ (not travel) much.

8 Complete the dialogue with the present perfect or the simple past form of the verbs in parentheses.

Anna ___Have___ you ever ___seen___ (see) one of the natural wonders of the world?

Ben Yes, I have. I **a** ____________ (visit) the Grand Canyon.

Anna Really? When **b** ____________ you ____________ (go) there?

Ben I **c** ____________ (go) last year when I was visiting my aunt and uncle in Las Vegas. They **d** ____________ (live) there for two years.

Anna What was it like?

Ben It was amazing. It's the best experience I **e** ____________ ever ____________ (have). I **f** ____________ (take) hundreds of pictures when I was there!

Quantity and Uncountable Nouns

9 Complete the sentences with *some*, *any*, *much* or *many*.

How ___many___ different countries have you been to?

a He didn't send ________ messages from New York – not one!

b I have ________ amazing pictures from my trip.

c We didn't buy ________ souvenirs – just one or two.

d How ________ food do you have in the suitcase?

e They don't have ________ money – only a few dollars each.

10 Complete the pairs of sentences with the correct words.

much / many

There isn't ___much___ to do in the evenings.

There aren't ___many___ things to do in the town.

few / a little

a I have ________ money.

b I have ________ $10 bills in my wallet.

a lot of / many

c There aren't ________ new teachers at the school.

d There are ________ new students.

3 The World around Us

1

2

3

4

VOCABULARY 1

Saving Environmental Resources

1 26 Look up the meaning of the phrases in the box in a dictionary. Then listen and repeat.

compost food scraps · install solar panels · insulate windows · mend old clothes · recycle packaging · ride a bike · save water · share car journeys · travel by public transportation · turn off lights · use rechargeable batteries

2 Write the phrases from the box in activity 1 that correspond to pictures 1-4.

1 ______________________

2 ______________________

3 ______________________

4 ______________________

3 Complete the quiz with phrases from activity 1. Then answer the questions.

QUIZ!

A Sharing ___*car journeys*___ is cheaper than having your own car. How much money can you save every year?

1 $50 **2** $2,000 **3** $3,000

B Which type of packaging is it most difficult to ______________?

1 plastic **2** paper **3** aluminum

C How many people ______________ to work every day in New York?

1 200 **2** 50,000 **3** 1 million

D Installing ______________ is an environmentally friendly way to generate energy. How many square meters of them are there in the world?

1 4 million **2** 90 million **3** 180 million

READING 1

1 Do you think it's possible to live trash-free? Why (not)?

____

A Life without Trash

How much trash do you throw away every day? Go on, be honest! If you're like most people, then you probably don't recycle that much. But could you imagine not producing any trash at all? Impossible? The Reid family – Michael and his wife Amanda and their daughter Natalie (14) and son Ryan (10) – decided to prove it was possible.

Like most people, the Reids didn't use to recycle much. Then, last January they decided to go trash-free for a year. Since then, they've reduced their waste to a minimum and Natalie is posting pictures and videos on Instagram to share their experience.

They've recycled as much as possible for the past few months. The town's garbage service collects paper, cans and plastic bottles and the Reids take glass, aluminum and cartons to a drop-off location. They compost vegetable waste, too. They've started growing a lot of their own fruits and vegetables. They've learned new skills, too – Natalie now makes her own soap, toothpaste and cheese.

Michael and Amanda have just taken a course to learn about repurposing things, or making new things from old items. Michael's already made a lamp from pieces of old metal and Amanda is making a chair for her bedroom from a bike. They've also started mending their old clothes instead of buying new ones.

'Getting new things is complicated,' explains Ryan. 'All my friends buy new cell phones, and electronic gadgets, but they all have a lot of packaging.' Both Natalie and Ryan now download all their music and movies from the internet and they're members of Freecycle.* 'I got my cell phone from there,' says Natalie. 'It's really cool. I also swap computer games with my friends. It's a good idea because we all have fun and we spend less.' For Ryan the hardest thing was not eating fast food. 'My friends go to burger joints a lot, but fast food has so much packaging!' Both the kids think it's possible to live a greener life and still have fun. 'With a bit of planning, you can do it,' they say.

The Reids are optimistic about the future. Since they started on January 6th, they've reduced their trash dramatically. They only have one small box of garbage. 'I think we're going to continue even after the year finishes,' says Michael. 'We're making a difference and that's a fabulous feeling.'

*Freecycle = an online organization where people offer things they don't use anymore to other members.

Amanda in the Reids' vegetable garden. The Reids have started growing their own fruits and vegetables.

2 🔊 27 Read and listen. Put the information in the order that it appears in the text.

a ☐ Natalie got her cell phone from Freecycle.

b ☐ Natalie makes her own soap.

c ☐ The Reids went trash-free.

d ☐ The family compost vegetable waste.

e ☐ They only have one box of garbage.

3 What kind of text is it?

a a human interest feature

b a tabloid article

c a letter to the editor

4 Read the text again. Then write T for *true* or F for *false*. Correct the false sentences.

a ☐ Natalie is writing a diary about their experience.

____

b ☐ The town's garbage service collects paper, cans and plastic bottles.

____

c ☐ Michael has made a table from old metal.

____

d ☐ Ryan goes to burger joints.

____

e ☐ They think they'll continue the project.

____

GRAMMAR 1

Review: Present Perfect + *for, since, how long*

1 Read the sentences below. Write (P) if the sentence indicates the period of time of an action; (PT) if the sentence describes an action from one point in time until the present; and (AT) if it asks about the amount of time of an action.

a ☐ How long have the Reids lived trash-free?

b ☐ They've reduced their garbage to a minimum since last year.

c ☐ They've recycled as much as possible for the past few months.

2 Look at the chart below. Check (✓) the correct information.

present perfect + *for, since, how long ...?*
They'**ve recycled** as much as possible **for** the past few months.
Since January, they **have reduced** their garbage dramatically.
How long have they **lived** trash-free?

a *How long + present perfect* asks about:
- ☐ the duration of a state or an activity.
- ☐ when in the past something happened.

b The *present perfect* with *since* or *for* talks about:
- ☐ a situation that started and finished in the past.
- ☐ a situation that started in the past and is still going on in the present.

c The *present perfect + for* talks about:
- ☐ a period of time.
- ☐ a point in past time.

d The *present perfect + since* talks about:
- ☐ a period of time.
- ☐ a point in past time.

TIP

We can also use *since* with the simple past.
I've learned a lot since I started this course.
Since I left school, I've worked in an office.

3 Write questions for the answers below. Use *how long* + present perfect.

a ______________________________
Jack has used solar panels in his house since he moved in.

b ______________________________
We have recycled packaging for two years now.

c ______________________________
The Reids have grown their own food since the beginning of this year.

4 Insert the time expressions from activity 3 in the chart below. Then include the following:

100 years 1995 20 minutes a long time I was born Monday nine o'clock three days

for	*since*
a period of time	**a point in time**

5 Complete the sentences with *for* or *since*. Underline the present perfect structure.

We've had our blog ___*for*___ six months.

a I have learned a lot ________ I started this project in May.

b They have grown their own vegetables ________ two years.

c Anna has tried to recycle more ________ last month.

d I've biked to school ________ January.

6 Look at the sentences in the chart below. Circle the verb tenses and underline the time expressions.

present perfect and simple past
a My neighbor recycled for three months last year.
b My neighbor has recycled for three years.
c How long have the Reids lived without trash?
d How long did the course about recycling take?

7 Notice that *how long* and *for* can be used with the present perfect and the simple past. Match the rules with the sentences from activity 6.

☐ *How long + present perfect* asks about the duration of an action that started in the past and continues up to the present.

☐ *How long + simple past* asks about the duration of an action in the past. This action is no longer happening.

☐ *for + present perfect* describes the amount of time an action which started in the past is still in course.

☐ *for + simple past* describes how long the action lasted in the past.

8 Complete the text with the correct form of the verbs in parentheses. Use the simple past or the present perfect.

My friend Suzy is really green. She ___*has recycled*___ (recycle) as much as possible for years. Last year she **a** ______________ (write) a great article for the school magazine about recycling. Since then, the students **b** ______________ (try) to recycle all the paper and plastic we use at school. We **c** ______________ (not throw away) any paper since then!
For the past year, Suzy **d** ______________ (buy) green presents for everyone. For my last birthday she **e** ______________ (buy) me some organic chocolate and a Fairtrade T-shirt. The chocolate **f** ______________ (be) delicious and I **g** ______________ (wear) the T-shirt often for a long time. Unfortunately, it **h** ______________ (shrink) when I **i** ______________ (wash) it last week.
Well, I'm going to try to be greener like Suzy! How about you? **j** ______________ (you / be) green-friendly this year?

9 **INTERFACE** Ask and answer questions about green habits. Use *how long*, *for* or *since*.

How long have you used recycled paper?

I've used it since the 5th grade.

GRAMMAR GUIDE page 54

LISTENING

Buy Nothing Day (BND)

1 Look at the pictures. What do you think Buy Nothing Day is?

a An event which highlights the environmental consequences of shopping.

b An event which encourages people to stop shopping completely.

2 28 Listen and check your answers.

3 28 Listen again. Then write T for *true* or F for *false*. Correct the false sentences.

a ☐ If you participate in Buy Nothing Day, you don't buy anything for 12 hours.
____

b ☐ Buy Nothing Day is on the same day as Black Friday.
____

c ☐ Buy Nothing Day is an international event that happens in many countries.
____

d ☐ At swap days, people sell items that they don't use.
____

e ☐ At workshops, people learned to make presents from old items.
____

f ☐ On Buy Nothing Day some participants write to supermarkets to ask them to use less packaging.
____

SPEAKING

Tech and the Environment

29 Judy and Marion are reading about ways tech can help the environment. Listen and complete the dialogue.

Marion, **a** ____________ the article about how technology can help the environment?

No, what does it say exactly?

It says that technological innovations may harm the environment if not used wisely, but they can certainly help solve some ecological problems we **b** ____________.

Very true... Think of renewable energy: recently, some eco-friendly tech advancements **c** ____________ place in the clean energy field, such as solar panels.

And the digital era? In the past ten years, at least, we **d** ____________ smartphones to take notes, companies **e** ____________ bills, newsletters, etc. over email; files have been stored in the cloud... less paper has been used!

... which means fewer trees **f** ____________ cut down and the result is: rainfall won't be affected and the atmosphere won't be unstable...

How about ridesharing companies which make it easier to get around without owning a car? Just call the service and off you go... as easy as that.

And vehicles are becoming more sustainable. Have you noticed the number of electric cars on the streets? It **g** ____________ over the last few years!

Hybrid cars **h** ____________ more common as well.

Yeah, lots of changes... for the better!

FUNCTIONAL LANGUAGE

Discussing Articles

Have you read / heard about...?
What does it say (exactly)?
It says...
Think...
How about...?
Have you noticed...?

Speaking Task

Write a dialogue between you and a friend.

Step 1

Think about different ways of helping the environment.

Turn faucet off while brushing your teeth.

Walk or bike to school.

Step 2

Write the information down to discuss it with your partner.

Step 3

In pairs, write your dialogue. Follow the conversation above as a guide.

Step 4

Take turns practicing your dialogue.

CULTURE

Electric Cars in Canada

Electric cars, or EVs, are a fast-growing alternative to gas everywhere in Canada as they run on electricity and have zero tailpipe emissions. These cars can be charged at public charging stations (some of them are free to use) or in the comfort of your home, after work, while doing something else. Many Canadians have reported saving a lot of money as the maintenance cost of these cars is low: the engine needs no lubrification, for instance. Studies in Canada show that EVs produce much fewer polluting emissions and can be a great way to reduce your carbon footprint. The Ministry of Environment and Climate Change in Canada points out that electric cars are becoming cheaper and a very good solution to fight climate change. The country plans to invest in more charging stations to make electric cars a more and more viable choice for Canadians. Supporting clean technology investments, in their view, will not only reduce GHG emissions but will also be fundamental for economic growth, the creation of new jobs and the possibility of taking Canadian businesses to the forefront of the clean-energy revolution.
However, some electric cars require an enormous charge to function properly. So, when purchasing an electric car, Canadians must consider all the options to not make an unwise investment which will show up on their monthly electricity bill. Some electric cars are still very expensive, especially because of the technology used to develop them.
In spite of that, using electricity to power an EV in Canada can reduce greenhouse-gas emissions a lot: around 60-90% per vehicle, making it competitive worldwide in the near future.

1 30 Read and listen to the information about *Electric Cars* and complete the chart below.

electric vehicles (EV) in Canada	
advantages	**disadvantages**

2 How popular are electric cars in your country?

____

____

3 What is being done in your country to produce clean and green energy? Share your findings with your friends.

____

____

VOCABULARY 2

Prefixes

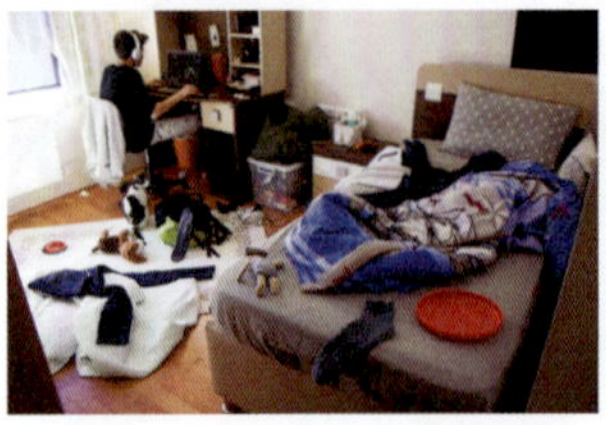

I need to reorganize!

I think I misunderstood.

I've overeaten!

Oh no! It's undercooked!

1 Look at the pictures. Then match the prefixes to the meanings.

a re-	☐ do something to excess
b mis-	☐ do something again
c over-	☐ do something less than necessary
d under-	☐ do something incorrectly

2 Look at the verbs in the box. Use your dictionary to check the meaning of any unknown words.

misinform misplace misunderstand
overcrowd overeat overpopulate recycle
reorganize replace replay undercook
underestimate underpay underuse

3 🔊 31 Listen and repeat.

4 Underline the correct words to complete the sentences

a The radio is broken. We need to **replace / misplace** it.

b There were too many people at the store, it was **overpopulated / overcrowded**.

c I have **replaced / misplaced** my bag. I can't find it anywhere.

d Don't **underestimate / misinform** Ellen, she's more intelligent than she appears to be.

READING 2

1 Look at the picture and the title of the text. What do you think this structure is for?

a Providing more places to live.

b Producing food for city inhabitants.

Feeding Our Cities

Our cities are overcrowded places. They are ecological nightmares because they use huge amounts of resources. Nowadays, more people live in cities than in the country, so one of the biggest problems is providing food. As food isn't grown in cities, it must be transported over long distances. Scientists have been aware of the problem for years, but they still haven't found a solution.

Professor Dickson Despommier, of Columbia University in the USA, is convinced that farms in skyscrapers could be the solution. In many cities, people have already built vertical gardens – gardens that grow up walls. Despommier's idea takes this one step further. The idea would be to replace traditional skyscrapers with special skyscrapers that contain farms. The farms would produce crops, chicken and fish in a controlled environment using existing technology. Not only that, they could recycle the water that people use. Solar power could provide all the heat and electricity.

This means that everyone in cities could get enough food and safe, clean water. Vertical farms could also be built in countries that don't have a lot of room for agriculture, such as Iceland, and countries with big populations such as India and China.

Despommier has designed a prototype, but he hasn't been able to build a vertical farm yet. He is sure his idea would be successful. He believes that at the moment technology is underused and we could make our cities more environmentally friendly and greener places to live with very little effort. It would surely be a mistake not to try.

2 🔊 32 Read and listen. Check your answer.

3 Read the text again and answer the questions.

a Do more people live in cities or in the country?

______

b Why does food have to be transported to cities?

______

c What does Despommier think is the solution?

______

d What things could the farms produce?

______

e Where would the heat and electricity for these farms come from?

______

GRAMMAR 2

Review: Present Perfect + *still, yet, already, just*

1 Look at the sentences in the chart. Underline the correct words to complete the rules below.

present perfect + *still, yet, already, just*
In many cities, people have **already** built vertical gardens.
Despommier has designed a prototype, but he hasn't been able to build a vertical farm **yet**.
Unfortunately, he **still** hasn't built the vertical farm.
Have scientists found a solution to the problem **yet**?
Despommier has **just** had a great idea which he plans to put into practice in no time!

a We use **yet / already** in positive sentences. It goes before the main verb.

b We use **yet / already** in negative sentences and questions. It always goes at the end of the sentence.

c We use **still / already** in negative sentences. It goes before the auxiliary verb.

d We use **just / still** between the auxiliary and the main verb. It means 'a short time ago.'

e We use **yet / just** to talk about something expected to happen. It means 'any time until now.'

f We use **already / still** to talk about something that hasn't happened / finished.

g We use **already / still** to talk about something that happened before we expected.

2 Complete the sentences below with *still, yet, already, just.*

a We have ______ taken 50 kilos of glass for recycling this year.

b Have you built the vertical garden ______?

c Peter ______ hasn't decided what to do with all that garbage.

d They haven't come to a decision ______. That should happen soon.

e They have ______ talked to the mayor about the Food Empowerment Project. Five minutes ago, in fact.

3 Look at Jack's list and write questions. Then answer the questions using the words in parentheses.

Has he joined Freecycle yet?

(already) *Yes, he has already joined Freecycle.*

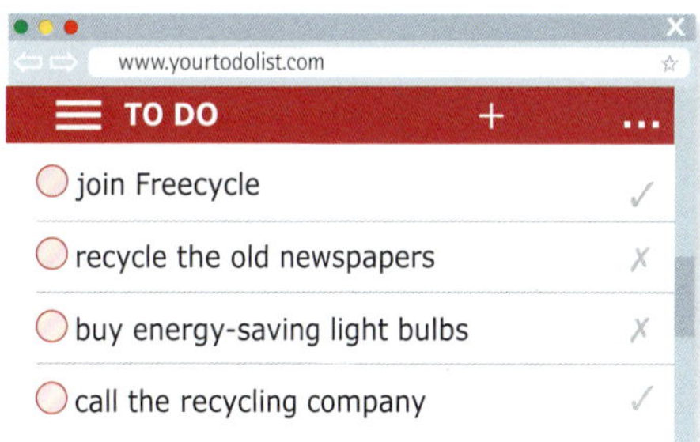

a ______

(still) ______

b ______

(yet) ______

c ______

(already) ______

TIP

Use the present perfect to ask for new information:
***Have** you **talked** to your teacher about the solar panel project yet?*
Use the simple past to mention when the action occurred in the past:
*Yes, I've already talked to him. We **discussed** it last week.*

GRAMMAR GUIDE page 54

CLIL

ART

Contemporary Protest Songs

Folk music is the traditional music of a country, region or community. Traditional folk music is played on local instruments, such as the bagpipes in Scotland or the sitar in India. However, in the 1960s, so-called 'contemporary' folk singers like Bob Dylan, Joni Mitchell and Joan Baez appeared in the USA. These folk musicians played guitars and sang about personal subjects like love and marriage, or about more social and political concerns like war and work.

When Bob Dylan released the song 'Blowin' in the Wind' in 1963, it soon became the anthem for the very active American Civil Rights Movement and the anti-war demonstrations taking place in the USA at the time. In the song, Dylan asks questions about war, peace and freedom. He sings that the answers to all our questions are 'blowing in the wind.' But who can catch the wind to find the answer?

Bob Dylan and Joan Baez in London, May 1965.

Singer Joni Mitchell performing in 1970.

1 🔊 33 Read and listen. Answer the question.

What things does Bob Dylan ask about in his song 'Blowin' in the Wind'?

____

____

2 Read the questions and choose the correct answers.

a What did the folk singers mentioned in the article sing about?

1 love and politics

2 nature and the environment

b What instrument did these folk musicians play?

1 guitar

2 saxophone

c When was 'Blowin' in the Wind' released?

1 1943

2 1963

d What did this song become the anthem for?

1 The American Civil Rights Movement

2 The American Space Program

VOCABULARY IN PICTURES

The Environment

compost food scraps

install solar panels

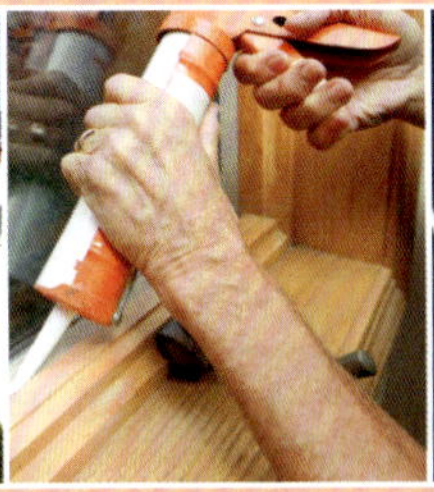
insulate windows

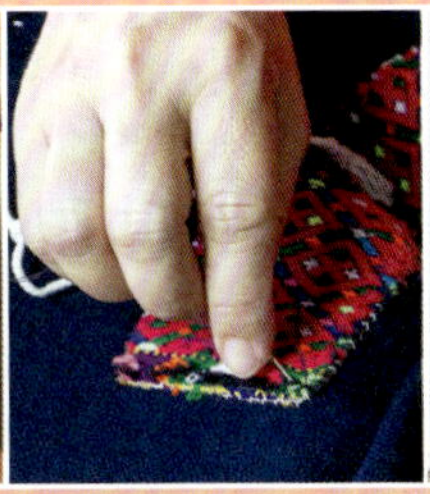
mend old clothes

recycle packaging

ride a bike

save water

share car journeys

travel by public transportation

turn off lights

use rechargeable batteries

Prefixes

misinform

misplace

misunderstand

overcrowd

overeat

overpopulate

recycle

reorganize

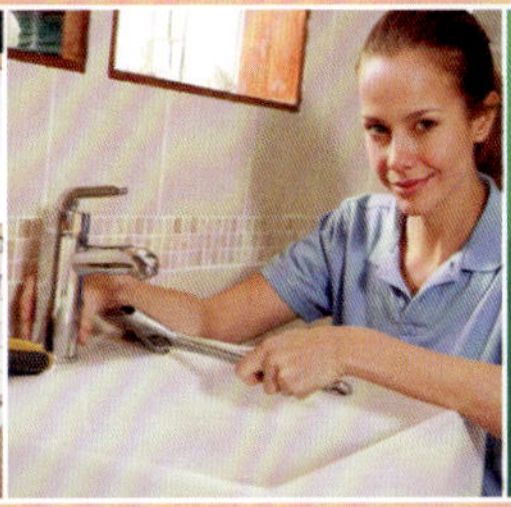
replace

replay

undercook

underestimate

underpay

underuse

GRAMMAR GUIDE

Present Perfect

+	I / You	**have ridden**	a bike.
	He / She / It	**has ridden**	
	We / You / They	**have ridden**	
–	I / You	**haven't ridden**	a bike.
	He / She / It	**hasn't ridden**	
	We / You / They	**haven't ridden**	
?	**Have** you **ridden** a bike? Yes, I **have**. No, I **haven't**.		

for, since, how long

How long have you lived in Boston?
I've lived in Boston **for** two years.
I've lived in Boston **since** 2015.

- we use *how long...?* to ask about the duration of an event or situation
- we use *for* with a period of time
- we use *since* with a point in time

for	since
five minutes	2015
five hours	5pm
three days	January
three weeks	this afternoon
a month	I was born
a year	Friday
a long time	last week

still, yet, already, just

I **still haven't recycled** the plastic bottles.
He **hasn't mended** his shoes **yet**.
Has he **mended** his shoes **yet**?
We**'ve already bought** rechargeable batteries.
Paul **has just left** the house.

- we use *still* and *yet* in negative sentences to talk about things we haven't done
- we also use *yet* in questions to ask if something has been done
- we use *just* to talk about something we've done a short time before the moment of speaking
- we use *already* in affirmative sentences to talk about things we have done

PROGRESS CHECK

Saving Environmental Resources

1 Match the columns to make expressions.

a compost	☐	water
b recycle	☐	car journeys
c save	☐	packaging
d mend	☐	food waste
e share	☐	solar panels
f install	☐	old clothes

Prefixes

2 Complete the sentences with the correct form of the verb and a suitable prefix.

a I didn't understand what he said – I ____________ (understand).

b I can't eat another thing! In fact, I've ____________ (eat).

c I want to organize this information again. I'm going to ____________ (organize) it tomorrow.

d Peter can't find his glasses. He has ____________ (place) them somewhere.

e They don't pay people enough. I think they ____________ (pay) them.

f I've lost my cell phone. I'll have to ____________ (place) it.

Review: Present Perfect + *for, since, how long*

3 Write questions for these answers. Use ***How long ...?***

a ______________________________

I have studied English for ten years.

b ______________________________

Mike has had his laptop for two weeks.

c ______________________________

Jim and Angela have lived here since 2016.

d ______________________________

I've wanted to be a biologist all my life.

4 Write sentences using the words in parentheses and *for* or *since*.

a I live here now. I moved here in 2013. (live / 2013)

____

b I am here now. I arrived at 9 o'clock. (be / 9 o'clock)

____

c We are here now. We arrived ten minutes ago. (be / ten minutes)

____

d Kate met Rachel five years ago. They are good friends now. (be / five years)

____

Review: Present Perfect + *still, yet, already, just*

5 Write sentences or questions.

a Sally / call / her father. (already)

____

b We / see / Paul. (just)

____

c Mark / not listen to / this song. (still)

____

d you / go to / the new burger joint ? (yet)

____

Grammar Buildup 3

1 2 3 4 5 6 7 8

6 Choose the correct answers.

The WWF has existed **a since / for** 1961 when a group of scientists, naturalists, businessmen and political leaders **b started / have started** the organization. The first office **c was / has been** in Switzerland. Over five million people have **d still / already** joined and together they **e achieved / have achieved** many things. It **f supports / is supporting** about 1,300 conservation and environmental projects around the world. In fact, **g for / since** 1985 WWF **h was investing / has invested** over $1.165 billion in more than 11,000 projects in 130 countries.

4 Good Friends

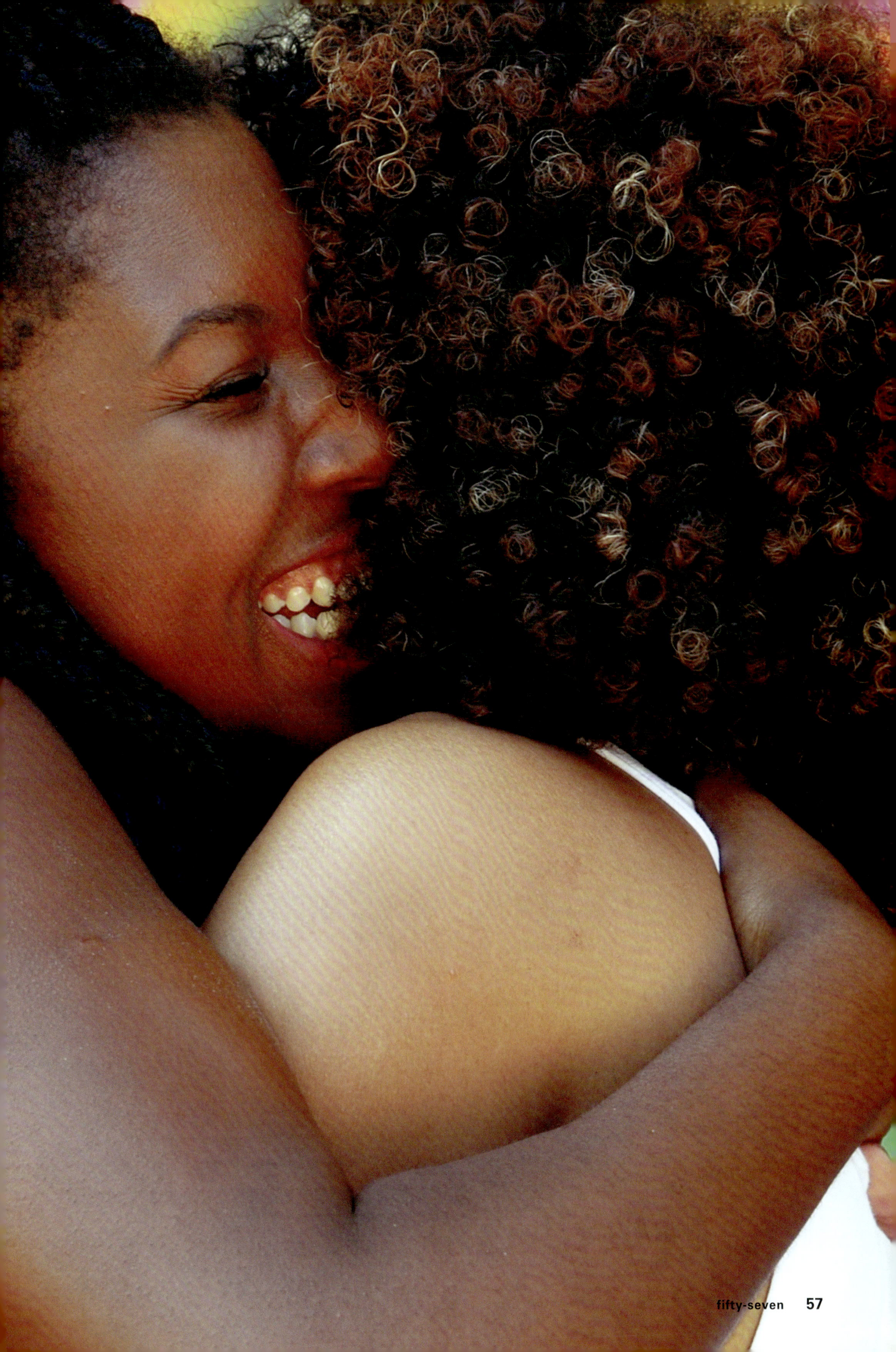

VOCABULARY 1

Making Friends

1 Match six of the phrases to the pictures. How do you say them in your language?

arrive early ☐ be late ☐ be polite ☐
be rude ☐ bring a present ☐
interrupt a conversation ☐ jump a line ☐
point at someone ☐ shake hands ☐
snap your fingers ☐
take off your shoes ☐ tell jokes ☐

2 🔊 34 Listen and repeat.

3 Which of the actions in activity 1 have you done today?

____

4 Choose the correct words.

a I **was late / interrupted their conversation / kissed my mother** because I woke up late.

b He asked me to **tell a joke / take off my shoes / jump the line** because they were dirty.

c I **arrived early / shook hands with / was rude to** Lionel Messi. He was really friendly.

d I **told a joke / took off my shoes / clicked my fingers**, but nobody laughed.

e He **was late / brought a present / arrived early**, so he helped us cook dinner.

f My teachers were talking so I couldn't **take off my shoes / be polite / interrupt their conversation**.

g Don't **tell a joke to / snap your fingers at / shake hands with** the waiter. It's very rude.

h He **jumped the line / told a joke / pointed at her** because he wanted to get on the bus first.

READING 1

1 🔊 35 Read and listen to the blog post. Match headings a-d with paragraphs 1-4.

a ☐ Chatting
b ☐ Visiting someone's house
c ☐ Having a meal
d ☐ Meeting people

2 Read the text again and answer the questions.

a What should you do when you meet someone for the first time in the UK?

____

b In which region is it mandatory to take our shoes off when we arrive?

____

c In which country is it acceptable to burp?

____

d Can you interrupt a conversation in the USA?

____

3 INTERFACE Work in pairs. What other cultural rules do you know?

> In India, you should only eat with your right hand.

CULTURAL FACT

In some countries it is polite to burp after a meal. Is it polite in your country?

Are you going on an exchange this year? Are you going to stay with a host family? Do you want to make new friends?

Then you need to know how to be polite, because being polite is different in different countries.

1 When you meet new people in Spain or France, you usually kiss women twice on the cheek. Men shake hands. People in the UK are more formal, so you should shake hands when you meet a stranger.

2 In the UK you don't have to bring a present, like flowers or chocolates, but people will think you are very polite if you do. In Germany, Austria and the UK you must not be late. It's very rude. In Mexico you should be late – it's normal. In the USA you must not arrive early. In central and eastern Europe and Scandinavia, you must take your shoes off when you arrive, so always wear clean socks.

3 In China you must never snap your fingers anywhere – it's very rude. However, it's OK to burp in China, in fact it's polite, but in most European countries you must not. In France you shouldn't tell jokes at dinner. The French take eating seriously.

4 In some countries it's OK to interrupt a conversation, but you shouldn't in the UK or the USA. You should wait until the other speakers have finished, especially if they are older than you.

Wherever you go, have fun. And remember: if you want to make friends, be polite!

GRAMMAR 1

Obligation, No Obligation, Prohibition, Advice

1 Complete the chart with the sentences below, according to what they express: obligation, no obligation, prohibition or advice.

- **a** You should shake hands when you meet a stranger.
- **b** You must not be late.
- **c** You must be polite everywhere.
- **d** In the UK you don't have to bring a present, like flowers or chocolates.

obligation	no obligation
prohibition	**advice**

2 Complete the rules below.

- **a** We use __________ to show **obligation**.
- **b** We use __________ to show there is **no obligation**.
- **c** We use __________ to show **prohibition**.
- **d** We use __________ to suggest something, to give **advice**.

3 Choose the correct words.

RULES FOR SUMMER CAMP

- **a** You **don't have to / must** be polite to the counselors.
- **b** You **must not / don't have to** talk in bed. People need to sleep.
- **c** You **must not / don't have to** make your bed. You can choose.
- **d** You **have to / don't have to** look after the key to your room.
- **e** You **must / must not** be late. Activities start at 8:30am.

4 Complete the dialogue using *must, have to, don't have to* or *must not.*

Jim: Can I go to the mall this weekend?
Mom: Yes, but there are some rules. You **a** __________ stay with your friends. You **b** __________ go anywhere on your own.
Jim: Right, Mom.
Mom: And you **c** __________ ride your bicycle into town, because there aren't any buses on Saturday.
Jim: Yes, Mom.
Mom: And you **d** __________ lose your keys or your new jacket.
Jim: Yes, Mom.
Mom: And you **e** __________ call me when you arrive.
Jim: OK, Mom.
Mom: But you **f** __________ buy me a present – only if you want to!
Jim: Thanks, Mom!

5 Underline the correct words to complete the text.

My Sister and My Best Friend

I'm really lucky because I **a shouldn't / don't have to** wait to talk to my best friend at school. My best friend is my older sister, Karen, and we share a bedroom. However, we do have some rules. For example, there are borrowing rules. I **b must not / don't have to** borrow her clothes and she **c has to / doesn't have to** ask me when she wants to use my smartphone. We also **d have to / should** follow other rules in our bedroom. We both **e must not / have to** keep our stuff tidy. We have one more rule. Because Karen's older than me, she **f doesn't have to / must not** go to bed when I do, but when she comes to bed, she **g doesn't have to / must not** wake me up if I'm asleep! Luckily she's really kind, so she never does. I **h should / don't have to** be more like her!

6 Look at the question in the chart. Check (✓) the correct information.

obligation – questions and short answers
Do I **have to** bring a present?
Yes, you do. / No, you don't.

In questions, *have to* is used instead of *must* and it indicates that …

☐ the obligation comes from somebody else and can't be changed.

☐ the obligation comes from somebody else but can be changed.

7 Write questions using *have to*.

young people / be / polite?

Do young people have to be polite?

a you / be home / before midnight?

____

b do / your homework / tonight?

____

c your dad / get up early / on Saturday mornings?

____

d visitors / bring presents / in your country?

____

8 **INTERFACE** Work in pairs. Ask and answer the questions in activity 7.

Do young people have to be polite?

TIP

For obligation (*have to* or *must*) in the past, always use *had to*.

I had to take off my shoes.

Did you have to do your homework?

9 Read about Joan and match the phrases.

When I was a child,…

a …I had to help mom with household chores.

b …I had to wake up at 6am to go to school.

c …I had to do my homework in the afternoon.

d …I had to walk my dog everyday.

☐ Now, I don't have a pet.

☐ Now, I live in my own apartment and do all the chores.

☐ Now, I wake up at 7am to go to work.

☐ Now, I have to work full-time and go to college in the evening.

GRAMMAR GUIDE page 68

LISTENING

My Gang

1 36 Listen and choose the correct words.

a Harry has **a best friend / a group of friends**.

b Maria has **a best friend / lots of different friends**.

2 36 Listen again and choose the correct answers.

a Harry and his friends like **going to parties / playing basketball / drawing and painting**.

b Alex is **approachable and sociable / funny / quiet and creative**.

c To join Harry's group of friends you must **love soccer / support Los Angeles FC / support LA Galaxy**.

d Harry and his friends like **dance music / hip hop / fast guitar music**.

e Maria has lots of friends from **secondary school / different places / primary school**.

f Marcus and Amelia are Maria's friends from **school / the beach / her neighborhood**.

g Maria believes friends **have to / should / don't have to** see each other every day.

h For Maria, it is important that her friends are **creative / funny / honest**.

3 **CLASS VOTE** Is it important that your friends like the same things as you?

SPEAKING

Friendship Survey

37 Mariah and her friend Emma are doing an online survey about friendship. Listen and complete the dialogue.

What about doing this survey about friendship, Emma? Let's see how much **a** __________ each other!

Ok, first question!

Do you think a friend **b** __________ always judge you?

Well, I think a real friend **c** __________ listen to you and give you support whenever necessary. After all, everybody makes mistakes.

What about this one: Does a friend **d** __________ tell you the truth even when it's hard for you to hear?

I think the truth is always better than a lie, but you **e** __________ choose your words carefully not to offend your friend. Real friendship **f** __________ about one person being the star and the other the servant.

I totally agree!

Look at this! They say here real friends **g** __________ check in with one another.

My mom always says friends are like plants. They have to be watered...

Very true... that's why we are bffs!

FUNCTIONAL LANGUAGE

Asking for / Giving Opinions

Do you think ... should / has to / must ...?
I think ... must not / must / should / shouldn't...
...say / says ....

Speaking Task

Write a dialogue between you and a friend.

Step 1

Think about online friendship or making friends abroad.

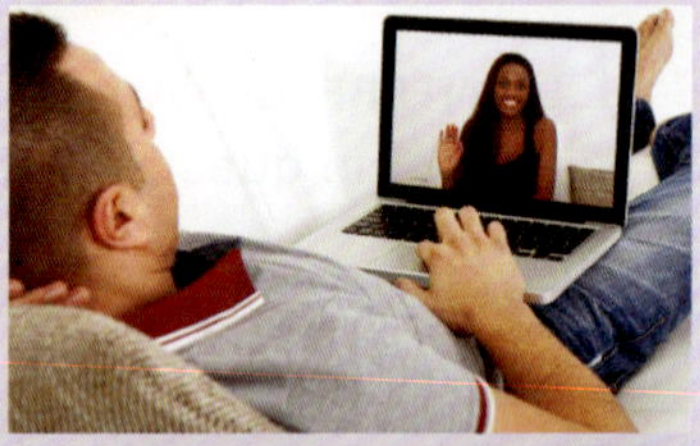

Step 2

Write about what should / must be done to maintain friendship ties in such contexts.

Step 3

In pairs: write your dialogue. Follow the conversation above as a guide.

Step 4

Take turns practicing your dialogue.

CULTURE

Being Friendly or Being Friends?

That is a tough question to answer, depending on where you are from. Western Indians believe real friends should be there for one another, for better or for worse. You will never be alone, you will have at least 10 offers from friends to join you in anything you do. Eventually, you will understand that you must go to your coleague's son's 1st birthday or his or her mother-in-law's 70th birthday. You must find no excuses not to join them for lunch or chai even after having just had a big meal (you don't have to call in advance) and you have to try to help your friend's brother's niece get a job wherever you work.

Something you shouldn't expect from your Indian friends is the use of 'please' and 'thank you.' For them, doing so means you are treating them as a business acquaintance, which is something they dislike. After all, you are friends! You shouldn't feel they are not treating you well because they do not use the so called 'magic words' of Western etiquette. The expectations friends have about one another do not rest only on the small things. Should you have an emergency, Indians feel it's quite appropriate to order you around. It may sound inconvenient, but, for them, that is loyalty. Although our culture may affect the way we see the world, it is fundamental to learn to separate the wheat from the chaff. In this sense, Indians are kind, empathetic, welcoming, passionate and extremely giving people, that is, friends.

1 38 Read and listen to the text. Then write T for *true* or F for *false*.

a ☐ Western Indians think friends don't have to be there for one another.

b ☐ In India, you are invited to lots of social gatherings.

c ☐ Indians use 'please' and 'thank you' all the time, especially among friends.

d ☐ In India, the expectations friends have about one another are very high.

e ☐ Indians are kind, empathetic, welcoming, passionate and extremely giving people.

2 What is it like to 'be friends' in your country?

____

____

____

____

3 What do you think about saying 'please' and 'thank you' between friends? Do you feel it is necessary? Why (not)?

____

____

____

____

VOCABULARY 2

Verb and Noun Collocations

1

2

3

4

5

1 Match the verbs in the box with the pictures.

give advice ☐	give presents ☐
have an argument ☐	have fun ☐
receive advice ☐	receive presents ☐
spend money ☐	spend time ☐
tell lies ☐	tell the truth ☐

2 39 Listen and repeat.

3 Choose the correct words.

a I love spending **money on / time with** my neighbor. We always have **an argument / fun**.

b I've tried to give my sister **presents / advice**, but she never listens to me.

c My cousin always tells me **the truth / lies**. She's extremely honest.

d John spent a lot of **money / time** on my birthday present. He's very generous.

e My brother told me **a lie / the truth** last night and we had a terrible **fun / argument**.

f He got a great **advice / present** from his uncle – a leather jacket.

4 Complete the sentences with verbs from activity 1.

Do you ever ___*give*___ advice to your friends? What about?

a When did you last ________ an argument with a friend?

b Is it ever OK to ________ a lie?

c How much time do you ________ with your parents on the weekends?

d What presents did you ________ for your last birthday?

e What are you going to do to ________ fun this weekend?

5 INTERFACE Work in small groups. Ask and answer the questions in activity 4.

READING 2

1 40 Read and listen to the questionnaire. Choose the best title.

a Friends or Family – What's More Important?

b You Must Not Tell Lies

c Friends – What Would You Do?

2 Read the questionnaire again and choose the best answers for you.

3 INTERFACE Work in small groups. Compare your answers. Do boys and girls think the same?

Questionnaire

a If you wanted to make friends with a new student in class, would you …

1 give him / her a present?

2 ask him / her to join in your study group?

3 ask a friend to talk to him / her?

b If it were your best friend's birthday, would you …

1 do nothing?

2 give her / him a present?

3 make her / him a cake?

c If you didn't like your friend's brother / sister, would you …

1 do nothing, because they're family?

2 tell your friend the truth?

3 ask your friend to stop spending time with his / her brother / sister?

d If your friend told you a lie, would you …

1 do nothing, because it's not important?

2 ask him / her to tell you the truth?

3 wait for him / her to apologize?

e If you had an argument with your best friend, would you …

1 apologize immediately?

2 start spending time with your other friends instead?

3 give him / her a present?

GRAMMAR 2

Second Conditional

1 Look at the following sentences. Circle the clause which indicates a *condition* and underline the one which indicates the *consequence* in case that condition becomes a fact.

a If I had an argument with a friend, I would apologize.

b If a friend told me a lie, I would be very upset.

c If I didn't like my friend's sister, I would avoid talking to her.

2 Complete the chart with the clauses. Then, choose the correct information as to the rules of the second conditional.

if clause	consequence

a The second conditional is used to express a particular condition in the future.

☐ There is NOT a real likelyhood for this condition to happen.

☐ There is a real likelyhood for this condition to happen.

b The structure of the second conditional is:

☐ if + simple present (condition) – will + verb base form (consequence) /

☐ if + simple past (condition) – would + verb base form (consequence).

3 Choose the correct words.

a What **would / did** you say if your best friend **were / would be** late to meet you?

b Robert **would go / went** to the movies with Mike if he **wouldn't / didn't** play soccer all the time.

c If he **told / would tell** me a lie, I **wouldn't be / wasn't** happy.

d **Would you tell / Did you tell** the truth if you **didn't / wouldn't** like a friend's sister?

4 Complete the sentences using the second conditional.

a I'm going to Paris this summer, but if I __________ (go) to London, I __________ (visit) my English friend.

b If Mike __________ (not have) a lot of homework, he __________ (go) out.

c If she __________ (have) more money, she __________ (buy) some new shoes.

d If we __________ (go) to the swimming pool instead of the movies, we __________ (have) more fun.

GRAMMAR GUIDE page 68

WRITING

A Formal Letter

1 41 Read and listen. Answer the questions.

a Who is Damien writing to?

____

____

b Why is he writing to them?

____

____

c What examples of formal language does he use?

____

____

Young Achievers
514 S. Magnolia St.
Orlando, FL 32806

123 6th St.
Melbourne, FL 32904
12 April

Dear Sir/Madam,
I am writing to nominate my friend Jemima Downside for a Young Achievers Award. Although Jemima is only 13, she has achieved a lot. Her father is ill and cannot work, so Jemima has to look after him while her mother is at work. She does the shopping and the cooking for her whole family as well as her homework every night. However, she never complains and is always happy and cheerful. Furthermore, Jemima has raised over $3,500 for Cancer Research by doing sponsored swims. In addition, she plays the drums in a local band and always gets excellent grades at school. Most importantly, however, Jemima is a fantastic friend. She is funny, thoughtful, loyal and trustworthy.
For all these reasons I think you should make Jemima a Young Achiever.
Yours faithfully,
Damien Rogers

LANGUAGE FOCUS

Linkers of Addition and Contrast

Although Jemima is only 13, she has achieved a lot.
However, she never complains.
Furthermore, Jemima has raised over $3,500.
In addition, she plays the drums **and** always gets excellent grades at school.

2 Look at the Language Focus box and complete the rules with the words in bold.

a We use __________ and __________ to show contrast.

b We use __________, __________ and __________ to show addition.

3 Rewrite the sentences using linkers.

a Tom is a bit eccentric. He's very approachable.

____

____

b She's very thoughtful. She's not very reliable.

____

____

c My sister is good at sports. She's very clever.

____

____

d John can speak five languages. He's now learning Arabic.

____

____

4 Write a formal letter (120-150 words) recommending a friend to be a Young Achiever.

Writing a Formal Letter

Step 1 > PLAN

Who do you want to recommend? What are his / her achievements? What is he / she like? Include other interesting details.

Step 2 > WRITE

Write a first draft. Divide your letter into four paragraphs. Use linkers.

Step 3 > CHECK

Check your work. Have you used linkers?

Step 4 > WRITE

Write your final copy and hand in your work.

VOCABULARY IN PICTURES

Making Friends

arrive early

be late

be polite

be rude

bring a present

snap your fingers

interrupt a conversation

jump a line

point at someone

shake hands

take off your shoes

tell jokes

Verb and Noun Collocations

give advice / receive advice

give presents / receive presents

have an argument

have fun

spend money

spend time

tell lies

tell the truth

GRAMMAR GUIDE

Obligation

I / You He / She / It We / You / They	**must** be polite. **have / has to** be polite.

- we use *must* and *have to* to show obligation
- in questions about obligation we only use *have to*
  Do I **have to** do my homework?

No Obligation

I / You	**don't have to** come.
He / She / It	**doesn't have to** come.
We / You / They	**don't have to** come.

- we use *don't have to* to show there is no obligation or that something isn't necessary
  She **doesn't have to** prepare dinner tonight.

Prohibition

I / You / He / She / It / We / You / They	**must not** be late.

- we use *must not* to show prohibition. It does not mean the same as *don't have to*
  You **must not** be late for school.

Advice

+	I / You	**should** go.
	He / She / It	
	We / You / They	
–	I / You	**shouldn't** go.
	He / She / It	
	We / You / They	
?	**Should** I / you **go**? Yes, I **should**. No, I **shouldn't**.	
	Should he / she / it **go**? Yes, he **should**. No, he **shouldn't**.	
	Should we / you / they **go**? Yes, we **should**. No, we **shouldn't**.	
?	**Do** I / you **have to** bring a present? Yes, I **do**. No, I **don't**.	
	Does he / she / it **have to** bring a present? Yes, he **does**. No, he **doesn't**.	
	Do we / you / they **have to** bring a present? Yes, we **do**. No, we **don't**.	

- we use *should / shouldn't* to give advice
  You **should** eat more fruit.

Second Conditional

if clause	consequence
If he told a lie,	what would you do?
If he told a lie,	I'd be angry.
consequence	***if* clause**
What would you do	if he told a lie?
I'd be angry	if he told a lie.

- we use the second conditional to talk about events in the present and future that are unlikely to happen
- to form second conditional sentences we use *if* + subject + simple past (for the situation), subject + *would / wouldn't* + infinitive without *to* (for the consequence)
- when the situation comes first, we use a comma
  If I **were** famous, I**'d** buy a big house.
- we don't use a comma if the consequence comes first
  Len **would be** sad **if** I **didn't tell** the truth.
- we form questions with (question word) + *would* + subject + infinitive without *to* + *if* + subject + simple past
  What **would** you **do if** you **had** an argument with your best friend?
- in the *if* clause, the verb *be* usually takes the form *were* for the first and the third persons
  If I **were** you, I wouldn't be rude to your friend.
- however, the form *was* is also used in everyday speech.
  If she **was** my friend, I would give her some advice.

PROGRESS CHECK

Making Friends

1 Complete the text with the correct form of the verbs in the box.

bring shake snap take tell off

When you meet your host family, remember this advice!

1 **a** __________ hands with the parents.

2 It's a good idea to **b** __________ a present for the mother of the family.

3 Look at what your exchange partner does. If he **c** __________ his shoes, you should, too.

4 It's OK to **d** __________ jokes to your host family.

5 When you're in a restaurant it is rude to **e** __________ your fingers at the waiter.

Verb and Noun Collocations

2 Match verbs a-e with nouns 1-5.

a	☐ give	1	an argument with / fun with
b	☐ tell	2	advice from / a present from
c	☐ spend	3	advice to / a present to
d	☐ receive	4	money on / time with
e	☐ have	5	lies to / the truth to

Obligation, No Obligation, Prohibition and Advice

3 Choose the correct words.

a A best friend **should / doesn't have to** always be honest and tell the truth.

b John **doesn't have to / must not** do any homework tonight. He did it all last night.

c I **have to / don't have to** call Jack. I talked to him at school today.

d You **have to / don't have to** keep Monica's secret. She thinks you're extremely honest.

Second Conditional

4 Write sentences using the second conditional.

you do / you saw your best friend stealing ?
What would you do if you saw your best friend stealing?

a you had an argument with your best friend / you apologize first ?
____

b Steve gave me a present / I / buy him lunch
____

c I / be very angry / my best friend weren't honest with me
____

d I were famous / I / still spend time with my friends
____

Grammar Buildup 4

1 2 3 4 5 6 7 8

5 Choose the correct answers.

Penny Hey, Mom says I can have a party.
Sian Great! You **a** _____ invite me. Please!
Penny Of course! Who else should I invite?
Sian You **b** _____ invite Glyn. I really like him.
Penny But you **c** _____ Bob, too.
Sian No. Glyn's **d** _____ than Bob.
Penny OK. And I have to invite Clara because I went to her party.
Sian Oh yeah. I didn't go. I was **e** _____ sick.
Penny It was a great party. Really amazing!
Sian If it were my party, I **f** _____ Brian. He's really funny.
Penny I'd ask Brian if I **g** _____ him, but we've never met.
Sian When **h** _____ the party?
Penny In two weeks.

a	1 don't have to	2 should
b	1 have to	2 shouldn't
c	1 like	2 have liked
d	1 funnier	2 more funny
e	1 enough	2 too
f	1 'd invite	2 'll invite
g	1 know	2 knew
h	1 will you have	2 are you going to have

Review 2

VOCABULARY

GRAMMAR

Complete the sentences with the correct words. Then find them in the word search.

1 Some habits help us live in a more sustainable way, like mending ___________, for example.

2 Fake news are created to ___________ people. Always double-check information on reliable sources.

3 He's ___________ and now he's feeling stuffed.

4 If you want to live in a sustainable world, you should ___________ your trash.

5 If Anthony rode his ___________ to the office more often, he would improve his health.

6 A wise way to save the environment is traveling by ___________ transportation.

H	V	H	A	Q	T	J	Z	T	W	Y	V	X	D	K
K	N	W	L	Y	M	L	Y	W	P	L	B	L	L	V
U	V	Q	K	F	P	U	B	L	I	C	O	J	K	B
U	P	S	P	P	R	K	W	H	D	Q	W	U	I	M
N	E	Y	O	L	D	C	L	O	T	H	E	S	E	T
D	G	F	B	V	T	I	B	M	N	O	C	C	J	T
E	A	E	J	D	U	M	V	Y	W	V	D	N	V	Q
R	Y	L	A	G	R	J	B	Q	Y	Z	A	M	Y	I
C	M	I	S	I	N	F	O	R	M	W	R	X	T	J
O	X	G	E	Z	O	O	V	E	R	E	A	T	E	N
O	W	P	W	A	F	J	I	W	M	X	L	W	R	B
K	I	S	Q	B	F	J	B	P	M	N	C	N	R	M
E	R	M	Y	G	E	E	I	O	U	L	W	R	K	Q
D	V	P	F	I	K	G	K	F	P	P	G	S	F	S
L	R	E	C	Y	C	L	E	C	F	O	H	S	P	C

7 To energy, we must ___________ the lights of a room when we're not there.

8 Some dishes at this restaurant have ___________ meat. Do you like it or do you prefer eating something different?

9 The little girl was singing out loud inside the plane, but she didn't mean to be __________ to the passenger.

10 Sandra had an __________ with Jane, but later they apologized to each other.

11 The student raised his hand and the teacher __________ at him.

12 You should always __________ hands with your interviewer. It's __________.

13 Nathalie prefers to __________ her allowance money on books and games.

14 If you go to Japan, take off your __________ before entering someone's house.

E H P U I Q U M R X J M H L N
J O K E S I T N U G N P F U A
S J R R A A S N D I O O G Q S
P J W F P S G Y E J Y L F E T
O X K G D O T V L A D I Y L V
I R D V M T V D Z C L T G P M
N A K D D U Q W P R M E U I A
T J C C U Q W S X T F Q I C X
E I B S I W X I D I A Z T N Z
D V Y H T J Y M E M A R N Y Y
X I T A R G U M E N T I K Q T
U J S K X A R S P E N D O X R
K H Q E B R H T B U L O Y U J
N G H D Z I D X F D Q A Q X C
O Y N S H O E S O F U R X O Z

15 Robert told a __________ to his host father, and both of them laughed a lot.

Review 2

VOCABULARY

GRAMMAR

Present Perfect + *for, since, how long*

1 Complete the chart with the time expressions in the box.

~~May 20th~~ ~~three years~~ weeks
several days the start of the month
we finished our exams yesterday
six hours 1995 a very long time

for	*since*
three years	*May 20th*

2 Write sentences using the present perfect and *for* or *since*.

a Bob (not have) a day off / three months.

b I (know) my best friend / we were three years old.

c My soccer team (not win) a game / last year.

d Susan (not talk) to Melanie / two months.

3 Write questions with *How long* ...?

Paul / work / at this school ?
How long has Paul worked at this school?

a you / have / your jeans ?

b she / be / your English teacher ?

c they / live / in France ?

d he / play / the violin ?

4 Write answers to the questions in activity 3. Use *for* or *since* and the time expression in parentheses.

(six years)
He has worked at this school for six years.

a (last week)

b (about eight months)

c (three years)

d (six years old)

Present Perfect + *still, yet, already, just*

5 Rewrite the sentences using the words in parentheses.

I've done this exercise. (already)
I've already done this exercise.

a My friends haven't seen that new movie. (still)

b I've spoken to Liam. (just)

c Have you called your parents? (yet)

d I have bought you a birthday present. (already)

e It's one in the afternoon and you haven't gotten dressed. (still)

f My cousins have moved to a new house. (just)

VOCABULARY

GRAMMAR

Obligation, No Obligation, Prohibition, Advice

6 Read the sentences. Then write O for *obligation* or N for *no obligation*.

Class must start at 9 o'clock. [O]

a Do you have to wear a school uniform? [ ]

b Students don't have to have lunch in school. [ ]

c Sara doesn't have to walk to school. [ ]

d Ivy must wear glasses to drive. [ ]

7 Complete the sentences with *must not* or *shouldn't* and the verbs in the box.

feed forget play ~~point~~ touch

'Have you seen that tall man over there?' 'Anna, you *shouldn't point* at him. It's rude!'

a It's Patrick's birthday next week. We ______________ to send him a card.

b Jack is only six so he ______________ that video game. The age rating is 14.

c You ______________ animals at the zoo.

d Soccer players ______________ the ball with their hands.

8 Complete the sentences with *should* or *shouldn't* and the verbs in the box.

~~arrive~~ eat put switch off talk

You *should arrive* ten minutes before the movie starts. It's annoying when people are late.

a You ______________ your cell phone before the movie starts.

b You ______________ quietly.

c You ______________ loudly to your friends during the movie.

d You ______________ your feet on the seat in front of you.

Second Conditional

9 Underline the correct words.

If I didn't / **wouldn't** work hard, I **didn't** / wouldn't pass my exams.

a If he **played** / **'d play** a musical instrument, he **chose** / **'d choose** the saxophone.

b Where **did** / **would** you live if you **moved** / **'d move** to another country?

c My parents **were** / **would be** delighted if I **went** / **'d go** to college.

d If you **had** / **'d have** $10,000, what **did** / **would** you spend it on?

10 Complete the first half of the sentences with the simple past or *would* / *wouldn't* + infinitive. Then match the sentence halves.

a [4] I *'d be* (be) extremely rich

b [ ] What ______________ you ______________ (say)

c [ ] If we ______________ (have) an argument,

d [ ] If I ______________ (not know) where I was,

e [ ] My parents ______________ (complain)

1 if someone jumped the line you were in?

2 if they didn't like the food in a restaurant.

3 we wouldn't be happy.

4 if I won the lottery.

5 I'd ask for directions.

You've Got a Friend in Me!

- **In your opinion, what is friendship? What makes someone a good friend?**
- **Have you ever heard of the *International Day of Friendship?* What is it about?**

1 What does it mean to be a good friend? Write A for *always* and T for *try not to.* Share your ideas with your class.

a ☐ Share the conversation so that you are both a listener and a talker.
b ☐ Brag about what you have or what you have done.
c ☐ Be aware of others' feelings: think before you speak.
d ☐ Argue if your friend doesn't agree with you about something.
e ☐ Be prejudiced: make any negative comments about someone's religion, country, skin color, or physical appearance.
f ☐ Fight your friends' battles instead of helping them deal with their own problems.
g ☐ Talk about your friends without their permission.
h ☐ Try to understand people by thinking about things from their point of view.
i ☐ Use your manners: say 'please' and 'thank you.'
j ☐ Praise your friends when they do something well.
k ☐ Do things for your friends without keeping score of who's done the most favors.

2 What do these images have in common? Discuss your ideas with your friends. Then match them with the quotes below.

a

b

c

☐ "Love is the only force capable of transforming an enemy into a friend." – Martin Luther King, Jr.
☐ "Friendship is the hardest thing in the world to explain. It's not something you learn in school. But if you haven't learned the meaning of friendship, you really haven't learned anything." – Muhammad Ali
☐ "It's all about freedom." – Benjamin Zephaniah

3 Match the sentences.

The *International Day of Friendship* is a day designed to bring up friendship and bridge the gaps between races, colors, religions and other factors which keep humans from enjoying each others' company.

a The *International Day of Friendship* was proclaimed by the United Nations (UN) in 2011 …

b The UN encourages governments, groups and organizations to host …

c The date suggested by the UN is July 30th, but many countries celebrate it …

d Studies point out that individuals…

☐ events that promote dialogue, acceptance and understanding between people of different backgrounds.

☐ on the first Sunday of August.

☐ with the objective of building communities and helping move towards world peace.

☐ with stronger relationships live longer.

4 Friendship keeps the world going! Do you know how to say 'friend' in other languages? Write the 'friend' words in the box next to their respective languages.

ami *dost* *Freund* *péngyou*
priyatel *tomodachi* *vriend*

a Mandarin: ______________________

b Dutch: ______________________

c French: ______________________

d German: ______________________

e Hindi: ______________________

f Japanese: ______________________

g Russian: ______________________

Can you add more words to the list?

A Recipe for Friendship!

How about preparing a 'friendship recipe'? Follow the steps below.

Doing

1 Think of a name for your recipe which includes the words *friend* or *friendship*.

2 Write how long it will take to prepare the 'dish.' (*Preparation time: ...*)

3 Mention the number of servings the recipe will provide. (*Serves …*)

4 List the ingredients you will need and their respective quantities or proportions. (*You will need ...*)

- **Suggested ingredients to choose from:** happiness, kindness, sharing, helpfulness, laughter, compassion, listening, patience, sensitivity, support, forgiveness, trust, honesty, conversation, understanding, affection, hugs, respect
- **Suggested quantities:** a cup of …, 1 tbsp (tablespoon) of…, 2 tsp (tea spoon) of…, a pinch of…, a sprinkle of…, a liter of…, 50g of…, a bag of…

5 Write how to prepare the dish. (*Method* or *Directions*)

- **Suggested verbs:** put, add, mix, stir, blend, pour, use, finish, serve, warm, bake

6 Include a photograph of the 'finished dish.'

Presenting

7 Tell your classmates what you took into consideration when you wrote your friendship recipe.

8 Hang the recipes in the school halls or post it on a student-friendly social media with the hashtag **#friendshipday**

Reflecting

9 Do you think your concept of friendship has changed? How?

10 After all this reflection on friendship, can you name the **three** most important qualities of a friend?

5 Followers of Fashion

1

2

3

4

5

6

7

VOCABULARY 1

Style Adjectives

1 Use your dictionary to look up the meaning of the adjectives in the box. Which can you use to describe the pictures?

The sneakers are very sporty.

casual	colorful	comfortable	
conventional	fashionable	formal	
glamorous	impractical	loose	
old-fashioned	sporty	tight	trendy

1 ______________________

2 ______________________

3 ______________________

4 ______________________

5 ______________________

6 ______________________

7 ______________________

2 42 Listen and repeat.

3 Complete the sentences with words from the box.

a I don't like wearing boring black and brown clothes – I prefer __________ designs.

b Those plain leather shoes are very __________ – I prefer more unconventional designs.

c My dad isn't allowed to wear __________ clothes at work. His office is very formal, so he wears a suit.

d My sister always follows the latest fashions. She never wears anything __________!

e This skirt is too __________ – I need a smaller size.

4 Choose the correct words.

My aunt loves shoes. She has so many pairs, it's unbelievable. She buys new shoes every week. She goes to the gym every day, so she has lots of sneakers, which are all **a sporty / old-fashioned**. They're also very **b trendy / conventional** because she always buys the latest designs by famous brands. Her favorite shoes are the high heels she wears on Saturday nights – they're really **c casual / glamorous** but so **d sporty / impractical**. I tried them on and I couldn't walk! Finally, she has her work shoes. She's a businesswoman, so she wears very **e formal / cool** shoes. She has to stand up a lot at work, so her shoes are **f comfortable / uncomfortable** – they can't be too **g conventional / tight**. What does she do? She owns a shoe store, of course!

READING 1

1 Read the text quickly and choose the best title.

a A short history of shoes

b FASHIONABLE FEET!

c High heels are bad for you

Look at the people around you.
Now look at their feet. What type of shoes are they wearing? What do the shoes have in common? Color? Material? Design?

The basic design of shoes has not changed much since they were first invented. Most shoes have a sole on the bottom, a heel at the back and an upper, the piece of material that covers the foot. However, fashion designers have found many creative ways to make shoes look different.

Let's start with heels. They can be low or incredibly high. In the 1950s, Italian designers created a glamorous new shoe: the stiletto, which has a very thin pointed heel. Shoemakers around the world loved the design and stilettos are still popular today. The ultimate pair must be the 40.5cm high stilettos produced by LadyBWear in the UK. Heels don't have to be thin to look different though: one American designer has created huge heels filled with water and toy goldfish! Of course, Lady Gaga is famous for wearing the 'heelless shoes' made for her by Noritaka Tatehana of Tokyo. These shoes have a high sole but no heel, so they're very difficult to walk in.

Shoe designers have also had creative ideas for soles. Platform boots became trendy in the 1970s when lots of glam rock bands such as Kiss began to wear them. Recently, shoe designer Christian Louboutin famously decided to paint the soles of all his shoes bright red to make them instantly recognizable and extremely glamorous. Soles can also be made to look unusual. What about a pair of grass flip-flops? The grass is real and you have to water it!

Finally, designers can make the uppers fashionable. Sports brand Nike has produced shoes that look like human feet. Then there are sneakers that look like melting ice cream! But if you want something really original, some websites allow you to design your own shoes.

With all these creative fashion ideas for shoes, it's not surprising that people begin to collect them. Well-known shoe collectors include Madonna and Sarah Jessica Parker. But no one has a bigger shoe collection than the woman who owned around 3,000 pairs: Imelda Marcos, the wife of a former president of the Philippines. She had so many shoes that she even opened a shoe museum in Manila! Many of the shoes in the exhibitions have never even been worn – it would have taken her over seven years to wear all her shoes!

READING STRATEGY

Notice how texts are structured to identify their *genre*. This helps you access previous knowledge about similar texts to predict the content and make the reading process more meaningful.

2 How is the information organized in the text above?

a It consists of a title, extensive data and a deep analysis in formal language.

b It contains a headline, a lead, topics, and the language is relatively informal.

3 What text genre does it illustrate?

a a newspaper / magazine / blog article

b a scientific journal article

4 43 Read and listen to the text. Then write T for *true* or F for *false*. Correct the false sentences.

a ☐ Designers try to make shoes that are unusual.

______

b ☐ Stilettos have only recently become popular.

______

c ☐ Noritaka Tatehana makes shoes for Lady Gaga.

______

d ☐ Nike makes shoes that look like human hands.

______

5 Scan the text and answer the questions.

a What is an upper?

______

b How high are the world's highest stilettos?

______

c Why are Noritaka Tatehana's shoes difficult to walk in?

______

d Where can you design your own shoes?

______

e Why do people collect shoes?

______

GRAMMAR 1

Relative Pronouns

1 Read the sentences below. Write if the words in **bold** refer to people (P), things (T), locations (L) or time (TI). Then write the words they refer to.

[T] *the stiletto* In the 1950s, Italian designers created the stiletto, **which** has a very thin pointed heel.

a [ ] ______ Sports brand Nike has produced shoes **that** look like human feet.

b [ ] ______ No one has a bigger shoe collection than the woman **who** owned around 3,000 pairs.

c [ ] ______ Italy is the country **where** fashion is a must.

d [ ] ______ Trendsetters **that** wear heelless shoes find them difficult to walk in.

e [ ] ______ Platform boots became trendy in the 1970s **when** rock bands began to wear them.

2 Based on the rules below, complete the chart.

a Relative pronouns are used to connect sentences. They refer to nouns (people, places, things mentioned previously).

b When we talk about people we can use *who* or *that*.

c When we talk about things we can use *which* or *that*.

d When we talk about places / locations, we use *where*.

e When we talk about time, we use *when*.

people
The woman ______ lives in that house owns a shoe store.
things
Chinese factories produce a lot of clothes ______ are sold in Europe.
time
An engineer invented the bikini in 1946, ______ Americans were testing atom bombs in the Bikini Atoll.
place
Milan is a city ______ many glamorous shoes are made.

3 Choose the correct words.

a Noritaka Tatehana is the man **who / which** designs shoes for Lady Gaga.

b The 1950s is **that / when** stiletto shoes became fashionable.

c The jackets **which / when** my brother bought were really expensive.

d She's the girl **that / which** I met at the party.

e Where's the scarf **who / that** I lent you last night?

f San Francisco is **that / where** my cousins live.

4 Match the columns to make sentences.

a That's the store
b I'm the person
c New Year's was
d Is that the dress
e He's the man
f That's the dog

[ ] that cost you $100?
[ ] where I bought my suit.
[ ] which bit me.
[ ] when I last saw him.
[ ] who called you yesterday.
[ ] that emailed me last week.

5 Complete the sentences with *who, which, where* or *when*.

You've probably bought a T-shirt or some jeans from H&M, but how much do you know about the popular clothes store? Read on to find out more.

Erling Persson is the man *who* started the company. Västerås in Sweden is **a** ______ the first store opened. 1947 is **b** ______ Persson opened his first store. There are now over 160,000 employees **c** ______ work for the company. H&M employs 100 designers **d** ______ work on the clothes. 4,553 is the number of stores **e** ______ the company owns. The things **f** ______ the company sells include clothes, shoes and cosmetics.

TIP

- In informal language, we can omit *which*, *who* or *that* when the pronoun refers to the **object** of the sentence. ***The shoes they are wearing*** *have a basic design.* (Notice that the shoes are the **object** of the verb 'wear'; in this case, we don't need to use *that* or *which*.)
- *Which*, *who* or *that* can never be omitted when they refer to the **subject** of a sentence. *It was* ***Lady Gaga who / that first wore 'heelless shoes'.*** (In this case, Lady Gaga is the **subject** of the verb 'wear,' so *who / that* cannot be omitted.)
- *Whose* is used to indicate possession. *Boots* ***whose*** *platform soles became trendy in the 1970s can be seen in lots of different styles.*

6 Read the text about fashion for teens and underline the appropriate relative pronouns. X refers to omission of the pronoun.

If your teen doesn't like the clothes **a that / X** are perfect for them in your opinion, you are not alone. He or she is not the only adolescent **b which / who** thinks you don't have a clue about fashion. Don't worry! As teens grow, fashion is one of the ways **c X / where** they use to express their feelings and show how they see the world. Teens **d who / X** undergo 'style-change' are just trying to express themselves.

7 INTERFACE Work in pairs. Ask and answer the questions using relative pronouns.

What's a food that you really don't like?
What's the name of a person who makes you laugh?

GRAMMAR GUIDE page 88

LISTENING

A Famous Designer

1 Look at the pictures. Who is the woman in the picture on the left? What is her job?

____

2 44 Listen to the first part of the interview. Check your answers.

3 45 Listen to the second part of the interview and answer the questions.

a Where did she grow up?
  1 in London 2 near London

b What sort of school did she go to?
  1 an expensive private school
  2 the local state school

c When did she become interested in fashion?
  1 as a teenager 2 as a grown-up

d Where did she study fashion?
  1 in Paris 2 in London

e Who modelled at her first fashion show?
  1 Kate Moss 2 Claudia Schiffer

f When did she start working for Chloe?
  1 1997 2 2001

g Who did she design a wedding dress for in 2000?
  1 Kate Moss 2 Madonna

h Why doesn't she use leather or fur?
  1 because she is against animal cruelty
  2 because they are very expensive

SPEAKING

Prom Night

46 Nathalie and Jude are talking about what to wear to their high school prom. Listen and complete the dialogue.

Jude, what are you planning to wear to the prom?

Well, I haven't made up my mind yet... you know, it's an **a** ______________ I'll hopefully look back and always remember...

Yeah, it asks for a very special **b** ______________! After all, it's not an average **c** ______________ like birthdays or holiday seasons...

It's our special day, but I don't want to feel **d** ______________ or wishing I had chosen something different...

What about a lacy black slip **e** ______________?

Well, I personally don't like black... I think a floral dress is perfect for a summer or **f** ______________!

The dance will take place on the grass, so we must choose our **g** ______________ carefully... no stilettos!!!

Maybe a **h** ______________...

Good idea!

In short, a lightweight dress, not too **i** ______________, and comfortable clothes! Perfect!

FUNCTIONAL LANGUAGE

Talking about Outfits

What are you planning to wear...?
I haven't made up my mind yet...
It's a special occasion...
What about...?
I personally don't like...
I think...
Maybe...

Speaking Task

Write a dialogue between you and a friend.

Step 1

Choose a special occasion to talk about. Some ideas:

A wedding party

A rock concert

A friend's birthday party

Make notes about what to wear for the occasion / event.

Step 2

Write the information down to discuss it with your partner.

Step 3

In pairs: write your dialogue. Follow the conversation above as a guide.

Step 4

Take turns practicing your dialogue.

CULTURE

Fashion Revolution in South Africa

South Africa is a melting pot of cultures and traditions and therefore has become an inspiration for many designers all over the world. Rather than just copying overseas trends, local designers look into what it means to be fashionable in South Africa. Following their inspiration, they choose fabric, beads and cultural aspects which can bring life to unique South African attire.

The ethnic look is a rule: *dashikis* – colorful garments worn by men and women in West Africa – come embellished in beads and are paired with pants. Many designers have also found ways to recycle by reusing clothes which allude to specific national and personal histories.

During Apartheid, *Loxion Kulka* – street slang for 'Location Culture' – was a term used to refer to townships (underdeveloped segregated urban areas). Nowadays, it is the hottest brand worn on the streets and reflects the lifestyle of urban Africa through apparel, shoes, accessories and handmade items.

African garments reveal something about heritage and perpetuation of local practices. Take *Seshoeshoe*, a printed dyed cotton fabric widely used for traditional African clothing. It is manufactured in different colors and patterns and, because it is quite popular, it is always in fashion.

That is South Africa: breaking waves in the industry and bringing the country's style to the world!

1 47 Read and listen to the article and answer the questions below.

a Why has South Africa become an inspiration for designers all over the country?

b What are *dashikis*?

c During Apartheid, what did *Loxion Kulka* refer to?

d What is *Loxion Kulka* today?

e What is *Seshoeshoe* fabric?

2 What is the latest fashion in your country?

3 Do you know any fashion trends inspired by traditional or local cultures? Do you like them? Why (not)?

VOCABULARY 2

Phrasal Verbs: Clothes

1 48 Use your dictionary to look up the meaning of the phrasal verbs in the box. Then listen and repeat.

separable:	give away	pick out	pick up
	put away	put on	take off
	throw away	try on	wear out
inseparable:	get into	go with	look for

2 Rewrite the words in **bold** using five of the phrasal verbs in the box.

This sweater's too small! I can't **fit into** it.
get into

a This T-shirt's really old – I'm going to **put it in the trash**. ____________

b I like this sweater. I'm going to **find out if it fits**. ____________

c I love sales. I always **find** good bargains in the stores. ____________

d Does this black jacket **look good** with these black pants? ____________

e I'm not going to wear this top often. I don't want it to **deteriorate**. ____________

3 Complete the sentences with the other phrasal verbs from activity 1.

a I don't know what to wear. Can you ________ something ________ for me?

b When my room's messy, my mom tells me to ________ my clothes ________.

c It's so hot in here. I'm going to ________ my jacket ________.

d Do you want this belt? I want to ________ it ________.

e It's cold. ________ your coat ________.

f I can't find any sneakers I like! Can you help me to ________ some?

TIP

Some phrasal verbs have multiple meanings (e.g. *pick up*), so always read the context to decide on the appropriate meaning.

READING 2

1 Look at the messages. What is happening on Saturday evening?

____

Skype

Hi, Anna!

Hi, Lucy.

Are you going anywhere Saturday evening?

Yeah, it's Jenny's party. Aren't you going?

Wow, how could I have forgotten! Are you wearing anything special?

I don't know. I might wear my new blue skirt. How about you?

I'm going to wear my new green dress.

I want to wear my black boat neck top, but I've lent it to someone. Was it you, by any chance?

Er... don't think so. Let me check, it might be somewhere in my messy closet.

Thanks, it'll be great if you find it. Otherwise I'll have to go to the mall to buy something to go with that skirt.

Remember that this Saturday is a national holiday, nothing will open!

Right, I must get it tomorrow, then!

But hey, your top's here. I've just found it!

Yay!

And how are you getting there on Saturday? Is anyone driving you?

Nope, no one will be home on Saturday.

I'll ask my dad if he can take us there.

Great, can you give me a ride?

Sure!

Thanks! Let's talk tomorrow to arrange it.

Yeap, bye!

2 49 Read and listen to the texts. Then write T (*true*) or F (*false*).

a ☐ Lucy is going to Jenny's party.

b ☐ Anna was planning to go to the party when Lucy called.

c ☐ Anna's wearing her black dress to the party.

d ☐ Anna's top was in Lucy's closet.

GRAMMAR 2

some, any, no Compounds

1 Look at the indefinite pronouns in **bold** in the sentences below. Write (P) for the ones which refer to *people*, (T) for those which refer to *things* and (L) for the ones which refer to *locations*.

a ☐ I'll have to go to the mall to buy **something** to match that skirt.

b ☐ Are you wearing **anything** special?

c ☐ I've lent my black top to **someone**.

d ☐ It might be **somewhere** in my messy closet.

e ☐ Is **anyone** driving you?

2 Look at the chart and complete the rules below with: *things* / *people* / *locations*.

I want to buy **something** really original.
I never go **anywhere** without my cell phone.
No one has a bigger shoe collection than Imelda Marcos.

a We use *someone*, *anyone* and *no one* to talk about ___________.

b We use *somewhere*, *anywhere* and *nowhere* to talk about ___________.

c We use *something*, *anything* and *nothing* to talk about ___________.

3 Underline the most appropriate indefinite pronouns in the sentences below.

a My uncle is participating in a fashion week event in New York. He's staying **somewhere / someone** near Central Park.

b **No one / Nothing** wears casual clothes at that school. It looks like they're all going to a party.

c I haven't bought **anything / anyone** for my mom's birthday. Do you think she'll enjoy a bright pink shirt?

d **Something / Someone** called you while you were in the shower.

e I've had **nothing / nowhere** to eat today. I must go grab something!

4 Complete the rules with the words in the box.

affirmative	negative	questions

a We use *some* and *no* compounds with ___________ verbs.

b We use *any* compounds with ___________ verbs and in ___________.

5 Complete the dialogue with the correct *some*, *any* or *no* compounds.

Amy I'm going out tonight for my dad's birthday and I need to buy a new pair of shoes. Do you know **a** ___________ that sells cheap shoes?

Jo Well, there's **b** ___________ in town. All the shoe stores are really expensive.

Amy Oh no. I've got to get **c** ___________. My old shoes are torn.

Jo Well, maybe I can lend you **d** ___________. What do you need?

Amy Some formal black shoes. **e** ___________ very trendy or glamorous – I want a simple design.

Jo I don't have **f** ___________ like that but I know **g** ___________ who does.

Amy Who?

Jo Kerry. She has lots of shoes. She'll lend you **h** ___________.

Amy Great idea. Let's call her.

6 Complete the sentences so they are true for you.

a ______ I know lives in ______.

b I have never been anywhere ______.

c ______ in my family plays tennis.

d There's nowhere to buy ______ in my town.

GRAMMAR GUIDE page 88

CLIL

ART

The Victoria and Albert Museum

The Victoria and Albert Museum, commonly known as the V&A, is a museum of art and design in London. It was established in 1852 and is named after Queen Victoria and her husband, Prince Albert. The museum's collections cover a wide variety of art forms from different historical periods and from all around the world. These include architecture, ceramics, painting, design and fashion, among many others. Visitors can see everything from medieval sculpture to oriental carpets.

Many famous British designers have their work on display in the popular fashion collection. There are designs by Vivienne Westwood, miniskirts created by Mary Quant and a selection of boots by Biba, the iconic London fashion boutique of the 1960s and 1970s. As well as contemporary clothes, there are fashion designs from previous centuries, including King James II's wedding suit from his 1637 marriage to Mary of Modena.

Special exhibitions are also held at the V&A. In 2007, there was an exhibition called Kylie – The Exhibition, a display of Kylie Minogue's extravagant costumes from her concert tours.

1 50 Read and listen. Answer the question.

Where can you find Vivienne Westwood's designs in the V&A?

____

2 Rearrange the letters to complete the crossword with collections you can see at the Victoria and Albert Museum.

Down

1 MICRECAS

3 STULCERUP

4 GISAPINTN

5 OHFSINA

Across

2 NISDEG

6 RETACRHICTUE

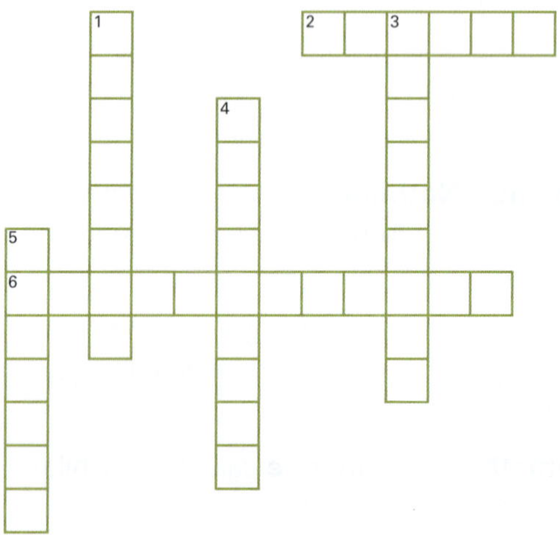

VOCABULARY IN PICTURES

Style Adjectives

casual

comfortable

colorful

conventional

fashionable

formal

glamourous

impractical

loose

old-fashioned

sporty

tight

trendy

Phrasal Verbs: Clothes

get into

give away

go with

look for

pick out

pick up

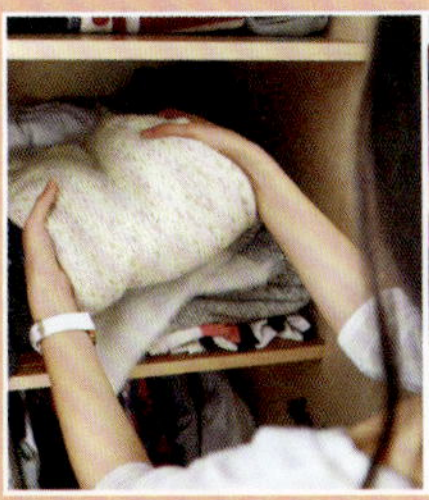
put away

put on

take off

throw away

try on

wear out

GRAMMAR GUIDE

Relative Pronouns

- We use relative pronouns to give extra information about people, places, time and things. We join two sentences using a relative pronoun.
  That's the man. He lives on my street.
  That's the man **who** lives on my street.
- We use *who* for people, *which* for things, *when* for time and *where* for places.

people	things	time	places
who	which	when	where
that	that	–	–

The man **who** lives in that house is from Athens.
Stella McCartney designs clothes **which** are fashionable.
I was living in Philadelphia **when** I met John.
That's the store **where** I bought my new shoes.

- We can use *that* instead of *who* or *which*.
  The man **that** lives in that house is from Athens.
  Stella McCartney designs clothes **that** are fashionable.

some, any, no Compounds

- we add *-one* to talk about people, *-thing* to talk about things and *-where* to talk about places

people	places	things
someone	**some**where	**some**thing
anyone	**any**where	**any**thing
no one	**no**where	**no**thing

- *some* is used with countable and uncountable nouns in affirmative sentences
  I want to go **somewhere** hot on vacation this year!
- *any* can be used in both negative sentences and questions
  I haven't bought **anything** all week.
  Has **anyone** seen that new movie yet?
- *no* can only be used in negative sentences
  There's **nothing** interesting on television tonight.
- we can also replace *-one* with *-body*.
  Somebody has stolen my bike.
  There's **nobody** here!
  Did **anybody** watch the news last night?

PROGRESS CHECK

Style Adjectives

1 Complete the sentences with style adjectives.

a I love Marilyn Monroe. She was so g__________.

b Heelless shoes look great but they're very i__________.

c I hate going to weddings because I have to wear f__________ clothes.

d My old sneakers are too t__________. I'll have to buy a bigger pair.

e My dad's very c__________. He even wears a suit on the weekend.

f My sister isn't very t__________. She isn't interested in fashion.

Phrasal Verbs: Clothes

2 Match the phrases to make sentences.

a Can I try	☐ out my jeans. I'll have to buy a new pair.
b I can't get	☐ away. Do you want it?
c Why don't you take	☐ up your clothes and put them in the wardrobe!
d I'm giving this T-shirt	☐ on these shoes, please?
e I've worn	☐ into these shoes. They're too small.
f Pick	☐ off your jacket? You look very hot!

Relative Pronouns

3 Use relative pronouns to join the two sentences.

I was born in a house. My father was born in the same house.

I was born in the house where my father was born.

a She's a designer. She designed my sister's wedding dress.

____

b This is a T-shirt. I wore it yesterday.

____

c We met in 1998. In 1998 we were 7 years old.

____

d I visited the museum. Your aunt works in this museum.

____

some, any, no Compounds

4 Complete the sentences with the correct compounds.

a Where are my sunglasses? I can't find them __________.

b I want to go __________ hot this summer. I need some sunshine.

c Did you get __________ nice for your birthday?

d I didn't know you were ill. __________ told me.

e The store is __________ near here. We'll have to go on the bus.

f I need to find __________ to wear to the job interview.

Grammar Buildup 5

1 2 3 4 5 6 7 8

5 Choose the correct answer.

Mila Hey, Karen.

Karen Hi, Mila. Hey, cool jeans. Where **a did you get / do you get** them?

Mila They were a present.

Karen Really! Who **b did give / gave** them to you?

Mila My grandma. Well, she gave me the money and I **c have bought / bought** them.

Karen Lucky you. Your grandma is really generous.

Mila Yeah, she **d gives / used to give** me presents for my birthday but now she gives me money. It's much better.

Karen When was your birthday?

Mila Last weekend.

Karen **e Did you have / Are you going to have** a party?

Mila No, I haven't had it **f already / yet**. Don't worry. I **g might / 'm going** to invite you.

6 Work and Money

1

4

2

3

VOCABULARY 1

The World of Work

1 Look at the words in the box. Use your dictionary to look up the meaning of any unknown words.

allowance ☐ application form ☐
apprenticeship ☐ benefits ☐ bonus ☐
conditions ☐ contract ☐ expenses ☐
job advertisement ☐ pay raise ☐
pension ☐ promotion ☐
wage ☐ work experience ☐

2 🔊 51 Listen and repeat.

3 Choose the correct words.

From: Diana
To: Greg
Subject: Good news! :-)

Hi, Greg!
Guess what? I have a part-time job! I'm a shop assistant at a bookstore in town. I'll only work there on Saturday afternoons, so I'll still have time for school and homework. I saw the **a pension / job advertisement** in the store window, so I went in and asked how to apply. I had to fill out **b a contract / an application form**, and then I had an interview this morning and they offered me the job. I'm going tomorrow to sign my **c contract / promotion**. The working **d expenses / conditions** are great (I get a free lunch!) and the **e wages / promotion** are quite good, too. And if I sell a lot of books, I'll get a **f salary / bonus**! Isn't that great?
Talk soon,
Diana

4 Complete the sentences with words from activity 1.

My brother wants a job with a good ___*pension*___, so he'll have enough money when he retires.

a My mom travels a lot for business. Her company pays all her ______________ such as flights and hotels.

b My parents give my older sister a monthly ______________ to buy clothes and pay for her cell phone.

c My mom has been given a ______________ at work. She's going to be a Senior Manager now.

d My brother's doing an ______________. He's training to be an electrician.

e My uncle gets great ______________ at his new job, including medical insurance and a company car.

f My dad's boss was so pleased with his work that she's given him a ______________. He'll get $3,000 more a year!

g I want to be a nurse so I'm going to get some ______________ at a hospital this summer.

READING 1

1 Look at the pictures and the title of the magazine article. What do you think Ben's job is?

a lifeguard b caretaker c soccer player

2 🔊 52 Read and listen. Choose the correct answers.

a Queensland is in **the USA / Australia**.

b The caretaker had to **swim / write a blog**.

c Ben is from **the UK / the USA**.

d Ben made **47 / 60** video diaries.

The BEST Job in the World

What do you think is the 'best job in the world'? Movie star? International soccer player? Politician? The problem is that you can't apply for these jobs. If you're a talented soccer player, you'll be successful. If you aren't, you won't. Music and acting are the same. If Shakira and Keira Knightley weren't good at what they do, they wouldn't be rich and famous.

However, in 2009 the Australian state of Queensland advertised what became known as 'the best job in the world', and people from all over the world could apply. The only job requirement was that applicants had to be able to speak English.

So what was the job? Caretaker of Hamilton Island, a tropical paradise in the Great Barrier Reef. Duties included sunbathing, walking on the beach and cleaning the swimming pool. But the most important tasks were to write a blog post once a week and to keep a video diary. The aim of the job was to promote tourism in Queensland.

The contract was for six months, and in return the caretaker received a generous salary of over €73,000 and lived in a multi-million dollar beach house. It was certainly a job with excellent working conditions.

Over 30,000 people filled out application forms for the post, and 16 of them had an interview. Queensland offered the job to Ben Southall, a 34-year-old charity worker from the UK.

However, the world's best job was also quite a difficult job. Ben often worked 19 hours a day, seven days a week. He visited 90 exotic locations, made 47 video diaries, and gave more than 250 media interviews – including one with famous TV presenter Oprah Winfrey. He spoke with local politicians, gave speeches, held meetings with travel industry representatives, and shook hands with thousands of tourists.

He wrote more than 75,000 words in 60 separate blog posts, uploaded more than 2,000 pictures and wrote more than 730 tweets. After he finished, Ben was so tired he needed a vacation!

Now Ben has a new job as Queensland's international tourism ambassador. He's still earning a great salary, and now he's traveling the world to promote the state. He's very busy again, but if he has time he'll write a book about his experience on the island. It should be an interesting story!

3 Read the text again. Then write T for *true* or F for *false*.

a ☐ Keira Knightley applied for a job as a movie star.

b ☐ The job applicants had to be English.

c ☐ The job was six months long.

d ☐ Only 16 people applied for the job.

e ☐ Ben doesn't earn a lot of money now.

4 Answer the questions. Write full sentences.

a Who advertised 'the best job in the world'?

____

b Why was the job created?

____

c Why was it called 'the best job in the world'?

____

d What was difficult about the job?

____

e What does Ben do now?

____

READING STRATEGY

Make connections between texts and your prior knowledge. This will enhance your text comprehension and make reading a more meaningful experience.

5 **INTERFACE** Work in pairs. Ask and answer the question.

What do you think is the best job in the world?

I think it's chocolate consultant! Can you imagine spending your day trying chocolate?

GRAMMAR 1

First and Second Conditionals

1 Read the sentences below. Underline the sentences which express conditions.

a If Ben has time, he'll write about his experience on Hamilton Island.

b If Shakira and Keira Knightley weren't good at what they do, they wouldn't be rich and famous.

2 Look at the chart and underline to complete the rules.

first conditional	
condition	**consequence**
If Ben **has** time,	**he'll write** about his experience.

second conditional	
condition	**consequence**
If they **weren't** good at what they do,	they **wouldn't be** rich and famous.

a We use the first conditional when we talk about **real and possible / unrealistic or not probable** situations in the future.

b We use the second conditional when we talk about **real and possible / unrealistic or not probable** situations in the future.

c The structure of the first conditional is *if* + verb in the **simple present / simple past** (condition) and ***would* / *will*** + base form of the verb (consequence).

d The structure of the second conditional is *if* + verb in the **simple present / simple past** (condition) and ***would* / *will*** + base form of the verb (consequence).

3 Read the sentences. Write P if the sentence is possible and NP if it doesn't reflect a current possibility.

a ☐ If my brother saves money, he'll buy a car.

b ☐ If I had a better job, I'd earn more money.

c ☐ I'd pass my exams if I worked harder.

d ☐ If my dad works hard he'll get a promotion.

4 Complete the first conditional sentences with the correct form of the verbs in parentheses.

a If my Dad __________ (work) hard, he'll get promoted.

b She __________ (not get) paid if she's late for work.

c If she __________ (not lend) you the money, I will.

5 Complete the second conditional sentences with the correct form of the verbs in parentheses.

a If she __________ (like) her job, she'd work harder.

b She __________ (get) a promotion if she worked harder.

c I'd have more money if I __________ (buy) fewer clothes.

PRONUNCIATION

Sentence Stress and Contractions

🔊 53 Listen and repeat the sentences. Which syllables have the main stress?

a If she's late for work, she'll lose her job.

b If I tell you the truth, you won't believe me.

c If he liked the car, he'd buy it.

6 Choose the correct answers.

I've always wanted to be a vet. It's my dream job. I know exactly what I have to do to become one. If I pass my exams when I'm older, I **a 'll / 'd** study sciences for the next two years. If I had time, I **b 'd / 'll** study English, too, but I don't think it's possible. If I **c want / wanted** to go to college, I **d 'll / 'd** need to get good marks, so I need to work hard. There won't be time for English. But that's OK. I **e 'll / 'd** read lots of novels this summer if I have any free time. If I **f have / had** enough money, I'd go to Africa this summer, but it's too expensive. I'd love to see wild lions. If I **g save / saved** my allowance, I'd be able to afford it. But I can't – I spend all my money on books!

7 Look at the charts. How do we form conditional questions? Check the correct information.

question	condition
What **will** you watch	if you **go** to the movies later?

question	condition
Where **would** you go	if you **went** to South America?

a ☐ In questions, *will* and *would* come before the subject.

b ☐ In questions, use *do* and *did* in conditions.

8 Choose the correct word.

a What **will / would** you study if you go to college?

b What **will / would** you say if you met the president of the US?

c Where will you go if you **go / went** on vacation this summer?

d What would you do if you **meet / met** David Beckham?

e If you **find / found** $50 in the street, what would you do?

9 Order the words to make questions.

a didn't / would / your town / you / live / Where / if / you / live / in ?

____

b will / you / go out / see / this weekend / if / you / Who ?

____

c Who / you / if / you / would / could / meet / meet / someone / famous ?

____

d choose / What / job / would / you / if / you / tomorrow / started / work ?

____

e What / million / you / if / would / you / had / do / one / dollars ?

____

10 **INTERFACE** Work in pairs. Ask and answer the questions in activity 9.

GRAMMAR GUIDE page 102

LISTENING

Part-time Jobs

1

2

3

1 Look at the pictures above and the phrases in the box. What tasks do you think the people in the pictures do at work?

do the washing up ☐
give customers advice ☐
make a playlist ☐ make coffee ☐
play music at a party ☐
sell clothes ☐ serve customers ☐

2 54 Listen to the radio show and match the speakers to the jobs.

a ☐ Jimmy (Speaker 1) 1 store assistant

b ☐ Charlotte (Speaker 2) 2 DJ

c ☐ Rob (Speaker 3) 3 waitress

3 54 Listen again and choose the correct answers.

a Jimmy plays music **in a disco / at parties**.

b Jimmy earns **$15 / $100** for each event.

c Charlotte works for eight hours every **Saturday / Sunday**.

d Charlotte **likes / doesn't like** getting an allowance from her parents.

e Rob enjoys selling **CDs / guitars**.

4 54 Listen again. Then write T for *true* and F for *false*.

a ☐ Jimmy makes sure people want to dance.

b ☐ Charlotte doesn't do the washing up.

c ☐ The customers at Charlotte's café are unfriendly.

d ☐ Rob's shop sells magazines.

e ☐ Rob earns a wage.

SPEAKING

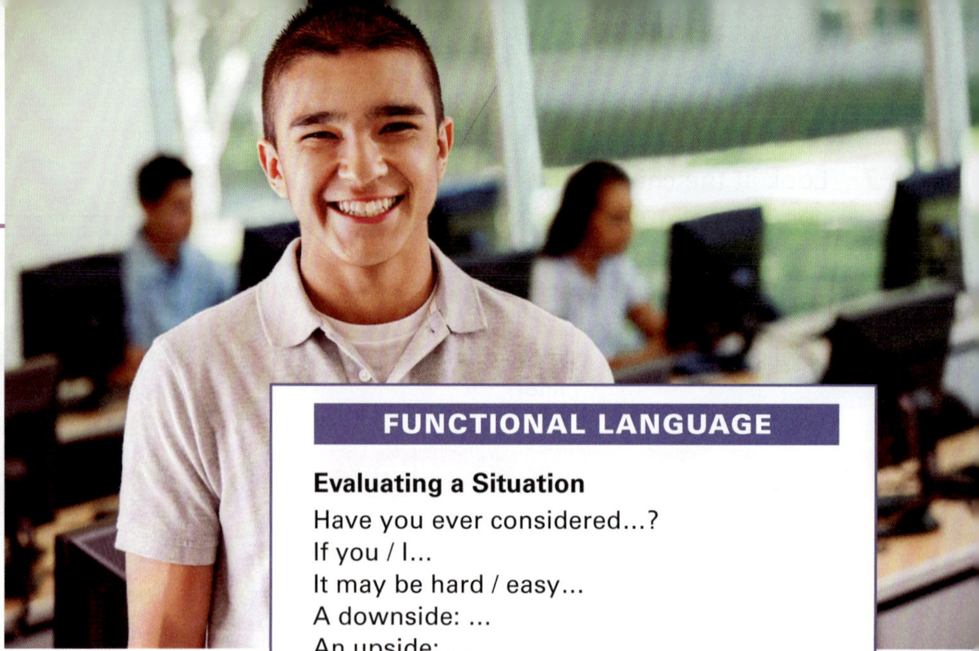

Looking for a Part-time Job

55 Bert, who is a high school student, is talking to his friend Joe about getting a part-time job. Listen and complete the dialogue.

Joe, have you ever considered **a** ________________ while in high school?

Not really. Have you?

In fact, yes! If I get a part-time job, **b** ________________ my own cash to spend. That's the best thing about it!

Well, that's true, but if **c** ________________ working now, your parents will probably ask you to help around the house. That means paying the five-letter word that everyone fears: BILLS.

Yeah, maybe **d** ________________ and other little things... no prob! If I do, **e** ________________ me to be disciplined and will help me appreciate what it's like to earn money.

It may be hard finding a job, but one thing is true: once you do, that's great **f** ________________!

That is catnip to future employers, especially **g** ________________ you worked part-time while still going to school! Another upside!

And you can **h** ________________ which can be quite helpful in future job opportunities!

Positively! I'm really excited...

A downside, though: remember you need **i** ________________ to not be held back a year.

FUNCTIONAL LANGUAGE

Evaluating a Situation

Have you ever considered...?
If you / I...
It may be hard / easy...
A downside: ...
An upside: ...
The best / worst thing about it is...

Speaking Task

Write a dialogue between you and a friend.

Step 1

Choose a part-time job or use your own ideas.

Job: part-time store assistant in a clothes store
Advantages: wage – it pays well
Best thing: discount on clothes
Disadvantages: long hours – very tiring

Job: vacation sports coach at a summer camp
Advantages: playing sports all day – it's great fun!
Best thing: being outside
Disadvantages: coaching young children – it can be difficult

Step 2

Think about what to say and suggestions your friend will give you.

Step 3

Work in pairs. Write your dialogue.

Step 4

Take turns practicing your dialogue.

CULTURE

Working Teenagers in the US

Many American teenagers look for part-time jobs in the US – to help support their families, to save for college or simply to earn some extra money for personal expenses. However, there are some facts which employers must consider when hiring a teen.

There are some rules the American Department of Labor sets for working teenagers, and these rules vary according to the age of the minor and the job involved. As a general rule, the Fair Labor Standards Act (FLSA) establishes an age limit (14 years of age) as the minimum age for employment, and also prohibits a minor from working in hazardous job positions such as work involving driving, operation of power-driven equipment and agricultural work.

It is also important to check working hours: 14-15-year-olds can only work 3 hours a day, 18 hours in a school week, 8 hours on a non-school day and 40 hours during a non-school week. Teens in that age-group are allowed to work from 7am to 7pm, and no later. However, students ages 16 and 17 can work unlimited hours. When they turn 18, they can work unlimited hours and hazardous jobs are not a problem.

Although the American law does not forbid teens from working, parents must monitor their children to make sure they are not spending too much time at work and leaving their studies behind.

1 🔊 56 Read and listen to the information. Then write T for *true*, F for *false* or NM for *not mentioned*.

- **a** ☐ American teenagers look for a part-time job for no specific reasons.
- **b** ☐ The Department of Labor sets rules for working teens starting at age 14.
- **c** ☐ Parents must sign a legal document giving permission for their teen to work.
- **d** ☐ 14-15-year-olds can only work 3 hours a day, 18 hours in a school week, 8 hours on a non-school day and 40 hours during a non-school week.
- **e** ☐ The American law forbids teens from working.
- **f** ☐ All part-time working students have good grades at school.

2 Can teens work in your country? What does the law say about it?

____

3 Do you think it is a good idea to have a part-time job while in high school? Why (not)?

____

VOCABULARY 2

Work Verbs

1

2

3

1 Match pictures 1-3 with verbs in the box. Use your dictionary if necessary.

apply for a job ☐	be unemployed ☐
claim expenses ☐	earn a salary ☐
fill in an application form ☐	get a job ☐
get a pension ☐	have a full-time job ☐
have an interview ☐	lose a job ☐
sign a contract ☐	work part-time ☐

2 57 Listen and repeat.

3 Match a-d with 1-4 to make sentences.

a ☐ My mom loves her job. She can claim

b ☐ Can you help me fill out

c ☐ My brother is

d ☐ My sister lost

1 unemployed. But he has an interview today.

2 this application form for a weekend job?

3 her job when the company closed down.

4 expenses for all her meals and travel.

4 Complete the questions with the verbs in the box.

applied earn get has

a My uncle always wears a suit when he ___________ a job interview.

b Do you want to ___________ a high salary?

c Have you ever ___________ for a job?

d Is it difficult to ___________ a job where you live?

READING 2

1 58 Read the leaflet and listen. What is an apprenticeship?

a a way to learn about a job and get experience

b a way to earn a lot of money

Try an Apprenticeship!

Finding a job can be difficult when you have no experience in the world of work. So before applying for a job, why don't you get some work experience while you're still at school?

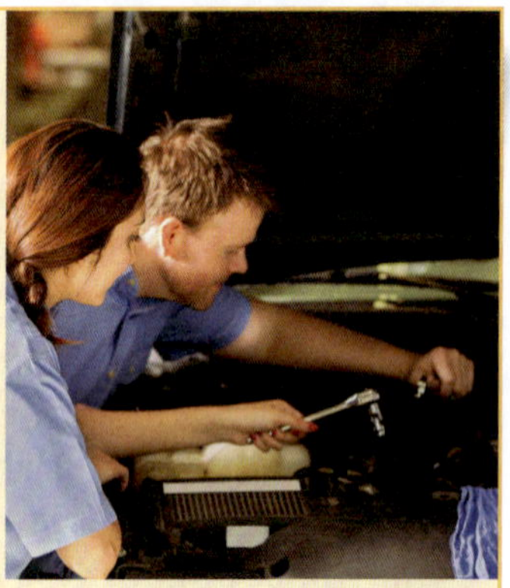

You Can Do a Summer Apprenticeship!

Summer apprenticeships might involve some training, as well as practical experience of working in a job you think you might enjoy. Your boss will supervise your work and help you learn new skills. There are lots of different job opportunities to choose from. Think about the skills you have and what types of jobs you might enjoy. Do you enjoy working with animals? You could apply to do an apprenticeship at the local zoo. Or if you love playing soccer and tennis, you might want to work as a sports coach for children at a summer camp.

Apprenticeships usually last for one month, and there are apprenticeship schemes all over the US for students aged 16-18.

**What are you waiting for?
Apply for an apprenticeship now!**

2 Read the leaflet again and answer the questions.

a What does an apprenticeship involve?

____

____

b Which jobs does the leaflet mention?

____

____

c Who can do an apprenticeship?

____

____

GRAMMAR 2

Gerunds and Infinitives

1 Read the sentences. Circle the verbs in the infinitive form and underline those in the gerund form.

- **a** Finding a job can be difficult when you have no experience in the world of work.
- **b** Do you enjoy working with animals?
- **c** You could apply to do an apprenticeship at the local zoo.
- **d** You might want to work as a sports coach.
- **e** Summer apprenticeships might involve practical experience of working in a job.

2 Look at the examples in the charts and then match them with the sentences below.

gerunds as the subject of a sentence
a **Finding** a job can be difficult.

gerunds after verbs
b Do you enjoy **working** with animals?

gerunds after prepositions
c Before **applying** for jobs, get some work experience.

infinitives after verbs
d Did you learn **to speak** Italian at school?

infinitives after adjectives
e He's happy **to meet** you at ten o'clock.

- ☐ No, I learned French instead.
- ☐ That's perfect! I'll be here on time.
- ☐ I sure do, especially dogs and cats.
- ☐ I know. It took me two years to find a new job after my long stay in Europe.
- ☐ Thank you for the suggestion. I'll start sending out my résumé.

3 Use gerund or infinitive forms of the verbs in the box to complete the sentences below.

be	live	see	travel	work

- **a** ___________ rich doesn't make you happy.
- **b** I want ___________ that movie.
- **c** ___________ long hours makes me feel tired.
- **d** ___________ in a house in New York is very expensive.
- **e** He'd like ___________ to Asia.

4 Complete the sentences with the correct form of the verbs in parentheses.

- **a** My dad really enjoys ___________ (play) golf.
- **b** I wanted ___________ (watch) the movie but it was too frightening.
- **c** I would really like ___________ (go) out tonight.
- **d** I can't afford ___________ (buy) a new pair of shoes.
- **e** I'm really looking forward to ___________ (see) Marvel's new movie.

5 Underline the correct verbs to complete the dialogue.

Sara Mom, can you help me? I don't know what to wear for my job interview. What about **a to wear / wearing** my new jeans?

Mom I'm not sure **b going / to go** in jeans will impress the interviewers. I think you need **c to wear / wearing** something more formal.

Sara Yes, I suppose you're right. **d To look / Looking** smart is all part of making a good impression, I guess. I'll wear my blue skirt.

Mom Yes and **e to be / being** on time for the interview is also important.

Sara Oh dear! I'm a bit late.

Mom Is that the time? It is difficult **f seeing / to see** how you will get there on time …

Sara Oh Mom! Would you like **g giving / to give** me a ride? I can't afford **h to take / taking** a taxi.

Mom Come on, of course I'll take you!

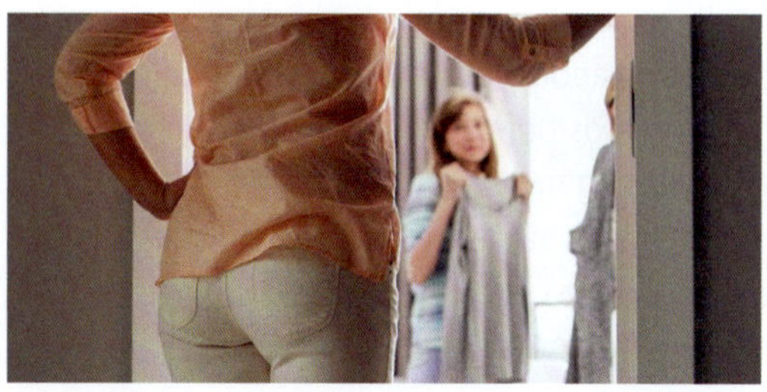

GRAMMAR GUIDE page 102

WRITING

A Letter of Application

1 59 Read and listen. Why is Louise writing to Universal Computers?

___

2 Read the letter again and answer the questions.

a What does Louise want to do in the future?

___

b How long has she been interested in computers?

___

c What relevant skills does Louise have?

___

d What personal qualities does she have?

___

e What does Louise ask for?

___

f What is she sending with her letter?

___

Dear Sir/Madam,

I am writing to apply for a work experience position at Universal Computers.

I am 14 years old and currently in 9th Grade at Highfields School. I am taking my exams in May and plan to continue studying at school for the next four years. In the future, I would like to study Business in college.

I have been interested in computers since I was eight years old. I can use Word, PowerPoint and Excel, and I am also learning to write computer programs. My favorite subjects at school are ICT and art, especially graphic design.

I am a hard-working and responsible person and I am sure that I would learn a lot from working with your company for two weeks.

I would be very grateful if you could send me more information about your company and the work experience position.

I am enclosing my résumé and a reference from my ICT teacher. I am available to attend an interview.

I look forward to hearing from you.

Sincerely,

Louise Greene

LANGUAGE FOCUS

Job Application Letters

Dear Sir/Madam,
I am writing to apply for...
I would be very grateful if...
I am enclosing...
I look forward to hearing from you.
Yours faithfully,

3 Order the words to make sentences.

a look / I / hearing / to / you / forward / from

___

b for / I / am / to / your café / apply / a job / writing / in

___

c some information / I / very grateful / if / would be / you could / send me

___

d I / my / am / résumé / enclosing

___

e available / am / I / attend / an interview / to

___

4 Write a letter applying for a work experience position at a company in your town (150-170 words).

Writing a Letter of Application

Step 1 > PLAN

Decide what company you want to write to. What relevant skills do you have? Think about what information you want from them and what to send with the letter.

Step 2 > WRITE

Write a first draft. Include information about your experience and personal qualities.

Step 3 > CHECK

Check your work. Have you concluded your letter appropriately?

Step 4 > WRITE

Write your final copy and hand in your work.

VOCABULARY IN PICTURES

The World of Work

allowance

application form

apprenticeship

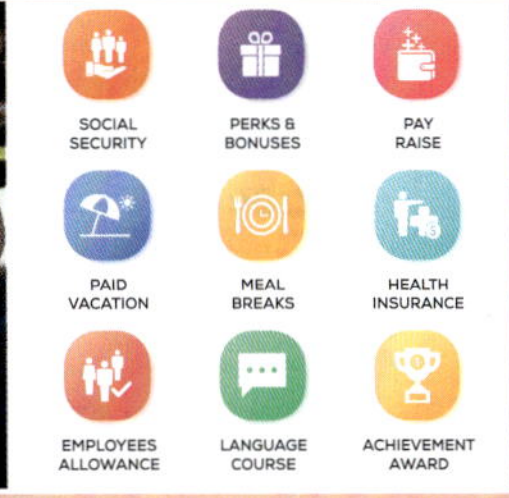

benefits

bonus

conditions

contract

expenses

job advertisement

pay raise

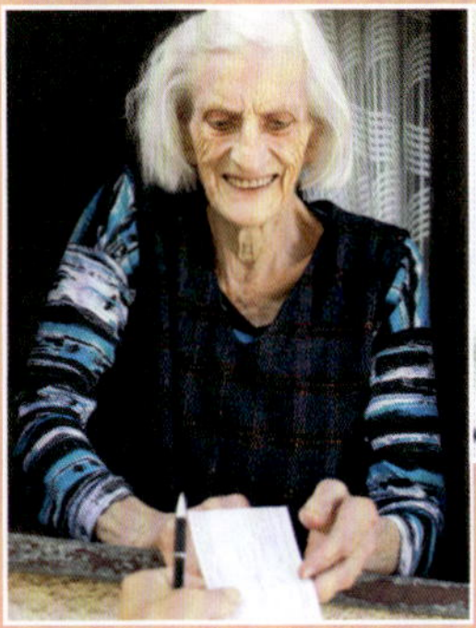
pension

promotion

salary

work experience

Work Verbs

apply for a job

be unemployed

claim expenses

earn a salary

fill in an application form

get a job

get a pension

have a full-time job

have an interview

lose a job

sign a contract

work part-time

GRAMMAR GUIDE

The First Conditional

situation	consequence
If you**'re** a great singer,	you**'ll get** a record contract.

consequence	situation
You**'ll get** a record contract	if you**'re** a great singer.

- we use the first conditional to talk about possible situations and their consequences
- we form the first conditional with *if* + subject + simple present (for the situation), and then subject + *will* / *won't* + infinitive without *to* (for the consequence)
  If we go to Madrid, **we'll stay** in a hotel.
  If he arrives late, **he won't get** a seat.
- we can put either the situation or the consequence first; if the situation comes first, we use a comma
  If you go out in the rain, **you'll get** wet.
- if the consequence comes first, we don't need a comma
  You'll get wet **if you go** out in the rain.

The Second Conditional

situation	consequence
If I **had** more money,	I **would buy** that dress.

consequence	situation
I **would buy** that dress	If I **had** more money.

- we use the second conditional to talk about imaginary or unlikely future situations and their consequences
- we form the second conditional with *if* + subject + simple past (for the situation), and then subject + *would* / *wouldn't* + infinitive without *to* (for the consequence)
  If I sold my car, **I'd buy** a motorbike.
  If they did more exercise, **they wouldn't** be so unfit.
- we can put either the situation or the consequence first; if the situation comes first, we use a comma
- if the consequence comes first, we don't need a comma

Gerunds and Infinitives

gerunds as the subject of a sentence
Making cakes is easy if you have a good recipe.

gerunds after verbs
I like **singing** in the shower.

gerunds after prepositions
After **watching** the movie, they had ice cream.

infinitives after verbs
Do you know how **to play** the piano?

infinitives after adjectives
She wasn't pleased **to see** the dog in the garden.

Gerunds as the Subject of a Sentence

- gerunds (the *-ing* form of the verb) can be the subject of a sentence
  Finding a job can be difficult.

Gerunds after Verbs

- some verbs are followed by a gerund
  I **enjoy playing** the trumpet.
  I **don't mind working** until 7pm
  Have you **finished eating**?

Infinitives after Verbs

- some verbs are followed by the infinitive
  I don't **want to talk** to you.
  We **expect to arrive** at ten o'clock.
  Did they **help to pay** for the car?
- be careful: some verbs can be followed by either a gerund or an infinitive but with slightly different meanings

Gerunds after Prepositions

- the gerund is generally used after prepositions
  I'm dreaming **about going** on vacation.
  She's good **at playing** the violin.
  I'm interested **in working** for you.

Infinitives after Adjectives

- the infinitive is generally used after adjectives
  I am **pleased to see** you.
  We were not **happy to be** there.
  I was **surprised to hear** that.

PROGRESS CHECK

The World of Work

1 Choose the correct word.

a Jo's **salary / apprenticeship** is $25,000 a year.

b My parents give me **a bonus / an allowance** if I help with the housework.

c My grandparents get their **pension / pay raise** every two weeks.

d My brother is looking for a job with good **conditions / expenses**.

e My dad doesn't get any **benefits / promotion** at work. He doesn't even get a pension.

Work Verbs

2 Complete the sentences with the words in the box.

claimed filled has lost signed worked

a My mother ________ a full-time job and looks after five children.

b Li has ________ a contract to play soccer in Europe.

c I ________ my job because I was late for work so often.

d My grandfather ________ part-time in the library after he retired.

e My dad ________ out an application form yesterday – I hope he gets an interview!

First and Second Conditional

3 Complete the sentences using the correct form of the verbs in parentheses.

a If I ____________ (become) a doctor, I'll earn a lot of money.

b If he saved his money, he ____________ (be) able to go on vacation.

c If you ____________ (not apologize), she won't talk to you.

d What ____________ (do) if you had $1 million?

e I ____________ (lend) you $25, if you promise to pay me back.

Gerunds and Infinitives

4 Complete the sentences with the verbs in gerund or infinitive.

a I enjoy __________ (play) golf with my dad. It's great fun.

b He spends so much time __________ (talk) on the phone.

c I've arranged __________ (meet) Monica at 8:30pm

d I don't want __________ (see) that movie. It looks boring.

e She's decided not __________ (leave) school next year.

Grammar Buildup 6

1 2 3 4 5 6 7 8

5 Underline the correct answer.

Ben Hi, Jan. You look great. Where **a are you going / do you go**?
Jan My grandma's having a party. She **b retires / 's retiring** today.
Ben Really?
Jan Yes, she's a cook. She **c 's worked / worked** in the same restaurant for 33 years. Today's her last day.
Ben Wow. So is she sad about retiring?
Jan No, she's really excited. She has lots of plans. She **d will / 's going to** travel and learn Italian.
Ben So where's the party?
Jan In the restaurant where she **e was working / works**.
Ben Who **f does organize / has organized** the party?
Jan Her boss. He's giving her a present, too.
Ben What is he going to give her?
Jan I don't know. But I hope it's not a cook book. If he **g will give / gives** her a cook book, she'll be really angry!
Ben Why?
Jan Because she **h 's going to / might** to write a cook book now that she's retired. It's one of her plans.

Review 3

VOCABULARY | **GRAMMAR**

Start

1

Maureen has finished college and now she's doing an _ _ _ _ _ _ _ _ _ _ _ _ _ _.

2

I love wearing very _ _ _ _ _ _ _ _ _ _ _ clothes when I'm relaxing at home!

7

I can't believe Seán has just _ _ _ _ his _ _ _ . He's an amazing professional!

8

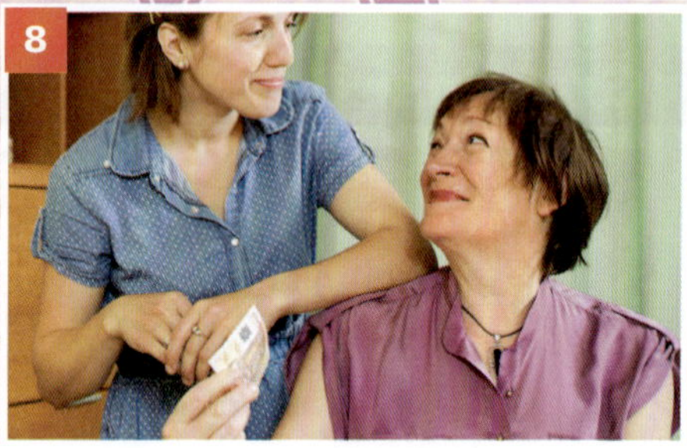

Lisa's just gotten her month's _ _ _ _ _ _ _ _ _ and she'll buy a new pair of jeans.

9

I don't know if I should _ _ _ _ _ _ _ the jeans or the cotton dress today.

10

Look at Ann's wardrobe, most of her clothes are _ _ _ _ _ _ because she goes to the gym every day!

15

They had to _ _ _ _ a contract in order to move to the new house.

Finish

3

... but when I visit a customer I must wear _ _ _ _ _ _ clothes.

4

After working hard for a long time, my cousin finally got a _ _ _ _ _ _ _ _ _ _.

6

These clothes in the ad look like they're from the 90s. They're so _ _ _ - _ _ _ _ _ _ _ _ _ _!

5

Grandpa has lived on his _ _ _ _ _ _ _ since he retired ten years ago.

11

My mom always _ _ _ _ _ _ _ _ her high heels as soon as she gets home.

12

Will _ _ _ _ _ _ a good salary at his new job.

14

We'd better _ _ _ _ _ these boots to make sure they're the right size.

13

Jimmi has just had a job _ _ _ _ _ _ _ _ _ today. He's confident he'll get hired!

Review 3

VOCABULARY | GRAMMAR

Relative Pronouns

1 Complete the sentences with *who, which, when* or *where.*

Alice Walker is a writer __*who*__ writes about social problems.

a The first day of primary school was ________ I met my best friend.

b That's the trash can ________ we recycle our garbage.

c That's my brother's friend ________ got into trouble with the police.

d A myth is a story ________ includes gods, heroes and magic.

2 Use a relative pronoun to join the two sentences.

I'm visiting my grandparents. They live in Texas.
I'm visiting my grandparents who live in Texas.

a We went to a beautiful beach. It had white sand and blue water.

____

____

b I met a famous actor. He's been in several movies.

____

____

c We went to a new gym. You could try all kinds of martial arts.

____

____

d It was New Year's. My dad fell in love with my mom.

____

____

3 Write complete sentences using the correct relative pronoun.

meet / was in *America's Got Talent* / I'll / the girl
I'll meet the girl who was in America's Got Talent.

a is the place / French /study / this / I

____

b is / got married / that / my parents / the year

____

c don't have / shoes / these / shoelaces / are

____

d created / was / Chanel /the jersey suit / the designer

____

some, any, no Compounds

4 Complete the sentences with the words in the box.

~~anything~~ anywhere no one nowhere someone something

I'm hungry. Do you have __*anything*__ to eat?

a I can't find my keys ________.

b Nathan was upset because ________ tried his cake.

c We're looking for ________ to wear for the wedding.

d While I was sleeping, ________ called.

e There's ________ better than home.

5 Underline the correct words.

My sister doesn't have **anything / nothing** to match her red pants.

a We wouldn't be here if we had **nowhere / anywhere** better to go!

b I have a bad headache. I need **something / nothing** to relieve it.

c There is **someone / anyone** at Kirsten's house she wants to introduce to us.

d In the future, **someone / no one** will need oil. All fuel will come from renewable sources.

VOCABULARY

GRAMMAR

The First Conditional

6 Write complete sentences in the first conditional.

If / I / go / abroad / I / make / new friends.
If I go abroad, I'll make new friends.

a If / he / take off / his sweater / he / be / cold.
____

b We / save / energy / if / we / switch off / the lights.
____

c If / you / not listen / you / not understand.
____

The Second Conditional

7 Turn the sentences in the first conditional into second conditional sentences.

We'll save a lot of water if we don't take a shower every day.
We'd save a lot of water if we didn't take a shower every day.

a If I'm rich and famous, I'll buy a helicopter.
____
____

b Lucy will work in a store if the conditions get better.
____
____

c If my sister finds a good job advertisement, she'll apply for it.
____
____

The First and Second Conditionals

8 Complete the sentences with the correct form of the verbs in parentheses. Use the first conditional or the second conditional.

I'll go (go) to the movies if it rains tomorrow.

a If my family won a lot of money, we__________ (move) to a new house.

b If I __________ (get) a good grade on the test, my parents will buy me a new bike.

c If I found a dog in the street, I __________ (keep) it.

9 Match the items to make sentences.

a I'll go by bike
b I'd get a part-time job
c If I wasn't happy at college,
d If you wear out those sneakers,

[ ] I'd drop out.
[ ] mom'll get angry.
[ ] if I needed money.
[*a*] if the weather is good.

Gerunds and Infinitives

10 Underline the correct words.

a He hopes **to arrive / arriving** before 9pm.

b I love **to play / playing** the piano.

c My mom avoids **to eat / eating** cheese.

d Tim was happy **to hear / hearing** the good news.

11 Complete the sentences with the correct form of the verbs in parentheses.

a I don't enjoy __________ (make) cakes.

b It's easy __________ (learn) French.

c My brother's good at __________ (play) baseball.

d Do you mind __________ (help) me clean the house?

7 Crime Doesn't Pay

1

2

3

4

VOCABULARY 1

Crime Verbs

1 Use your dictionary to look up the meaning of the verbs in the box. Then write C if the actions are done by *criminals* and P for actions done by the *police*.

arrest a suspect ☐ be guilty ☐
be innocent ☐ catch a thief ☐
commit a crime ☐
do community service ☐ go on trial ☐
go to prison ☐ investigate a crime ☐
look for clues ☐ pay a fine ☐
question a suspect ☐ solve a crime ☐
suspect someone ☐

2 🔊 60 Listen and repeat. Which expressions can you use to describe pictures 1-4?

1 ______________________

2 ______________________

3 ______________________

4 ______________________

3 Underline the correct words.

One of the most mysterious crimes in history were the Jack the Ripper murders. Five women were killed in east London, UK, during three months in 1888. The police never **a committed / solved** the crimes. They **b looked for / caught** and found many clues and **c suspected / questioned** suspects but nothing helped them.
The detective who **d committed / investigated** the murders, Inspector Frederick Abberline, never **e suspected / caught** the murderer – he never even **f solved / arrested** anyone. No one ever **g paid a fine / went to prison** for the murders.
Even today we have no idea who was **h innocent / guilty** of the terrible crimes.

READING 1

1 Look at the poster. What kind of animals do people smuggle?

____

Watch Out for ANIMAL SMUGGLERS!

Imagine this situation. You're at the airport waiting to collect your suitcase. A man is standing next to you. He picks up a large leather suitcase from the baggage carousel. His bag moves.
What do you think?
a There must be something alive inside his bag.
b It's none of my business.

You look closely at the suitcase. It moves again.
What could it be?
a It can't be a person. It might be an animal.
b I don't know and I don't care.

He picks up the bag and looks around him. He looks nervous.
Who is he?
a He might be an animal smuggler.
b Sorry, I have no idea.

The bag moves again.
What do you do?
a Call a customs officer.
b Nothing.

THE CORRECT ANSWER TO ALL THESE QUESTIONS IS A.

Animal smuggling is cruel. Many of the animals that people smuggle are endangered species that should not be removed from their natural habitat. A large number of them die during the journey because they travel in boxes, suitcases, or even inside people's clothes.

Animal smuggling is a crime. Buying and collecting smuggled animals is illegal. Punishments can include heavy fines and imprisonment.

Animal smuggling is increasing. It's the second most portable illegal activity in the world. Only drug smuggling makes more money.

Help us stop animal smuggling! If you see something suspicious, REPORT IT!

Sleeping Snakes in a Suitcase

Customs officers in Jakarta arrested two men suspected of having animals in their suitcases. The men were trying to fly from Indonesia to Dubai. When airport officials looked in the men's bags, they found 40 pythons. The snakes had been given drugs to make them sleep. The suspects were questioned by airport authorities and the pythons were taken to the animal quarantine center at the airport.

Tiger Smuggling in Thailand

Police caught a 31-year-old woman trying to smuggle a baby tiger into Thailand. The tiger cub was inside a suitcase with a toy tiger. Although the woman had drugged the animal to keep it quiet, airport officials noticed that one of the two tigers was moving when they scanned her suitcase. The smuggler went to prison for six years.

2 🔊 61 Read and listen. Check your answer to activity 1.

3 Write T for *true* or F for *false*. Try to correct the false sentences.

a ☐ Many smuggled animals are very rare.
____

b ☐ The journey kills many animals.
____

c ☐ Animal smuggling is more profitable than drug smuggling.
____

d ☐ Criminals smuggle dangerous animals.
____

e ☐ Customs officials arrested the snake smugglers in Dubai.
____

f ☐ The woman was smuggling two tigers into Thailand.
____

GRAMMAR 1

Modals of Deduction and Possibility

1 Read the sentences below. Do they express *deduction* (D), *possibility* (P) or *impossibility* (I)?

- **a** ☐ There must be something alive inside his bag.
- **b** ☐ It can't be a person.
- **c** ☐ It might be an animal.
- **d** ☐ He may be an animal smuggler.
- **e** ☐ It could be a dangerous snake.

2 Look at the sentences in activity 1 again. Complete the rules with the words in the box.

can't	isn't true	it is possible
might	must	believe

- **a** We use the modal verbs *may*, __________ and *could* + base form of a verb when we think __________ that something is true.
- **b** __________ + base form of a verb is used when we __________ something is true.
- **c** __________ + base form of a verb is used when we are sure something __________.

3 Match the deductions to their meanings.

- **a** He must be a smuggler.
- **b** He might be a smuggler.
- **c** He can't be a smuggler.

☐ I'm certain he's not a smuggler.
☐ I think it's possible he's a smuggler.
☐ I'm certain he's a smuggler.

4 Read sentences a-f and match them with the deductions below.

- **a** She speaks French and has a French passport.
- **b** She used to live in Paris.
- **c** Joanne hates dogs! A dog bit her when she was a child.
- **d** I think Sheila likes dogs, but I'm not sure.
- **e** I think I saw him on television yesterday.
- **f** He's in that new movie we saw last week!

☐ That can't be Joanne's dog.
☐ He must be a famous actor.
☐ She may be French.
☐ He might be an actor.
☐ She must be French.
☐ That could be Sheila's dog.

5 Choose the correct words.

- **a** He **must / can't** be guilty. He's never committed a crime in his life!
- **b** There **could / must** be a dog in that bag. It's moving.
- **c** You **must / can't** be hungry. It's four o'clock and you haven't had lunch.
- **d** He **might / can't** be American. He speaks English.
- **e** Ask John. He **can't / might** know the answer.
- **f** This movie's terrible. You **might / can't** like it.

6 Look at the pictures of stolen items. Then complete the sentences with the most appropriate modal verb.

- **a** The speakers __________ be Jane's. She never listens to music.
- **b** The sunglasses __________ be Pete's. Jane never wears them.
- **c** The money __________ be Jane's, but it __________ be Pete's too.
- **d** The camera __________ be Pete's. He doesn't have one.
- **e** The e-book reader __________ be Pete's or Jane's. They both love reading.
- **f** The earrings __________ be Jane's. She bought a pair like those last year.

7 62 Listen to the sounds. Then write T for *true* or F for *false*.

a 1 ☐ It might be New Year's Eve.
2 ☐ It can't be a celebration.
3 ☐ It could be fireworks for the Fourth of July.

b 1 ☐ He can't be happy.
2 ☐ He must be happy.
3 ☐ He may have heard some good news.

c 1 ☐ It can't be a cat.
2 ☐ A thief might be trying to steal something from the house!
3 ☐ It must be a cat.

d 1 ☐ It might be a restaurant.
2 ☐ It must be a library.
3 ☐ Someone may be cooking dinner.

8 Choose the correct words.

Jack Hey, look! That's Andy Samberg, the actor.
Cath Who?
Jack Andy Samberg. He's in *Brooklyn Nine-Nine* on TV.
Cath No, it **a can't / must** be him!
Jack Why not? He **b might / can't** live near here.
Cath No way! Andy Samberg lives in California.
Jack Well, he **c must / could** be here making a movie.
Cath He **d can't / may** be Andy! He's wearing glasses.
Jack He **e must / might** wear glasses in real life. Hey, look! He's coming this way.
Andy Excuse me. I don't know this area. I **f must / can't** be lost. Can you help me?
Jack Of course. Are you Andy Samberg, the actor?
Andy Yes, I am. Do you watch *Brooklyn Nine-Nine*? You **g must / can't** miss it!

9 INTERFACE Think of a friend. What are they doing now? Write sentences giving evidence and using modal verbs. Then discuss your sentences with a partner.

What is Carlos doing now?

He must be on vacation in Key West, because he went there on Sunday. He might be at the beach.

GRAMMAR GUIDE page 120

LISTENING

Crime News

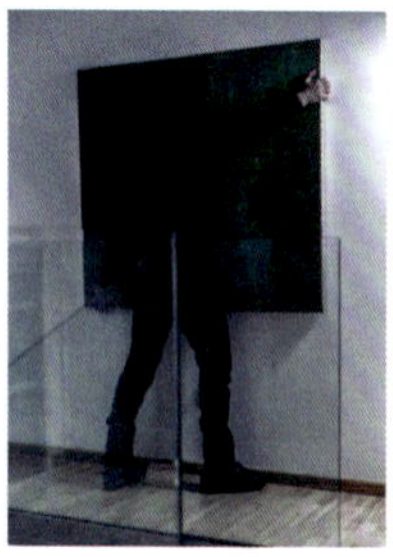

1 63 Listen to the three news stories. Put the robberies in the order you hear them.

a ☐ art theft
b ☐ jewelry theft
c ☐ a bank robbery

2 63 Listen again and answer the questions.

a Where was the bank robbery?
____

b What happened to the bank robbers?
____

c How long was the painting missing for?
____

d Who did the painting belong to?
____

e What did Horatio Mandeville steal?
____

f How many times has he been found guilty before?
____

3 63 Listen again and complete the sentences.

a Police investigated the bank robbery for __________ days.

b Mrs. Johnson was found __________ by the court.

c The painting was stolen from Paul Chambers' __________.

d Security guards found the painting after __________ minutes.

e The diamonds were worth more than __________ euros.

f Mandeville got out of prison __________ weeks ago.

SPEAKING

Witnessing a Crime

64 David is telling James how his bike has been stolen. Listen and complete the dialogue.

I'm so upset today...

Why? What **a** ______________?

My bike was stolen last night.

How come? **b** ______________ did it happen?

I **c** ______________ home to go to the gym. I left it in front of the gate for a few minutes to get my gym clothes in my bedroom.

d ______________

e ______________! I heard a noise and looked out of my window. A man was riding away on my bike!

Wow! That's absolutely incredible. I **f** ______________ someone would do that. It **g** ______________ be someone from another neighborhood.

h ______________. Anyway, I called the police and went to the station to talk to them.

Good for you – it's really important to report crimes. I hope the police find your bike.

FUNCTIONAL LANGUAGE

Describing a Crime	Reacting
What happened?	That's incredible!
Where...?	It can't be true.
I...	It might / may / could...
... the police.	It must...

Speaking Task

Write a new dialogue between you and a friend.

Step 1

Choose a fact file or use your own ideas to describe a crime you have witnessed.

CRIME: robbery at a supermarket
CRIMINALS: three thieves
EQUIPMENT: masks
ACTIVITY: stealing cash
ACTION: told the security guards

CRIME: mugging outside a restaurant
CRIMINALS: one man
EQUIPMENT: none
ACTIVITY: stealing a woman's handbag
ACTION: called the police and an ambulance

CRIME: animal smuggling
CRIMINALS: two smugglers
EQUIPMENT: a suitcase
ACTIVITY: smuggling a snake onto a plane
ACTION: told customs officials

Step 2

Describe what you saw.

I saw a robbery last night at...
The thief stole ...
I called ...

Think about what your friend says.

You're joking! Tell me more.
What happened next?
I can't believe it.

Step 3

Write your dialogue.

Step 4

Take turns practicing your dialogue.

CULTURE

Cybercrime in India

Life has become much easier since technology started playing a role in our lives. The use of the internet has brought lots of advantages: paying bills, buying tickets for shows, booking hotels, among others. However, anyone can fall prey to online fraud and lose their confidential information, money and even reputation due to revenge, for instance.
India, being the home to IT innovation, has a strong internet and programming culture. However, this can also have a downside, because just as you have a huge army of amazing IT specialists, you also have a lot of cyber criminals with sufficient skills to break many security barriers. Malicious internet activities are called *cybercrimes*, which in India means 'unlawful acts where the computer is used either as a tool or a target or both.' Due to the rapid spread of this kind of criminal activity, there is a separate law for crimes committed on the internet.
Here are some examples of cybercrimes:

Against the Person
In this category, offenses include: *cyber stalking*, that is, threating people using computer technology such as emails, webcams, etc.; *hacking*, that is, accessing a computer system without permission; *defamation*, that is, using the net to damage a person's good reputation; *child pornography*, that is, using the net to spread, create or access materials which exploit minors.

Against the Government
Cyber terrorism, which refers to the use of information technology to cause disruption and fear among the population.
The list increases every day and the punishment also varies depending on the offense, from a fine to imprisonment. Therefore, certain precautions should be taken by netizens when using the web to avoid this terrible threat called cybercrime.

1 🔊 65 **Read and listen to the information about cybercrime in India and answer the questions.**

a What advantages has the use of internet brought?

____

b What does *cybercrime* mean in Indian law?

____

c What crime mentioned in the text relates to entering someone's computer or personal accounts?

____

d What example of crime against the government is given? Explain.

____

e Is there a punishment for cybercrime in India? Which?

____

2 **Is there a law for cybercrime in your country? For which offenses? What is the punishment?**

____

3 **How do you think a cybercrime law can prevent offenses against people without threatening our freedom of expression?**

____

VOCABULARY 2

Crimes and Criminals

1 Use your dictionary to look up the meaning of the words in the box.

burglar burglary kidnapper
kidnapping murder murderer
pickpocket pickpocketing robber
robbery theft thief vandal vandalism

2 🔊 66 Listen, check and repeat.

3 Copy and complete the chart using the words in activity 1.

crime	criminal
burglary	*burglar*

TIP

Thieves rob places and steal things.
The thief robbed a bank and stole $200,000.

4 Complete the sentences with words from the chart.

a A ____________ stole my bike from outside school.

b I think ____________ is the most serious crime. Killing someone is unacceptable!

c A ____________ stole my cell phone from my pocket when I was on the train.

d The police caught the ____________ after he released the victim. No one knew where she was for days!

e I think graffiti is a form of ____________.

f I saw three ____________ running away from the bank yesterday. They stole $100,000!

g There has been an increase in ____________ recently. Someone broke all the windows at the city hall.

h Be careful with your wallet on the bus. ____________ is a real problem here.

READING 2

1 🔊 67 Look at the title and the pictures. What do you think the text is about? Read, listen and check your answer.

____

Preserving a Burglary Scene

Detectives investigating crimes look for clues like fingerprints which can identify the criminals. Why? Because police officers know that all criminals sometimes make mistakes.
Check out what you *must* and *must not* do in case of a burglary.

1 Call the police immediately.
Besides making sure you get immediate help and some advice on how to preserve the crime scene, you must report the crime under your name in order to testify for the state if it prosecutes the burglar.

2 Don't move things around!
If you ever get home and realize your house's been broken into, although you might feel like immediately looking for your precious belongings, be careful! You must not touch some key items like internal door handles, faucets and windows if you want the police to ever catch the criminals.

3 Look for the suspect's movements.
One of the most important things to help police locate the criminals is to have clues of how they entered and left the place. In order to help with that, you have to notice if there are any signs of open doors and windows or footsteps, and you must not close any doors or windows before the police arrive.

4 Keep unauthorized people out.
In order to preserve all evidence that you have taken care of in the previous items, avoid letting strangers into the house.

2 Read the text again and answer the questions.

a What text genre is it?

1 a how-to list **2** a news report

b What must you do with entry and exit points?

1 leave them as they are

2 close them all for safety

c What should you do in case someone offers help?

1 Let them help tidy your house.

2 Don't let them in and accept help in other ways.

GRAMMAR 2

Review: *must / must not*

1 Read the sentences below. Circle the ones showing *prohibition* and underline those which express *obligation* or *duty*.

a When witnessing a crime, you must report it to the police.

b Criminal offenses must be punished.

c The police must not search your home without a search warrant.

d If the police want to search your home, they must do it in your presence.

e As a witness, you must not hide any details from the police.

2 Look at the chart below. Check (✓) the correct information as to the rules of *must* and *must not*.

obligation / duty	deduction	prohibition
You *must* report the crime.	The suspect *must* be from another neighborhood.	You *must not* carry a gun without permission.
The police *must* investigate that murder.		

a ☐ *Must* can only be used to express obligation.

b ☐ *Must not* is used to express prohibition.

3 Read the sentences below. Write (O) if *must* expresses obligation and (D) if it expresses deduction.

a ☐ A crime scene reconstructionist must keep his or her report confidential.

b ☐ Jonathan Blair must be the robber. He has already gone to trial for bank robberies.

c ☐ All staff must wear safety equipment to access the area.

d ☐ The robbers must have hidden the money … But where?

4 Underline the correct words in the paragraph below.

www.legaltips.com

How to Sue for Defamation

Libel is the act of publicly offending someone, in written form, and lying about facts of this person's life. If you ever feel that you have been *libeled* or *defamed*, you can take the case to court. But in order to do that, you **a must / must not** only prove that what was written about you is a lie, but you **b must / must not** also prove that the person who wrote it actually knew that it was false. The text **c must / must not** also be a statement of fact that can be proven, and not just a personal opinion. Besides that, the text **d must / must not** cause damage to your reputation to be considered libel. It **e must / must not** be something that only hurts your feelings or makes you feel bad.

5 INTERFACE Talk to a classmate about crimes and punishment. Use *must* and *must not*.

I think a person must be responsible for his or her acts.

In my opinion, the person who accuses must provide evidence.

GRAMMAR GUIDE page 120

CLIL

ART

Graffiti – Inside or Outside the Law?

Graffiti is an Art

If art is a painting or a drawing that is created to be beautiful or to express ideas, then graffiti is art.
Major art museums, collectors and celebrities pay thousands of dollars for works by famous graffiti artists such as the English artist Banksy.
When Banksy painted a mural of two Hollywood actors near a London underground station, art critics said that it could be worth $400,000.
But the transportation authorities disagreed: it was their property and Banksy didn't have their permission, so they painted over the mural.

Graffiti is a Crime

In 2006, New York City tried to forbid any person under 21 from possessing spray paint or permanent markers. However, art students took the issue to court and won, legitimizing graffiti art in the city.
The Chicago Transit Authority now sues graffiti writers to recover the clean-up costs, and in some cases, the authors have to clean up the graffiti as well. The agency loses about $1 million in 'vandalism' costs each year.

Banksy, Los Angeles, 2010

A wall with graffiti and murals in East London

A political message and art in a graffiti in Berlin, 2016

1 68 Read and listen. Is graffiti considered an art form or is it a crime?

____

____

2 Complete the sentences with the words in the box.

critic graffiti mural Museum works

a The art __________ said that the painting was worth $400,000.

b A __________ is a painting that is painted on a wall.

c The Los Angeles County __________ of Art has a beautiful collection of paintings.

d Leonardo da Vinci's *Mona Lisa* is one of the most famous __________ of art in the world.

e Many people think that __________ isn't art – it's vandalism.

3 Do you think graffiti is a form of art and expression or a form of crime? Why?

VOCABULARY IN PICTURES

Crime Verbs

arrest a suspect

be guilty

be innocent

catch a thief

commit a crime

do community service

go on trial

go to prison

investigate a crime

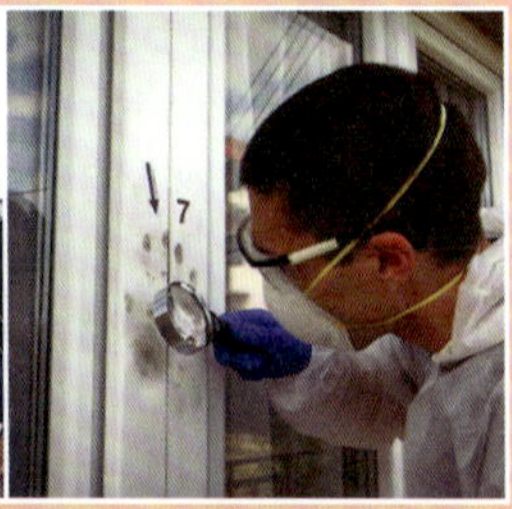
look for clues

pay a fine

question a suspect

solve a crime

suspect someone

Crimes and Criminals

burglar

burglary

kidnapper

kidnapping

murder

murderer

pickpocket

pickpocketing

robber

robbery

theft

thief

vandal

vandalism

GRAMMAR GUIDE

Modals of Deduction

modals of deduction
You **must** be tired after your journey.
He **can't** be guilty – he's the most honest person I know.

- we use *must* and *can't* for deduction
- *must* and *can't* take the same form for all subject pronouns
- we use *must* when we are certain about something because there is a logical explanation for it
  John has walked 20 miles today. He **must** be tired.
- we use *can't* when we are certain that something is impossible
  You **can't** be hungry now – you had a pizza and cake for dinner!

Modals of Possibility

modals of possibility
He **might** be Jessica's brother.
It **may** be sunny tomorrow.
She **could** be at the gym.

- we use *might*, *may* and *could* when something is possible or probable but not certain
  Joanne didn't answer the phone. She **might** have turned it off.
  My wallet isn't in my bag – I **may** have left it at the restaurant.
  The door is open. They **could** be in the house.
- *might*, *may* and *could* take the same form for all subject pronouns

must / must not

obligation
To press charges, you **must** go to the police station.
He **must** appear in front of a jury.
They **must** stay in court until the end of the trial!

- we use *must* for obligation

prohibition
You **must not** interfere with crime evidence.
He **must not** touch what the burglars touched.
They **must not** cross the line.

- *must not* is used for prohibition
- to talk about something that is not an obligation nor a prohibition, we use *don't / doesn't have to*
  You **don't have to** call the police if it was just theft. You can report it over the internet.

PROGRESS CHECK

Crime Verbs

1 Match the phrases to make sentences.

a The man who stole the painting is going
b The vandals have to do
c He had to pay
d The police are suspecting
e Interpol has arrested
f A security guard caught
g The school security officers suspect

☐ five men for drug smuggling.
☐ the ambassador was kidnapped.
☐ a woman stealing books.
☐ a freshman graffitied the bathroom stalls.
☐ community service for six months.
☐ to prison for ten years.
☐ a $100 fine because he parked his car illegally.

Crimes and Criminals

2 Which criminals do these crimes?

a theft ______________
b vandalism ______________
c kidnapping ______________
d murder ______________
e pickpocketing ______________
f robbery ______________
g burglary ______________

Modals of Deduction and Possibility

3 Choose the correct modal verb.

a He **must / can't** be Australian. He doesn't speak English.
b She **might / can't** be Ann's sister. They look quite similar.
c It **could / must** be his book. It has his name in it.
d He **can't / may** like football. I can't remember.
e He **can't / might** be the robber. He's too tall.
f You **must / can't** be thirsty. It's very hot outside.

Review: *must / must not*

4 Write O if the sentence refers to an *obligation*, P if it's a *prohibition* and D if it's a *deduction*.

a ☐ You must not take plants to a foreign country.
b ☐ We must carry an ID card at all times.
c ☐ He must have bought those flip-flops in Brazil.
d ☐ You walked past the store so you must have seen the robbers.
e ☐ They must get a vaccine for yellow fever to go to Costa Rica.
f ☐ She must not go out in the sun without sunscreen. Her skin is too sensitive.

Grammar Buildup 7

1 2 3 4 5 6 7 8

5 Underline the correct answer.

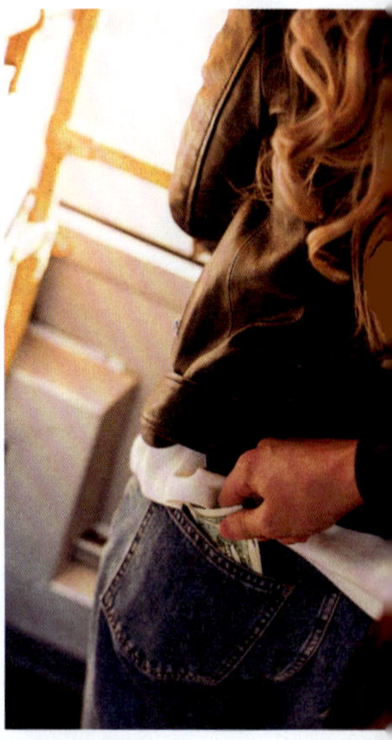

The police **a are / have** investigating a recent increase in pickpocketing on trains in Chicago. In February, 157 people had their wallets **b stealing / stolen** on trains, and 70 more **c reported / report** their cell phone stolen. Last week, Edna Thomas witnessed a pickpocket in action on the Purple Line. 'One man **d got / has got** on the train at the same time as me. He looked ordinary – he **e has worn / was wearing** a pair of jeans and a T-shirt. The train was full so he **f stand / stood** up. Suddenly, I saw him move his hand slightly. When he got off at the next stop, the woman next to him **g was noticing / noticed** that her purse was missing.' 'He **h must / can't** have stolen it,' she said.

8 Communicate

1

Joanna17: I'm buying a new car! I'm so excited – I'm going to buy it tomorrow.

2:16 PM Nov 6th

2

"The single biggest problem in communication is the illusion that it has taken place."

George Bernard Shaw (1856-1950)

3

4

RECEIPT

==============================

Carter's Fruit and Vegetable Shop

2 APPLES	$0.70
5 BANANAS	$2.00
1kg POTATOES	$1.00

==============================

TOTAL: $3.70

Date: 12/05/2019 Time: 10:27

THANK YOU FOR YOUR BUSINESS

5

Smoked salmon paté

450g smoked salmon, chopped in small pieces
1 tsp chopped fresh thyme
Juice of 1 small lemon
2 tbsp butter
85g soft cream cheese

1 Mix the smoked salmon, thyme and lemon juice in a food processor.
2 Add the butter and cheese. Season with paprika.
3 Process again until the mixture is smooth.
4 Chill in the fridge overnight. Serve with fresh bread.

VOCABULARY 1

The Written Word

1 Match text genres 1-8 with words in the box. Use your dictionary to check the meaning of the other words.

advertisement ☐ article ☐ blog ☐
cartoon ☐ dictionary entry ☐
instruction manual ☐ label ☐
quote ☐ receipt ☐ recipe ☐
review ☐ travel guide ☐ tweet ☐

2 🔊 69 Listen and repeat.

3 Choose the correct words. Then answer the questions in pairs.

a Do you know any **quotes / advertisements** by Shakespeare?

b Do you usually follow **recipes / receipts** when you cook or do you invent your own?

c Do you usually read **blogs / articles** in a newspaper or do you only look at the **cartoons / labels**?

d Do you usually read the **dictionary entry / instruction manual** when you buy a new gadget or do you try to work it out on your own?

e Do you usually read the **reviews / labels** before you see a movie?

f If you take a gap year, will you write a **blog / tweet**?

6

Colin Firth Wins an Oscar!

After the huge success of his movie *The King's Speech*, it was no surprise that Colin Firth won the Oscar for best actor for his starring role as King George VI. Since the movie was released in January 2011, it has made over $400 million dollars at the box office. Firth is currently working on new projects.

WINNER: Firth with his Oscar

7

R

ride1 /raɪd/ (past tense **rode** /rəʊd/; past participle **ridden** /ˈrɪd(ə)n/) verb
1 to sit on an animal, especially a horse, and control its movements as it moves along: *John used to ride his horse every weekend, but he doesn't have time now.*
2 to travel in a car, train, plane, etc. especially as a passenger: *They were riding on the subway when the train broke down.*
3 to take part in a race on a horse, bicycle, motorcycle etc.: *Peter is going to ride in the race tomorrow. I hope he wins!*

8

BARGAIN BREAKS WITH TAYLOR'S TRAVEL

Need a vacation but can't afford an expensive trip abroad? **Think again ...** you can with Taylor's!

With a week's vacation in Europe starting at just $200 per person including flights and accommodation. Your dream destination could be cheaper than you ever thought possible.

Call 0345 761987 TODAY to find out more!

READING 1

1 Look at the texts. Which one do you think looks the most interesting? Why?

____

____

____

READING STRATEGY

Identify the genre of a text in order to know what to expect from it.

2 70 Read and listen to the texts. Write T for *true* or F for *false*. Then give reasons for your answer.

a ☐ Text 1: Joanna has bought a new car.

____

b ☐ Text 6: The movie *The King's Speech* hasn't been a success.

____

c ☐ Text 8: Taylor's Travel sells expensive vacations.

____

d ☐ Text 7: The dictionary entry only gives information about the meaning of the word.

____

e ☐ Text 4: Someone spent $3.70 on fruit and vegetables.

____

f ☐ Text 2: George Bernard Shaw thinks that communication is easy.

____

____

____

g ☐ Text 5: You have to make the salmon paté one day before you want to eat it.

____

3 Find the words or phrases in the texts for definitions a-e.

a a false or wrong belief or idea (text 2)

____

b cut into tiny pieces (text 5) ______________

c metro (text 7) ______________

d a place to stay (text 8) ______________

e the main part in a play, movie or TV series (text 6) ______________

4 CLASS VOTE What do you think? Do you agree with the quote (text 2)?

GRAMMAR 1

Tense Review

1 Read these sentences. Match the verbs in bold to their respective tense uses.

a John **used to** ride his horse every weekend, but he doesn't have time now.

b You **thought** I might not want your flowers.

c The flowers you bought **have lasted** all this time.

d The biggest problem in communication is the illusion that it **has taken place**.

e **I'm buying** a new car!

f Firth **is** currently **working** on his new movie.

g Some men never **think** of buying flowers.

h They **were riding** on the subway when the train broke down.

i **I'm going to buy** a new car tomorrow.

j We**'ll** definitely **watch** the movie!

☐ simple present for habits

☐ present progressive for an action happening now

☐ simple past for an action in the past

☐ past progressive for an action in progress in the past

☐ present perfect for an action that started in the past and continues until now

☐ present perfect for an action at an indefinite time in the past

☐ *used to* to talk about a past habit

☐ *going to* to talk about a future plan

☐ present progressive to talk about a future arrangement

☐ simple future to talk about a future prediction

The Present

2 Underline the most appropriate verb form to complete the paragraph.

Nowadays, the internet **a is / is being** one of the most popular forms of communication. More than one billion people in the world regularly **b use / are using** computers and smartphones every day. Nobody **c knows / is knowing** exactly how many people have internet access, but experts **d believe / are believing** it is around 29% of the world's population. Chat rooms and social networking sites **e become / are becoming** more and more popular among all age groups. At the moment, IT specialists **f try / are trying** to improve internet connections to make our experience better.

3 INTERFACE Complete the sentences about yourself. Then ask and answer questions about them in pairs.

a I often...

b I ... every day.

c I don't usually...

d At the moment I'm...

e These days I'm...

f I'm not ... now.

What do you do every day?

The Past

4 Complete the text with the correct form of the verbs in parentheses. Use the simple past, past progressive or present perfect.

The inventor Guglielmo Marconi ___*sent*___ (send) and **a** __________ (receive) the first radio signal in Italy in 1895. Marconi **b** __________ (work) in Italy when he **c** __________ (invent) the first radio transmitter, but he couldn't get money there to develop it, so he **d** __________ (go) to Britain.

Radio technology **e** __________ (grow) considerably since its early development. The first radio station **f** __________ (start) broadcasting in 1902. Nowadays there are millions of stations. For the past few years it **g** __________ (be) possible to listen to the radio online.

The Future

5 Choose the most appropriate verb tenses.

Frank: I've had an argument with my friend. I **a 'll meet / 'm meeting** her later, but I'm a bit nervous.
Jessie: Where are you going to meet?
Frank: I'm not sure. We **b will probably meet / are probably meeting** at school.
Jessie: I think you should meet somewhere quiet, then you can talk.
Frank: Good idea, I **c will text / am texting** her soon and arrange to meet at a café.
Jessie: Do you know what you want to say to her?
Frank: Yes, I've thought about it, I know what I **d am saying / am going to say**. I think I **e will apologize / am apologizing** for forgetting her birthday.
Jessie: Good idea.
Frank: And I've bought some flowers. I **f am giving / am going to give** them to her.
Jessie: Good luck! Don't forget to take her the flowers.
Frank: Don't worry. I **g won't forget / am not forgetting**. Thanks.

6 Complete the sentences with the correct form of the verbs in parentheses. Use *will*, *be going to* or the present progressive.

a Scientists predict that in the future communication ____________ (be) even faster. They say people ____________ (not have to) speak face to face if they don't want to.

b I ____________ (meet) Bill later, I've just arranged it. We ____________ (write) our article for the school newspaper together.

c I ____________ (not do) anything at all next weekend, I haven't made any arrangements at all. I ____________ (relax)!

d Experts say that the internet ____________ (grow) even bigger over the next few years and soon people ____________ (not be able) to imagine life without it.

TIP

The simple present is also used to talk about timetables in the future.
The train to London leaves at 18:50.
The movie finishes in 15 minutes.

GRAMMAR GUIDE page 134

LISTENING

Communications Quiz

1 Look at the words in the box. What do they all have in common?

hieroglyphics homing pigeons newspapers alphabet microphone postal service printing press telegraph telephone typewriter

____

2 71 Listen to the quiz and choose the correct answers.

a The … developed the first alphabet.
1 Egyptians 2 Phoenicians

b The first use of homing pigeons was in …
1 England 2 Greece

c The … established the first postal service.
1 Romans 2 Chinese

d The printing press was invented in Europe in …
1 1450 2 1650

e Henry Mill patented the … in 1714.
1 telephone 2 typewriter

f Emile Berliner invented a box that could reproduce … in 1876.
1 sound 2 images

3 71 Listen again. Then write T for *true* or F for *false*.

a ☐ The Greeks started using homing pigeons around 1775BC.

b ☐ The first message sent by pigeon was about an invasion.

c ☐ The first daily newspaper appeared in 1650 in Germany.

d ☐ Emile Berliner invented the microphone.

SPEAKING

Good News

72 Josh is talking to his dad about a prize he won at the school art competition. Listen and complete the dialogue.

Dad, guess what?

What???

My group **a** ______________ the *Recycle and Create* art competition at school!

CONGRATS! I'm sure you deserved it! You **b** ______________ a great student! How many students took part?

Around 100, I guess! We were all evaluated based on creativity, percentage of use of recyclable and environmentally friendly materials.

I **c** ______________ how hard you and your friends **d** ______________ to collect all those bottles and cans and create a wonderful panel.

Yeah, and now we know how important **e** ______________ to reintroduce all that 'trash' in the cycle of life...

f ______________ so proud of you, son! **g** ______________ an exhibition of the projects, isn't there?

Yeah, **h** ______________ open till the end of next month.

Great! So, your mom and I can visit it next Friday. What **i** ______________?

FUNCTIONAL LANGUAGE

Talking about News and Sympathizing

What happened?
How was it?
You did a great job!
Congrats!
You deserved it!

Speaking Task

Write a new dialogue between you and a friend.

Step 1

Choose a situation or use your own ideas.

"I've failed my exams."

"I have tickets for the music festival!"

Step 2

Think about what you say.

I've had some bad news. I...
There's some good news, too. I...

Think about how your friend responds.

Oh no! How terrible.
Congratulations, that's wonderful news!

Step 3

Write your dialogue.

Step 4

Work in pairs. Take turns practicing your dialogue.

CULTURE

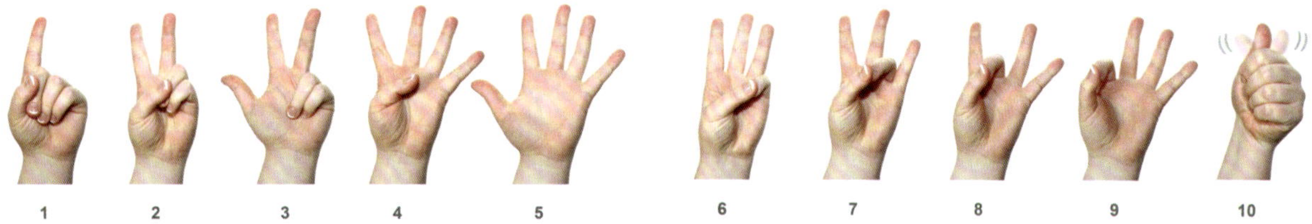

American Sign Language

American Sign Language (ASL) has been one of the primary means of communication for the hearing impaired since the 1800s. At that time, Thomas Hopkins Gallaudet, an American deaf educator, helped develop a language and co-founded the first institution for the education of the deaf in the US, which is now known as the American School for the Deaf.

Millions of Americans use sign language as their native language. The deaf community is very large and the chance to interact in their own language is very important for them, especially if you understand that the language you speak represents your country's identity. Those who use sign language also love to see their language used before their eyes.

Besides, sign language can help bridge the gap between those who can hear and those who are hearing impaired.

Nowadays, the practice of teaching hearing children sign language is becoming popular all over the country. Studies have shown that learning ASL brings many educational benefits such as having the opportunity to gain cultural heritage of the deaf community, which includes various forms of cultural expressions, such as visual poetry, theater and folklore. Another key factor is learning about values, beliefs, social and educational aspects of the deaf community, which will certainly help understand other cultures as well.

1 🔊 73 Read and listen to the text. Then write T for *true* or F for *false*.

a ☐ ASL has been the only means of communication of the hearing impaired for a long time.

b ☐ Thomas Hopkins Gallaudet, whose son was deaf, helped develop a language for the deaf community.

c ☐ Sign language can help bridge the gap between those who can hear and those who are hearing impaired.

d ☐ Nowadays, the practice of teaching hearing children sign language is not popular in the country.

e ☐ ASL provides no educational benefits.

2 What do you know about sign language in your country? Find as much information as you can about it.

____

____

____

3 Would you like to learn your country's sign language? Why (not)?

____

VOCABULARY 2

Adjectives with *-able* and *-ible*

1 Complete the definitions with the adjectives in the box.

acceptable bearable flexible reasonable reliable responsible ~~visible~~

A person or thing that you can see is *visible*.

a A person who can deal with a lot of responsibility is ________.

b A person you can rely on is ________.

c A person who shows reason is ________.

d A person who adapts quickly to new situations is ________.

e A situation that you can bear is ________.

f A situation or thing that you can accept is ________.

2 Match the adjectives from activity 1 with their opposites in the box.

inflexible invisible irresponsible ~~unacceptable~~ unbearable unreasonable unreliable

acceptable – unacceptable

____

____

____

____

____

____

3 🔊 74 Listen, check and repeat.

4 Complete the sentences with words from activity 2.

Lucy never does anything she says she will do. She's very *unreliable*.

a We complained because their behavior was ________, and ________ – they completely destroyed the house.

b The magician made the rabbit ________ – you couldn't see it at all!

c This situation is awful. It's really ________ – I just can't tolerate it anymore.

d John is very ________. He doesn't like changes.

e My mom said I couldn't go to the party – she's so ________.

READING 2

1 Look at the cartoon self-portrait. What three questions would you ask the cartoonist?

____

____

2 🔊 75 Read and listen. Did you have similar questions?

3 Read the text again. Then write T for *true* or F for *false*. Correct the false sentences.

a ☐ Doug Savage has created a webcomic.

____

b ☐ Doug had a creative job.

____

c ☐ He has always read comics.

____

d ☐ Doug draws his cartoons on the computer.

____

e ☐ He has drawn 1000 cartoons.

____

The Man Behind the Chickens

Cartoonists are some of the most adaptable and creative people when it comes to communicating a complex idea in a small space. Doug Savage is best-known for his Savage Chickens webcomic – each cartoon is drawn on one single sticky note! Here he tells us all about himself.

Why do you draw chickens?
I drew cartoons a lot when I was younger, but when I started working in an office, I slowly lost the ability to draw. When I started drawing cartoons again, chickens were the only thing that I remembered how to draw!

When did you start drawing chickens?
I started drawing the chickens in autumn 2004 and I began posting them online in January 2005.

Why did you decide to start a webcomic?
I wasn't enjoying my office job because it wasn't very creative, so I was looking for some sort of artistic activity. A lot of people were starting blogs at the time. I thought it would be fun to create one too, so I started putting my comics on the web.

Did you read comics when you were younger?
Yes, I did. As a child, I read all of the comic strips I could find at the local library – especially Peanuts. I've always enjoyed authors who combine art and storytelling, such as Richard Scarry, Dr. Seuss and Raymond Briggs.

What do you draw on?
I draw on actual yellow sticky notes, just like the ones you can find in an office. Then, I scan them and edit the images on the computer.

What inspires you?
Everything, but mostly human behavior. People are so funny, and the world can be a very silly place.

What has been your biggest achievement so far?
A collection of my cartoons has been published in a book, which is incredible. But I'm also very proud of all the work that I've created over the past few years. I'm amazed that I've drawn over 1600 cartoons!

What are your plans for the future?
I hope to publish more books and do more animation. And I'm always experimenting with new techniques, so I'd like to try more painting and maybe even write a graphic novel. I want to keep trying new things!

GRAMMAR 2

Tense Review: Question Forms

1 Read the sentences below. Underline the auxiliaries when provided.

- **a** Why do you draw chickens?
- **b** When did you start drawing chickens?
- **c** Who inspires you?
- **d** What has been you biggest achievement so far?

2 Complete the chart below with the questions from activity 1.

question forms	
Use the auxiliary when the subject is present in the question	Don't use the auxiliary when the subject is the question word

3 Order the words to make questions.

- **a** you / write / will / a blog post / later today ?
  ____
- **b** what / you / were / reading / when / arrived / your teacher ?
  ____
- **c** you / what / do / did / before / you / came to school ?
  ____
- **d** send / you / yesterday / did / any emails ?
  ____

4 Complete the questions with the correct form of the verbs in parentheses.

- **a** What ____________________ (your friends / do) when you arrived at school?
- **b** ____________________ (you / ever / make) a podcast?
- **c** ____________________ (your friends / arrive) at school yet?
- **d** Have you made any arrangements for this weekend? What ____________________ (you / do)?
- **e** ____________________ (you / buy) a new bike later this year?

GRAMMAR GUIDE page 134

WRITING

A Blog Post

1 🔊 76 Read, listen and answer.

What is the advantage of social networking sites?

____

What is the Best Way to Communicate?

I've been thinking about the different ways we communicate. On my blog today, I'm discussing the best method of communication. In the past, people only used to be able to communicate in person or by letter. However, nowadays there are many different ways to communicate, such as email, phone and chat rooms. As I see it, different forms of communication are more appropriate at different times.

For example, it's better to spend time with your friends in person because you can enjoy their company. What's more, the best way to solve problems is face to face. However, when you are out and you need to give someone some information, then the quickest and easiest option is to send a text message. Finally, email and social networking sites are a good way of keeping in touch with a lot of people, especially if they live far away.

To conclude, in my opinion you should choose the best way to communicate depending on the circumstances.

What do you think?

Joanne

2 Rewrite the sentences using the words in the box.

as a result finally firstly ~~furthermore~~ I believe on the other hand secondly whereas

Sending texts is easy. It is cheap. (linker of addition) *Sending texts is easy. Furthermore, it is cheap.*

a Some teenagers stay up too late sending messages. (opinion expression)

____

____

b Texts are easy to send. Some people send far too many. (linker of result)

____

____

c Making phone calls can be expensive. Sending texts is cheap. (linker of contrast)

____

____

d There are several advantages to sending texts. Texts are cheap. You can send them from anywhere. They don't take long to write. (3 linkers of sequencing)

____

____

e On the one hand, texts are easy to send. They can become addictive. (linker of contrast)

____

____

LANGUAGE FOCUS

Checking Your Work

a Check that you have used correct grammar, word order, spelling and punctuation.
b Check that you have used linkers.
c Check that you have used appropriate expressions to give your opinion.

3 Write a blog post (150-170 words). Too many young people are addicted to social networking.

What is your opinion?

Writing a Blog Post

Step 1 > PLAN

Decide your opinion. What are the advantages and disadvantages of social networking?

Step 2 > WRITE

Write your first draft. Write three paragraphs. Think about what to include in each paragraph.

Step 3 > CHECK

Check your work. Have you used linkers and sequencing words?

Step 4 > WRITE

Write your final copy and hand in your work.

VOCABULARY IN PICTURES

The Written Word

advertisement

article

blog

cartoon

dictionary entry

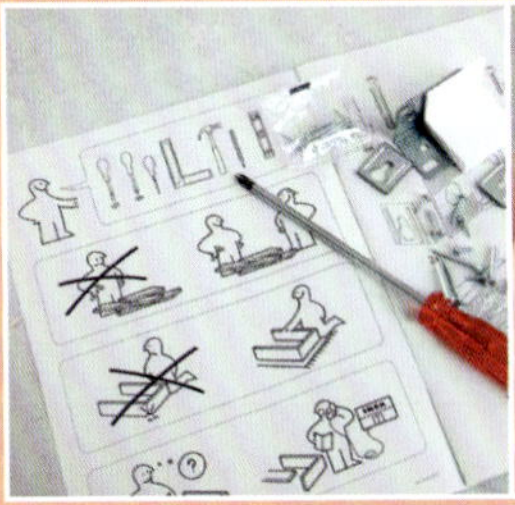
instruction manual

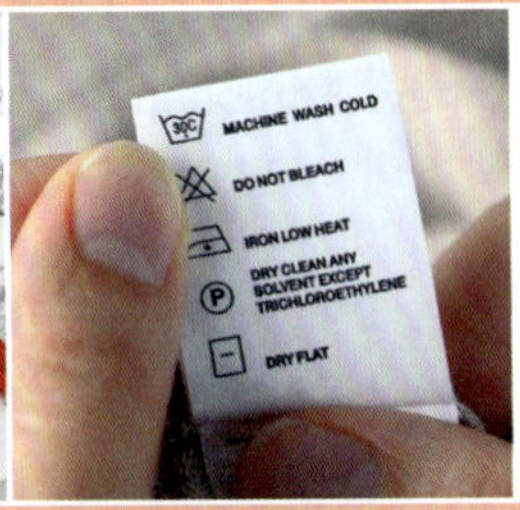

label

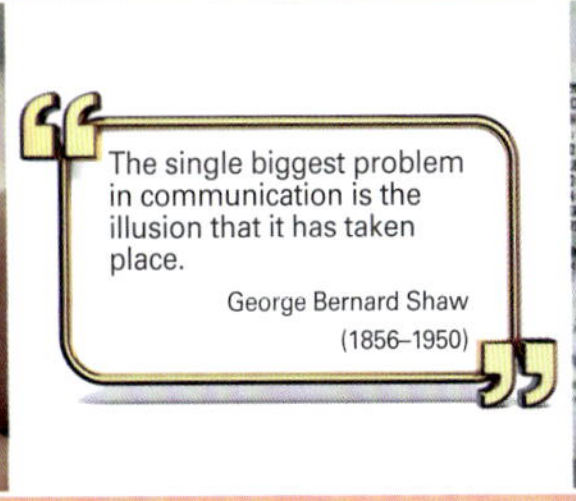

quote

receipt

recipe

review

travel guide

tweet

Adjectives with *-able* and *-ible*

acceptable

bearable

flexible

inflexible

invisible

irresponsible

reasonable

reliable

responsible

unacceptable

unbearable

unreasonable

unreliable

visible

GRAMMAR GUIDE

Tense Review

simple present	
+	I **play** basketball.
–	He **doesn't like** rock music.
?	**Do** they **eat** dinner at 7pm? Yes, they **do**. / No, they **don't**.

present progressive	
+	I'**m waiting** for the bus.
–	He **isn't talking** to Louise.
?	**Are** they **worrying** about the exam? Yes, they **are**. / No, they **aren't**.

present perfect	
+	I **have spoken** to Jenny.
–	She **hasn't bought** a new car.
?	**Have** you **seen** Brad Pitt's new movie? Yes, I **have**. / No, I **haven't**.

will	
+	I **will** go to college in London.
–	She **won't** be late.
?	**Will** they **move** to a new house next year? Yes, they **will**. / No, they **won't**.

simple past	
+	I **lived** in France for two years.
–	She **didn't watch** the tennis match.
?	**Did** he **read** the book? Yes, he **did**. / No, he **didn't**.

past progressive	
+	I **was listening** to a CD.
–	She **wasn't reading** a book.
?	**Were** they **playing** soccer? Yes, they **were**. / No, they **weren't**.

be going to	
+	**I'm going to** watch a movie.
–	He **isn't going to** sell his car.
?	**Are** you **going to** speak to John? Yes, I **am**. / No, **I'm not**.

question forms
What is your name? How long have you been interested in music? What sports did you play when you were younger? What are you doing now? What are you going to do next? Will you go on vacation next year?

PROGRESS CHECK

The Written Word

1 Complete the sentences with the words in the box.

advertisements articles headlines instruction manual recipe

a When I read a newspaper, I look at the ______________ first to get an idea of what all the ______________ are about.

b I don't usually watch the ______________ on TV because most of them are boring.

c This soup tastes horrible – I should have used a better ______________.

d I don't understand how to work my smartphone. Have you seen the ______________?

Adjectives with *-able* and *-ible*

2 Choose the correct adjectives to complete the sentences.

a She's late again! That's completely **acceptable / unacceptable**.

b He wouldn't share his pizza with me – he's so **reasonable / unreasonable**.

c He didn't see me in the street yesterday – maybe I'm **invisible / visible**!

d My sister is absolutely **bearable / unbearable** – she's so noisy, and she always steals my clothes.

Tense Review

3 Choose the correct answers.

a Yesterday I **read / have read** the newspaper.

b I think I **will send / are sending** an email tomorrow if we **don't / didn't** hear from Pete.

c I usually **listen / am listening** to the radio every morning before school.

d They know this cartoonist. They' **re / ve** read her cartoons before.

4 Complete the text with the correct form of the verbs in parentheses.

If you **a** ______________ (love) computer games, you **b** ______________ (be) happy to hear that an exciting new games console **c** ______________ (release) next month. Designed by Fusion, the console **d** ______________ (have) lots of innovative new features. Fusion **e** ______________ (design) other consoles in the past, including the BS-20 which **f** ______________ (sell) in Europe.

5 Write questions for these answers.

a ______________________________

Yes, I have written lots of articles.

b ______________________________

No, I won't use that recipe.

c ______________________________

No, I wasn't reading that travel guide when you arrived.

6 Write questions. Then answer them.

a what / you / do / yesterday ?

____

b what / you / do / next weekend ?

____

c how long / you / have / your cell phone ?

____

d what / you / do / now ?

____

Grammar Buildup 8

1 2 3 4 5 6 7 8

7 Choose the correct answers.

How much **a do you know / are you knowing** about text messages? Also known as SMS, the first one **b was sent / is sent** in December 1992 by engineer Neil Pepworth. Since then, text messaging **c is becoming / has become** popular all over the world.

Text messages **d are / have been** an easy way to communicate, especially when it's difficult to make phone calls. Sending text messages can be dangerous though: some people **e admitted / are admitting** to sending text messages while driving.

Text messages **f are still developing / will still develop**. You can now send photos and videos by text message.

Who knows what **g is happening / will happen** in the future?

Review 4

VOCABULARY

GRAMMAR

Start

1

In order to assemble the shelves, you must read the **instruction manual** / **label**.

2

He was arrested for **robbery** / **theft** after stealing that woman's bag.

8

The detective is **searching for** / **investigating** a crime.

7

I can barely see the glass in this picture. It's almost **visible** / **invisible**.

9

This definition is so precise, it looks like a dictionary **entry** / **description**.

10

To find out how to wash it, read the **recipe** / **label**.

15

Destroying the bus stop was pure **vandalism** / **theft**.

Finish

3

Ethan is **irresponsible** / **reliable**.
He doesn't take care of any of his belongings.

4

This back pain is just **unbearable** / **bearable**!
I need a painkiller to continue working.

6

The manager had to go on **trial** / **vacation** for not paying the staff's wages.

5

Officer McLaughlin is **interviewing** / **questioning** the suspect now.

11

She's an experienced climber. She's totally **reliable** / **unreliable**!

12

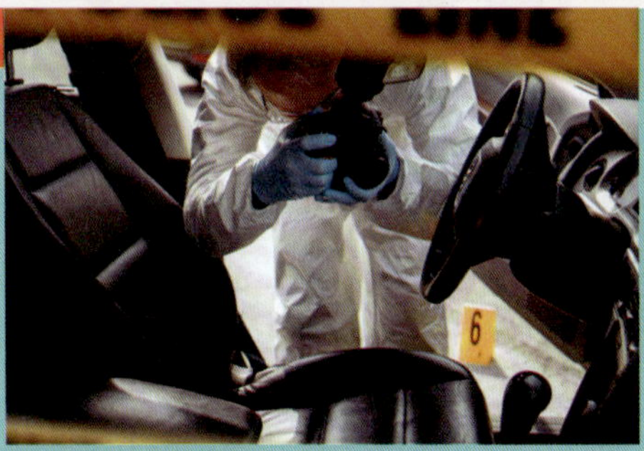

The forensic scientist is looking for **clues** / **tips**.

14

You can find out how much tax is being charged if you read the **recipe** / **receipt**.

13

Always carry your bag in front of you to avoid **robbery** / **pickpocketing**.

Review 4

VOCABULARY

GRAMMAR

Modals of Deduction and Possibility

1 Look at the pictures and the information in the chart and write the corresponding names.

a

Rick

b

____

c

____

	Larry	Rick	Steve
height	1.92m	1.95m	1.60m
weight	90 kilos	75 kilos	110 kilos
hair	brown	blond	black

2 Read the chart in activity 1 again and complete the sentences with *must*, *might* or *can't*.

The short man *can't* be Larry because he's tall.

a The short man ________ be Rick either because he's 1.95m tall.

b The man has brown hair. It ________ be Larry.

c The tall man ________ be Larry.

d The man weighs more than 100 kilos. It ________ be Larry or Rick.

3 Underline the correct words.

Ruth isn't at school. She **can** / **may** be on vacation.

a What's that noise? I'm not sure, but it **might** / **must** be the dog.

b It **can't** / **must not** be 11pm. It's light outside.

c Eva is making a snack. She **must** / **could** be hungry.

d My friends aren't here. They **could** / **can** be late.

4 Rewrite the sentences using *must*, *might* or *can't*.

Where's Elisa? Perhaps she's at home.
Elisa might be at home.

a Ali's lived in England. I'm sure he speaks English.

____

b Luke was with me all day. I'm sure he isn't guilty.

____

c They're not answering the phone. Maybe they're asleep.

____

must / *must not*

5 Match the parts to make rules.

a To win at *Monopoly*,

b If you want the Police to catch the thief,

c In order to apply for scholarship,

d To board the plane,

[ ] you must not carry sharp items.

[*a*] you must buy a lot of properties.

[ ] you must have excellent marks.

[ ] you must not eliminate any clues left.

VOCABULARY

GRAMMAR

Tense Review

6 Write the correct tense for the verbs in bold.

They often **train** before school.
simple present

a Last night I **dreamed** about a ghost.

______

b We**'re going to** have a party soon.

______

c He **was walking** home when he met an old friend.

______

d They**'ve lived** here since 2015.

______

e She **does** her homework every day.

______

f I**'m reading** a great short story.

______

g You**'ll become** rich and famous one day.

______

7 Now match the tenses in activity 6 with their uses.

a [*a*] used for an action or event in the past

b [ ] used for an action or event that started in the past and continues until now

c [ ] used for talking about a future plan

d [ ] used for an action or event which is true at the present time or which happens regularly as a habit

e [ ] used for talking about a future prediction

f [ ] used for an action or event which is happening now

g [ ] used for an action or event in progress in the past

8 Complete the sentences using the simple past, past progressive or present perfect.

We *were* (be) late so we *didn't eat* (not eat) breakfast this morning.

a I ______ (send) you a text message when I ______ (drop) my phone.

b I ______ (visit) the Guggenheim Museum in New York but I ______ (see) the Guggenheim Museum in Bilbao.

c He ______ (not ride) his bike since he ______ (have) an accident.

9 Write complete sentences using the correct future tense.

When / I / (be) / older / I / travel around the world
When I'm older, I'll travel around the world.

a We / (meet) / at the club / at 9pm

______

b That child / (cry) / soon

______

c He / probably / (be) / an engineer / after finishing college

______

10 Write complete questions. Then write short answers.

you / often / argue / with your friends? ✔
Do you often argue with your friends? Yes, I do.

a you / take a shower / yesterday / when / the phone ring? ✓

______

______

b your friends / study / at college next year? ✗

______

______

c you / know / your best friend / since primary school? ✓

______

______

Not a Job, a Vocation

- **What do you enjoy?**
- **What are you good at?**
- **What do you value most in your life?**

1 Before choosing a career path, it is fundamental to find out about your interests, likes and dislikes. Read the chart below and check (✓) the items that apply to you. Add extra information, if necessary.

interests	skills	personal qualities
At school or in your free time, do you enjoy:	Are you good at:	Do you:
☐ art?	☐ ICT?	☐ work well in a group?
☐ sports?	☐ science?	☐ plan ahead?
☐ pets?	☐ math?	☐ help people around you?
☐ socializing?	☐ communication?	☐ have original ideas?
☐ surfing the net?	☐ creative work?	☐ meet deadlines?
Other: ______	☐ sports?	☐ listen to people with different views?
	☐ crafts?	Other: ______
	Other: ______	

2 Interview a friend. Ask him the questions from activity 1. Do you and your friend share the same interests / skills and personal qualities?

Are you good at math?

I'm terrible at math, but I'm really good at crafts!

3 The theory below was developed by American psychologist John Holland. In his view, there are 6 types of vocational personalities which could make people predisposed to certain jobs / occupations. Match the types to the descriptions provided.

a realistic ("doers")
b investigative ("thinkers")
c artistic ("creators")
d social ("helpers")
e enterprising ("persuaders")
f conventional ("organizers")

☐ They like to work with people, helping them whenever needed. They are caring, warm and look for close relationships with others.

☐ They enjoy people's company but want to be in charge of the situation. They are good 'talkers' and are always trying to persuade people to do what they want. They are leaders who value money, status and power.

☐ They like to work with things and are very competitive. The outdoor type, they like working with tools and machines. They are not very good at socializing.

☐ These people like to work with ideas and express their feelings. They are usually very creative as they use their imagination a lot. However, they dislike rules and regulations.

☐ They prefer to think and observe. Logics and concepts are important so science is the field they often enjoy.

☐ They like rules and regulations and emphasize self-control. They are usually well-organized but have little or no imagination.

4 **Read the job titles and write the most suitable type of vocational personality for each group of professionals.**

a artist, actor, dancer, designer, DJ: ____________

b nurse, librarian, physiotherapist: ____________

c chemist, mathematician, pharmacist: ____________

d lawyer, manager, journalist: ____________

e secretary, clerk, supervisor: ____________

f farmer, truck driver, builder, carpenter: ____________

Finding Out the Class's Vocational Types

Imagine you are a vocational counselor and you are going to interview a classmate. You will also be interviewed, so that the whole class can find out what vocational types each one represents and how each one of you can help build a collaborative society.

Doing

1. Interview your classmate, asking questions about his or her interests, personal qualities and skills.
2. Individually, evaluate what vocational type(s) your classmate fits the most.
3. Get together again and discuss your results.
4. Write your conclusion after hearing his or her opinion.

Presenting

5. Elect a representative to build a chart to tally up the results for the whole class.
6. Each pair presents their result to the whole class, making a brief comment as to why you've reached that conclusion.
7. After the last pair has spoken, the representative sums up how many students represent each category and presents the results to the class.
8. Organize a discussion on the rates at which each category appeared in the final results:
   - Are any of the categories absent?
   - Is there a category that has disproportionate results?
   - If you were to start a new town, or colony in space, how would you organize things considering your different vocations?

Reflecting

9. In what ways are your interests, personal qualities and skills similar to most of your classmates'?
10. Do you think all people can fit into only one of these categories? Why or why not?
11. What have you learned about yourself by doing this project?

Irregular Verbs

Infinitive	Simple Past	Past Participle
127 **be** /bi/	was / were /wɑz/, /wɜr/	been /bin/, /bɪn/
begin /bɪ'gɪn/	began /bɪ'gæn/	begun /bɪ'gʌn/
break /breɪk/	broke /broʊk/	broken /'broʊkən/
bring /brɪŋ/	brought /brɔt/	brought /brɔt/
build /bɪld/	built /bɪlt/	built /bɪlt/
buy /baɪ/	bought /bɔt/	bought /bɔt/
choose /tʃuz/	chose /tʃoʊz/	chosen /'tʃoʊz(ə)n/
come /kʌm/	came /keɪm/	come /kʌm/
do /du/	did /dɪd/	done /dʌn/
drink /drɪŋk/	drank /dræŋk/	drunk /drʌŋk/
drive /draɪv/	drove /droʊv/	driven /'drɪv(ə)n/
eat /it/	ate /eɪt/	eaten /'it(ə)n/
fall /fɔl/	fell /fel/	fallen /'fɔlən/
find /faɪnd/	found /faʊnd/	found /faʊnd/
fly /flaɪ/	flew /flu/	flown /floʊn/
forget /fər'get/	forgot /fər'gɑt/	forgotten /fər'gɑt(ə)n/
get /get/	got /gɑt/	got /gɑt/, gotten /'gɑt(ə)n/
give /gɪv/	gave /geɪv/	given /'gɪv(ə)n/
go /goʊ/	went /went/	gone /gɔn/
have /hæv/	had /həd/	had /həd/
hear /hɪr/	heard /hɜrd/	heard /hɜrd/
know /noʊ/	knew /nu/	known /noʊn/
learn /lɜrn/	learnt / learned /lɜrnt/, /'lɜrnəd/	learnt / learned /lɜrnt/, /'lɜrnəd/
leave /liv/	left /left/	left /left/
lose /luz/	lost /lɔst/	lost /lɔst/
make /meɪk/	made /meɪd/	made /meɪd/
meet /mit/	met /met/	met /met/
pay /peɪ/	paid /peɪd/	paid /peɪd/
put /pʊt/	put /pʊt/	put /pʊt/
read /rid/	read /red/	read /red/
run /rʌn/	ran /ræn/	run /rʌn/
say /seɪ/	said /sed/	said /sed/
see /si/	saw /sɔ/	seen /sin/
sell /sel/	sold /soʊld/	sold /soʊld/
sing /sɪŋ/	sang /sæŋ/	sung /sʌŋ/
sit /sɪt/	sat /sæt/	sat /sæt/
speak /spik/	spoke /spoʊk/	spoken /'spoʊkən/
take /teɪk/	took /tʊk/	taken /'teɪkən/
teach /titʃ/	taught /tɔt/	taught /tɔt/
tell /tel/	told /toʊld/	told /toʊld/
think /θɪŋk/	thought /θɔt/	thought /θɔt/
wear /wer/	wore /wɔr/	worn /wɔrn/
win /wɪn/	won /wʌn/	won /wʌn/
write /raɪt/	wrote /roʊt/	written /'rɪt(ə)n/

Workbook

CONTENTS

Starter

Jobs and Life Events

1 Find in the word spiral the name of 18 jobs.

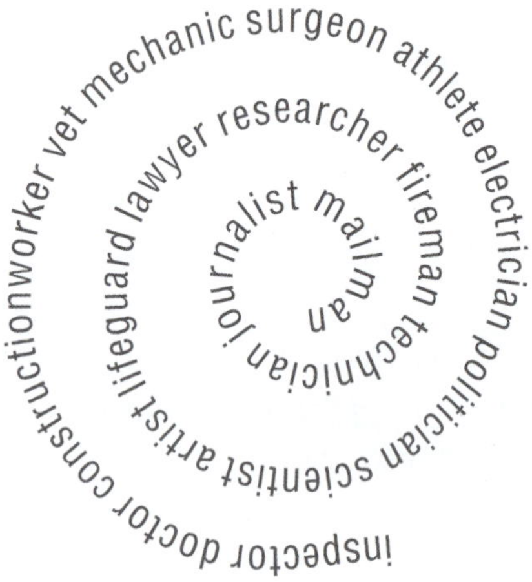

2 Match the columns to find at least 8 life events. Items can have more than one match.

a be	a house
b get	school
c start	drive
d learn to	born
e leave	home
f buy	children
g have	a job
	married

3 Write down the life events found in activity 2.

____

____

____

____

____

____

____

____

____

____

____

Clothes and Accessories

4 Number the clothes and accessories in the pictures according to the words in the box.

1 boots	2 dress	3 jacket	4 pants
5 shirt	6 skirt	7 sneakers	8 T-shirt

5 Complete the names of the clothes and accessories with the missing letters.

a c ___ ___ ___

b ___ e a n ___

c s ___ ___ ___ ___ ___ r

d s ___ ___ ___ f

e s ___ ___ ___ ___ s

Prepositions

6 Underline the most appropriate preposition to complete the sentences.

a Is this bus heading **toward / over** town?

b This is a very interesting town: let me show you **across / around**.

c She could see a figure **along / through** the fog.

d Keep your hands **into / away from** the hot stove!

e Please put the bowl **into / along** the sink.

f The ship sailed **under / along** the coast.

make and *do*

7 Complete the sentences with the words in the box.

a decision a mistake charity work homework money

a Many students find it difficult to do __________ under pressure.

b Sometimes you'll have to make __________ between something bad and something worse.

c Everyone makes __________ every now and then.

d There is no easy way to make __________.

e The high school students are raising funds to do __________.

should / shouldn't

8 Underline the words to complete the sentences.

a You **should / shouldn't** research your family tree. It would be so interesting!

b You **should / shouldn't** definitely follow your dream. It's really worth doing it.

c You **should / shouldn't** conquer your fear. There is no reason to be afraid.

d You **should / shouldn't** pass by those who need your help. Be compassionate.

e You **should / shouldn't** find time for studying. You'd feel more confident at school.

f You **should / shouldn't** be afraid to say no. Only you know what's best for you.

will and *be going to*

9 Order the words to make sentences.

a new book / a / think / bestseller / her / I / will become

____

____

b reopen / summer / That store / definitely / before / will

____

____

____

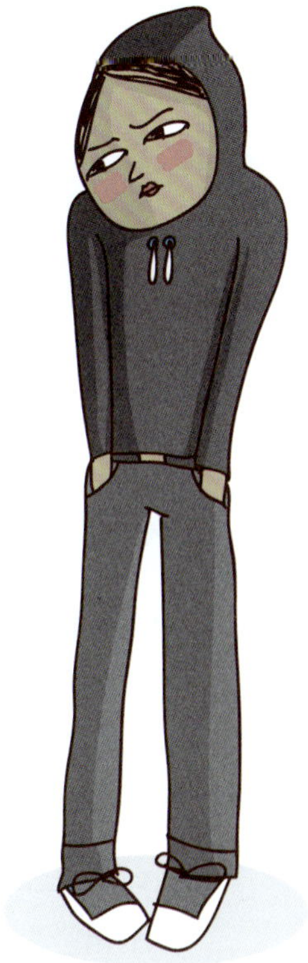

c class / going to / We / afternoon / this / have / English / aren't

____

____

____

d a retreat / spend / the weekend / going to / at / They're

____

____

____

e because / acting classes / won't take / too shy / I'm / I / the

____

____

First Conditional

10 Match the columns to make sentences.

a If you go to bed late	if the forecast is for bad weather.
b We won't go	if we agree to some rules.
c If you miss the flight	we'll have time to watch some TV.
d Everybody will be more comfortable	you'll have to buy another ticket.
e If you finish doing your homework soon	you'll feel tired in the morning.

11 Write down the sentences formed in activity 10. Use commas when necessary.

a ______________________________

____

b ______________________________

____

c ______________________________

____

d ______________________________

____

e ______________________________

____

1 Changing Lives

VOCABULARY 1

Life-changing Events

1 Complete the words with the vowels.

g _e_ t _i_ n t _o_ t r _o_ _u_ b l _e_

a b ___ c ___ m ___ r ___ c h

b g ___ ___ b r ___ ___ d

c c h ___ n g e s c h ___ ___ l s

d m ___ v ___

e t ___ k ___ ___ g ___ p y ___ ___ r

f s t ___ r t y ___ ___ r ___ w n b ___ s ___ n ___ s s

2 Match the phrases with what the people say.

a [3] win an award
b [ ] settle down
c [ ] drop out of college
d [ ] have an accident
e [ ] go for a job interview
f [ ] retire
g [ ] make new friends

1 'We're getting married next month. We've already bought a house.'

2 'What can you offer this company?'
'I'm very hard-working and I speak several languages.'

3 'And the winner of *Teenager of the Year* is Damien Arrowsmith.'

4 'I've moved into the house next door.'
'Would you like to come round for a coffee?'

5 'I'm only 19 but I've stopped going. It was too boring. I want to get a job and save some money to travel.'

6 'I'm 62 now. I've stopped working. I spend all my time in my garden.'

7 'What's wrong with your leg?'
'It's broken. I fell off my motorcycle.'

3 Complete the sentences with the words in the box.

become rich	change schools	~~go abroad~~	move	start my own business	take a gap year

I don't want to go to college here. I want to _go abroad_ to study, perhaps to the UK.

a I don't want to work for anyone. I want to ___________.

b My parents want to ___________ and live downtown. Then it will be much quicker for them to get to work.

c Some teenagers dream they can ___________ as famous musicians or sports stars.

d Two of her friends left the school, so she decided to ___________, too.

e When I leave school, I'm going to ___________ before I go to college.

GRAMMAR 1

Simple Past (Review) and *used to*

1 Complete the sentences with the simple past form of the verbs in parentheses.

A lot of people in my class ___*took*___ a gap year before college. (take)

a She's very shy so she __________ new friends during her trip. (not make)

b The science teacher often __________ about rockets when we were in 8th grade. (talk)

c __________ Maria __________ about becoming famous before being famous? (dream)

d My little brother __________ into some serious trouble at school. (get)

e I __________ much about the trade on my first job interview. (not know)

f At what age __________ your grandparents __________? (retire)

2 Complete the questions and answers using the simple past form of the verbs in parentheses.

Q: Why ___*did she get*___ (she get) so upset?

A: Because Eddie ___*didn't invite*___ (not invite) her to his party.

a **Q:** How much money __________ (you win)?

A: I __________ (win) $500.

b **Q:** Why __________ (you be) late for school this morning?

A: I __________ (not be) late. I __________ (arrive) at eight fifteen.

c **Q:** When __________ (they break up)?

A: They __________ (break up) about a year ago.

d **Q:** Where __________ (he lose) his cell phone?

A: He __________ (leave) it on the bus, I think.

e **Q:** Why __________ (you take) the last chocolate cookie?

A: I __________ (not take) it. Martin __________ (take) it.

3 Underline the correct words.

We always **<u>used to</u>** / **didn't use to** go on vacation to Guatemala but this summer we went to Peru.

a Caroline **used to** / **didn't use to** have long hair but she had it cut last week.

b I **used to** / **didn't use to** like sports very much because I wasn't very good at it.

c There **used to** / **didn't use to** be a swimming pool here but they built one last year.

d My parents **used to** / **didn't use to** hate camping, but they love it now.

e One hundred years ago, most women **used to** / **didn't use to** go to college or work outside the home.

4 When his family moved from Los Angeles to a village near the sea, Chris's life changed a lot. Complete the sentences using *used to* and *didn't use to*.

Before Chris…	Now Chris…
lived in a small apartment on a busy street	lives in a big house with a garden
had a small room with a view of a parking lot	has a big room with a view of the sea
met his friends at the shopping mall	meets his friends at the beach
spent all his free time playing computer games	spends all his free time surfing

a He ___*used to live*___ in a small apartment on a busy street.

He ___*didn't use to live*___ in a big house with a garden.

b He __________ a small room with a view of a parking lot.

He __________ a big room with a view of the sea.

c He __________ his friends at the beach.

He __________ his friends at the shopping mall.

d He spends all his free time surfing now but he __________ all his free time playing computer games.

5 Write questions using *used to* and the words in parentheses.

(you / get) into trouble a lot when you were young?
Did you use to get into trouble a lot when you were young?

a (people / spend) more time cooking 20 years ago?
____

b What (you / do) in your free time when you were a teenager, Granny?
____

c (your / brother) annoy you when he was younger?
____

d Where (you / go) to school before you moved to this town?
____

e What (you / watch) on TV when you were six years old?
____

6 Complete the dialogue with *used to* + the verbs in parentheses.

Grandma: I was born here 93 years ago. It **a** *used to be* (be) much quieter here in those days. It was a village, not a town, and there weren't many cars. Do you know, even the policeman **b** ________ (ride) a bike.

Ellie: What **c** ________ (you / do) in your free time? **d** ________ (you / watch TV)?

Grandma: Oh no, dear. We didn't have a television. But we sometimes **e** ________ (go) to the movie theater in Salinas. They **f** ________ (show) lovely black and white movies. Nice and romantic!

Ellie: What kind of music **g** ________ (you / listen to), Grandma?

Grandma: Well, people didn't have those things you put in your ears.

Ellie: You mean ear phones?

Grandma: Yes, dear. We just **h** ________ (listen) to the radio. And I **i** ________ (spend) a lot of time talking to my friend May.

Ellie: On the phone?

Grandma: No, no, dear. People didn't use those horrible cell phone things. We **j** ________ (visit) each other's houses.

7 Complete the text with the correct form of the verbs in parentheses. Use the simple past or *used to* + verb.

Lily Thompson *was* (be) a millionaire in the first half of the 20th century. She **a** ________ (live) in a big apartment in the middle of New York. She **b** ________ (not drive) because her chauffeur **c** ________ (drive) her everywhere. She **d** ________ (go) to Italy and France on vacation and she **e** ________ (wear) designer clothes. She **f** ________ (not work) and she **g** ________ (not have) any money worries. But things **h** ________ (not be) always like this for Lily. Before being a millionaire, she **i** ________ (work) in a café as a waitress. She **j** ________ (buy) cheap clothes and she **k** ________ (not go) abroad for her vacations. So when **l** ________ (things change) for Lily? One day in 1926 a customer in her café **m** ________ (not have) enough money to give Lily a tip so he **n** ________ (give) her a race ticket instead. That lucky ticket **o** ________ (win) Lily a million dollars and **p** ________ (change) her life forever.

VOCABULARY 2

Verb + Preposition

1 Underline the correct phrase.

Some people always **argue about** / **dream about** being rich and famous one day.

- **a** We always **wait for** / **look forward to** our camping trip during summer vacation.
- **b** I don't **argue with** / **agree with** you about this but we can still be friends.
- **c** I need to **listen to** / **talk to** you about something important.
- **d** Don't **worry about** / **dream about** Karen's health. I am sure she will be better tomorrow.
- **e** Do you want to **depend on** / **participate in** an exciting new project?

2 Complete the sentences with the prepositions in the box.

about on ~~to~~ to to with

My mother loves listening *to* music.

- **a** I usually agree ________ my best friend about most things.
- **b** She's a great person to have on the team. You can always depend ________ her.
- **c** I'm looking forward ________ seeing you next weekend.
- **d** My brother always worries ________ school tests.
- **e** When I'm worried I sometimes talk ________ my aunt Alice.

3 Match the phrases with what the people say.

- **a** [4] agree with someone
- **b** [ ] argue about something
- **c** [ ] depend on someone
- **d** [ ] dream about something
- **e** [ ] look forward to something
- **f** [ ] participate in something
- **g** [ ] wait for someone
- **h** [ ] worry about someone

1 'I'd love to sail around the world in my own boat one day.'

2 'I have tickets for the concert on Saturday. It's going to be great!'

3 'It was really interesting.'
'No, it wasn't. It was really boring!'

4 'That book was really terrible.'
'Yep, you're totally right.'

5 'There's an athletics meet tomorrow. I'm going to be in it because I'm on our school athletics team.'

6 'We need you on the team. We can't succeed without you.'

7 'Where is she? It's 4:20 and I got here at 4pm. She's late!'

8 'Why does he want to climb that mountain? It's very dangerous. He might fall.'

4 Complete the sentences with the phrases in the box.

agree about argue with depend on ~~dream about~~ talk about wait for worry about

I often *dream about* learning to fly a plane.

- **a** If I'm staying out late, I call my parents so they don't ________________ me.
- **b** If you're late, I'll ________________ you – but only for 15 minutes.
- **c** We have the same taste in music so we always ________________ which bands are the best.
- **d** He always does what he says he will do. We can ________________ him.
- **e** I don't want to ________________ that test. I know I did very badly on it.
- **f** When I ________________ my father about politics he always wins because he knows more facts.

GRAMMAR 2

Subject and Object Questions

1 Write if the underlined question words refer to the subject (S) or object (O).

[O] Who did you see in the park?
a [ ] What did you buy at the store?
b [ ] What happened at the store?
c [ ] Who told you about the party?
d [ ] What do you usually have for breakfast?
e [ ] Who's making that noise?
f [ ] What makes you laugh?
g [ ] Who do you know in this picture?

2 Order the words to make questions. Write *S* if the question word is a subject and *O* if it is an object.

[O] about / did / talk / What / yesterday / you ?
What did you talk about yesterday?

a [ ] movie theater / outside / the / did / meet / Who / you ?
______

b [ ] bag / fell / just / now / out of / What / your ?
______

c [ ] does / family / in / the / usually / washing up / Who / your ?
______

d [ ] about / did / dream / last / night / What / you ?
______

e [ ] family / in / makes / most / noise / the / Who / your ?
______

f [ ] at the / movie / end / happened / of / that / What?
______

g [ ] do / talk to / when / Who / worried / you / you're ?
______

3 Write *who* questions from these sentences.

You listened to someone.
Who did you listen to?

Someone spoke to you.
Who spoke to you?

a You looked at someone.
______

b Someone smiled at you.
______

c She waved at someone.
______

d He spoke to someone.
______

e Someone gave you that number.
______

f Someone stole the money.
______

4 Write *what* questions from these sentences.

He took something out of that bag.
What did he take out of that bag?

a Something happened on the way to school.
______

b She bought something from the store.
______

c He is hiding something from us.
______

d Something frightened them.
______

e They are stealing something.
______

f Something fell out of the sky.
______

5 Write subject or object questions using *who* or *what* for the underlined information.

Picasso painted *Guernica*.
Who painted Guernica?

Picasso painted *Guernica*.
What did Picasso paint?

a Shakespeare wrote *Hamlet*.
______

b Shakespeare wrote *Hamlet*.
______

c Walt Disney created Mickey Mouse.
______

d Walt Disney created Mickey Mouse.
______

e Mark Zuckerberg started Facebook.
______

f Mark Zuckerberg started Facebook.
______

GRAMMAR CHECK

1 Read the text and circle the correct answers.

Even when he was a young child, Ben Adams **a** ______ surfing and skateboarding. He was also very interested in fashion and **b** ______ designing his own surfing and skating clothes. When he was only 15, he **c** ______ a prize for his T-shirt designs, and during the summer, he **d** ______ to work for Fashion First in New York. At 16, he **e** ______ out of school and started his own clothes company, Skate and Surf. He is now 17 and a multimillionaire. We interviewed him at his home in Malibu, California.

What **f** ______ *when you dropped out of school?*
My Mom was worried but my Dad wasn't.

What did your teachers say?
They **g** ______. I **h** ______ in all the classes except physical education.

Did you **i** ______ *to get into trouble?*
I'm afraid so, but the teachers all like me now!

What **j** ______ *when you left school?*
I missed being with my friends at first, but now I have a new bunch of friends.

	A	B	C
a	loves	loved	was loving
b	enjoyed	did enjoy	enjoys
c	wind	winning	won
d	used to go	was going	went
e	was dropping	used to drop	dropped
f	did you happen	happening	happened
g	didn't care	cared not	didn't use to care
h	dreamt	was dreaming	used to dream
i	use	used	usually
j	did you miss	you missed	you do miss

2 77 Listen and check your answers.

LISTENING

1 78 Listen to a radio show. Check (✓) the things you hear about.

- [x] problems at school
- [ ] moving
- [ ] arguments with parents
- [ ] surfing
- [ ] changing schools
- [ ] starting a business
- [ ] traveling
- [ ] New Year's Eve
- [ ] the internet
- [ ] writing newspaper articles
- [ ] working in a restaurant
- [ ] teaching children

2 78 Order these events in Eddie's life. Number them 1 to 10. Be careful! There are two extra events which did not happen.

a ☐ He applied to college.
b 1 He argued with his parents about school work.
c ☐ He dropped out of school.
d ☐ He flew to Australia.
e ☐ He got a job at a surf shop.
f ☐ He opened his own restaurant.
g ☐ He put an advertisement in a local newspaper.
h ☐ He started giving surf lessons in Carmel.
i ☐ He started to earn $200 a day.
j ☐ He worked in a restaurant.
k ☐ His parents stopped speaking to him.
l ☐ The bank agreed to lend him money.

EXTENSION

Underline the correct words to complete the text.

Bethany Hamilton was born in Hawaii in 1990 and **a grew up / was growing up** near the ocean. Young Bethany **b used to spend / was spending** all her time in the water and she **c used to learn / learned** to surf before she could walk.
At the age of eight, she **d starts / started** to compete seriously. By the time she was 12, she was the world's number two under-eighteen surfer. She **e was planning / is planning** to become a professional and her sponsors **f were helping / helped** her with her plan.
Then at the age of 13, Bethany's life **g changed / was changing** forever. She **h surfed / was surfing** off the Hawaiian island of Kauai with her friend Alana Blanchard and Alana's brother and father. Bethany **i had / was having** a rest. She **j was lying / is lying** on her surfboard with her arms hanging in the water. Suddenly a shark **k attacked / was attacking** her and **l used to pull / pulled** her left arm off just under her shoulder. Her friends helped her get back to the shore, but Bethany **m lost / was losing** 60% of her blood. She **n was / is** lucky to be alive today.
But Beth **o didn't give up / doesn't give up** surfing. She told reporters that she had to work on her fear of sharks and that she sometimes still **p gets / is getting** scared. But one year after the attack, she **q was starting / started** competing again. Today Bethany **r surfed / surfs** in world championships and **s was winning / wins** prizes. She also **t helps / helped** other victims of shark attacks through her charity, Friends of Bethany. She **u wrote / writes** her story, *Soul Surfer*, in 2004. There's also a movie of the book but Bethany **v doesn't star / wasn't starring** in it.

VOCABULARY PLUS

College Degrees

1 ____________

2 ____________

3 ____________

4 ____________

5 ____________

6 ____________

7 ____________

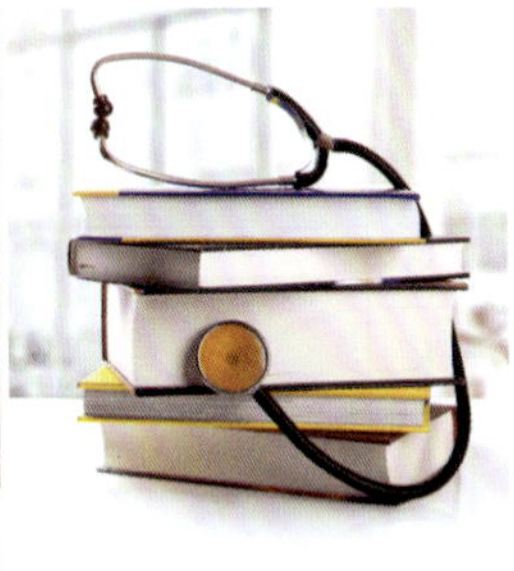

8 ____________

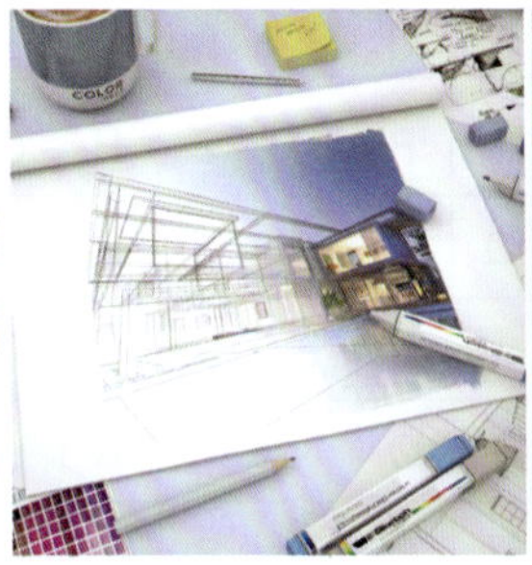

9 ____________

10 ____________

1 79 Label the pictures with the words in the box. Then listen and repeat.

architecture business
computer science engineering fine art
law media studies medicine
nursing teacher training

2 Underline the correct words.

She wanted to be a journalist so she studied **medicine** / **media studies**.

- a You learn how to design buildings when you get **a law** / **an architecture** degree.
- b If you enjoy looking after sick people, why don't you get a degree in **engineering** / **nursing**?
- c My dad loved designing machines so he studied **engineering** / **business**.
- d I'm terrible at drawing so I'd never get a **fine art** / **computer science** degree.
- e Jack loves reading about famous criminals and their cases. He should study **teacher training** / **law**.

3 What degree should they get? Write the correct words.

My brother wants to be a nurse.
nursing

- a My sister wants to be a doctor.
  ____
- b I'd like to start my own business.
  ____
- c My best friend would like to be a teacher.
  ____
- d My cousin is interested in working in TV.
  ____
- e My neighbor is always on his computer writing new programs.
  ____

4 Complete the sentences for you. Try to use words from activity 1.

- a I'd love to study
  ____
- b I wouldn't like to get a degree in
  ____
- c A lot of people in my school are going to study
  ____

2 Incredible Journeys

VOCABULARY 1

Travel

1 Find ten words related to travel in the word search.

T	P	O	S	T	C	A	R	D	S	Y
R	A	C	Z	I	R	D	Z	H	Q	O
A	E	B	X	Q	F	V	U	R	S	G
I	Q	G	U	I	D	E	B	O	O	K
N	G	N	G	J	O	N	M	A	U	B
A	R	R	I	V	E	T	B	C	V	M
P	A	C	K	O	P	U	B	O	E	X
O	V	S	T	T	Z	R	W	B	N	E
K	I	U	S	L	T	E	P	U	I	S
S	U	I	T	C	A	S	E	S	R	X
J	O	U	R	N	E	Y	L	K	S	K

2 Match a-h with 1-8 to make travel phrases.

a send — **8** postcards
b buy — **1** a journey
c come back — **2** a bus
d get off — **3** a suitcase
e have — **4** a guidebook
f meet — **5** home
g pack — **6** adventures
h plan — **7** people

3 Complete the sentences with the words in the box.

journey ~~people~~ train suitcase adventures postcards guidebook

Have you ever met nice *people* while you were camping?

a I always send __________ to my friends when I go on vacation.

b My sister always packs her __________ a week before she leaves!

c I need to buy a __________ so I can plan my trip.

d We got on the __________ at nine this morning.

e You have to plan your __________ before you leave.

f We had a lot of __________ when we traveled around India.

4 Match the travel phrases in the box with the sentences.

arrive buy souvenirs have adventures ~~meet people~~ set off plan a journey

'Hi. Do you speak English?'
'Yes, I am Australian! Do you need help?'
meet people

a I have my passport, ticket and money. Now I must go. Goodbye, everyone.

____

b Let's fly to Rome. Then we can get the train to Bari. From there we can get a boat to Patras, in Greece.

____

c Let's get a T-shirt that says I LOVE LONDON and a statue of Big Ben!

____

d On one Greek island there wasn't any room in the hostel, so we slept on the beach.

____

e That was a long journey, but we're here now. Fantastic!

____

GRAMMAR 1

Review: Present Perfect and Simple Past

1 Write *SP* (simple past) or *PP* (present perfect) next to each sentence.

[*PP*] Kim has gone to China.

a [ ] He went three weeks ago.
b [ ] Karen lived in Paris from 2001 to 2008.
c [ ] Karen didn't enjoy her time there.
d [ ] She's told me a lot about those years.
e [ ] Have you ever lived outside of Europe?
f [ ] I've traveled all around the world.
g [ ] I haven't been to South America.
h [ ] Where did you go for your last vacation?

2 Write pairs of sentences using the present perfect and the simple past form of the verbs in parentheses.

Luis ___*has lost*___ (lose) his glasses. (present perfect)
He ___*left*___ (leave) them on the bus yesterday. (simple past)

a **1** You ______________ (change)! (present perfect)
2 You ______________ (have) long hair the last time I saw you. (simple past)

b **1** Maria ______________ (break) her leg. (present perfect)
2 She ______________ (do) it on her skiing vacation last month. (simple past)

c **1** My parents ______________ (buy) a new car. (present perfect)
2 They ______________ (get) it yesterday. (simple past)

d **1** They ______________ (paint) the house. (present perfect)
2 Adam ______________ (choose) all the colors. (simple past)

e **1** We ______________ (write) a letter to Sylvia. (present perfect)
2 We ______________ (send) it this morning. (simple past)

f **1** I ______________ (spend) all my allowance. (present perfect)
2 I ______________ (buy) lots of new clothes during the weekend. (simple past)

3 Underline the correct words.

I've never **been** / **gone** to Switzerland. What's it like?

a Jack Where's Tom?
Kay He went out an hour ago.
Jack Where's he **been** / **gone**?

b How many times have you **been** / **gone** to Segovia?

c Have you **been** / **gone** to the Guggenheim Museum in Bilbao?

d They're having a fantastic time in Australia. They've **been** / **gone** for six months.

e Vicki isn't here. She's **been** / **gone** to the movies with her friends.

f I'm at home on my own. Everyone's **been** / **gone** for a walk by the river.

4 Circle the correct answers.

I _____ to Italy last summer.

1 have been **2** (went) **3** have gone

a They _____ that dog for about three months.
1 had **2** hasn't had **3** have had

b 'Did you get those jeans for your birthday?'
'Yes, I _____ .'
1 have **2** did **3** did get

c 'Do you like duck?' 'I don't know. I _____ it.'
1 never ate **3** didn't eat
2 've never eaten

d 'Has Jen learnt the vocabulary for her test yet?'
'No, she _____ .'
1 haven't **2** didn't **3** hasn't

e Sue can drive us to the airport. She _____ her test yesterday.
1 did pass
2 has passed
3 passed

5 **Write questions using the present perfect or the simple past.**

What time ___*did you go*___ (you / go) to bed yesterday?

___*Has Mark already finished*___ (Mark / already / finish) reading that long book?

a (they / meet) any nice people on their last vacation?

____

b What (Jen / say) to you last Tuesday?

____

c How many times (Lily / lose) her glasses this week?

____

d Where (you / buy) those amazing shoes?

____

e How long (you / know) your friend Carmen?

____

f (Josie / call) you at four o'clock?

____

g How much money (they / raise) since March?

____

h (Lucy / ever / go) to New York?

____

6 **Complete the dialogues with the present perfect or the simple past form of the verbs in parentheses.**

Beth ___*Have you ever been*___ (you ever be) to Italy?
John Yes, we **a** ______________ (have) a vacation in Pisa three years ago.
Beth **b** ______________ (you / fly) there?
John No, we **c** ______________ (drive).

Liz Where's Ben? **d** ______________ (you / see) him anywhere?
Pete Yes, he **e** ______________ (go) to the gym five minutes ago.
Liz What about Luke?
Pete I don't know. I **f** ______________ (not see) him since lunchtime.

Ann Do you know Penny's brother?
Jim I **g** ______________ (see) him a few times at parties, but I **h** ______________ (never speak) to him. **i** ______________ (you / ever / talk) to him?
Ann Yes. I **j** ______________ (meet) him after the game on Saturday. He's really nice.

7 **Write questions for the answers. Only use the present perfect or the simple past.**

Have you ever been to Berlin?
Yes, I have, once.

a ______________________________
At four o'clock.

b ______________________________
No, I haven't.

c ______________________________
Yesterday.

d ______________________________
Since Monday.

e ______________________________
For three years.

f ______________________________
No, never.

g ______________________________
Two months ago.

h ______________________________
No, he didn't.

VOCABULARY 2

Extreme Adjectives

1 Complete the extreme adjectives with the vowels. Then match them with the normal adjectives in the box.

bad big cold frightening ~~good~~ happy hot small tired

_a_ m _a_ z _i_ n g ______ *good* ______

a ___ w f ___ l ______

b b ___ ___ l i n g ______

c d ___ l ___ g h t ___ d ______

d ___ n ___ r m ___ ___ s ______

e ___ x h ___ ___ s t ___ d ______

f f r ___ ___ z ___ n g ______

g t ___ r r ___ f y ___ n g ______

h t ___ n y ______

2 Circle the correct words.

Can we open the window? It's … in here!

1 (boiling) **3** tiny
2 freezing

a It's a movie about a man who kills people. It's … ! Don't go and see it.

1 enormous **3** terrifying
2 tiny

b Can you lend me a sweater and a hat, please? I'm … .

1 enormous **3** tiny
2 freezing

c My parents gave my sister a puppy for her birthday. She's … with it.

1 terrifying **3** awful
2 delighted

d My feet are much bigger than yours. I can't wear these … shoes of yours!

1 awful **3** freezing
2 tiny

e You look … . Why don't you go to bed early tonight?

1 delighted **3** exhausted
2 amazing

f This book is … . You'll love it.

1 amazing **3** delighted
2 awful

3 Complete the sentences with the correct extreme adjectives from activity 1.

It's ___*boiling*___ today. The temperature is about 40° C.

a She was ______ when she received two free tickets to the concert.

b I wrote the number on a ______ bit of paper and now I can't find it.

c We can't camp in Scotland in the middle of winter. It will be ______.

d Look at the size of that elephant. It's ______.

e Our vacation in Greece was ______. I loved it and I want to go back next year.

f We were swimming near the boat when we saw a shark. The shark was ______.

g The cake and the flowers are for me? Really? That's so lovely. Thank you so much. I'm ______.

h The average temperature in January in Novosibirsk, Siberia's largest city, is –24° C. It's ______.

i The average temperature in August in Jeddah, Saudi Arabia, is 40° C. It's ______.

j The Leshan statue of Buddha in China is 71 meters high. His shoulders are 28 meters wide. It's ______.

k While we were on the boat, there was a storm. The waves were eight meters high. People were crying. It was ______.

l The world's smallest monkey is the pygmy marmoset. Adults are only about 11cm long and weigh 120 grams. They are ______.

GRAMMAR 2

Review: Quantity and Uncountable Nouns

1 Write C (countable) or U (uncountable) next to the nouns.

[*U*] tea

a [ ] money
b [ ] water
c [ ] candy
d [ ] people
e [ ] information
f [ ] space
g [ ] socks
h [ ] noise
i [ ] fruit
j [ ] ideas

2 Complete the questions with *much* or *many*.

Health Quiz

How *much* fruit do you eat a week?
How a _______ hours of sleep do you get a night?
How b _______ time do you spend in front of the TV?
How c _______ glasses of water do you drink a day?
How d _______ times a day do you clean your teeth?
How e _______ sport do you do a week?
How f _______ tea or coffee do you drink a day?

3 Match the sentence beginnings with the endings.

a [*5*] I can't make this cake because there isn't
b [ ] We went to the beach, but there wasn't
c [ ] The doctor says I mustn't drink
d [ ] You can have a party, but please don't invite too
e [ ] There are a lot of boys in this class, but there are only
f [ ] There were a lot of potatoes, but there was only
g [ ] There aren't any potatoes, but there is

1 a lot of meat.
2 a little meat.
3 many people.
4 much sun.
5 any butter.
6 a few girls.
7 a lot of coffee.

4 Complete the sentences with *much*, *many*, *a little* or *a few*.

Let's put *a few* olives on this pizza.

a I'm not very sporty, but I like to do _______ exercise every day.

b Let's buy _______ apples for the picnic. I usually eat one after lunch.

c Don't eat too _______ candy. It's bad for you.

d I can't get her an expensive present because I don't have _______ money.

5 Circle the correct answers.

There wasn't ______ space in the car for our bags.

1 many 2 some 3 (much)

a There are just ______ vegetables in the fridge.
1 a few 2 a little 3 any

b Do you have ______ good ideas about raising money?
1 a little 2 any 3 much

c We saw ______ beautiful birds near the coast.
1 a little 2 some 3 any

d Did you buy ______ fruit at the market?
1 a lot of 2 many 3 a few

e Jack didn't know ______ people at the party.
1 much 2 many 3 a little

f We need ______ information about train times.
1 much 2 a few 3 some

6 Write true sentences about you, your friends, your family or your home.

My sister doesn't eat any *fish*.

I have just bought some *new computer games*.

a __________ doesn't eat any __________.

b __________ have just bought some __________.

c We only have a few __________.

d There is only a little __________.

e __________ don't have much __________.

f __________ doesn't have many __________.

GRAMMAR CHECK

1 Read the text and circle the correct answers.

I **a** ______ to South America three times in my life. Last year, we **b** ______ to Argentina. We **c** ______ to dance the tango in Buenos Aires and bought **d** ______ souvenirs at San Telmo. We **e** ______ La Recoleta cemetery and found the tombs of **f** ______ famous people. Then we **g** ______ the sunset at Palermo. Mar del Plata was amazing, but we didn't spend **h** ______ time there. We only saw **i** ______ seals there, but we'll stay longer next time. What **j** ______ when you went to Argentina?

	1	2	3
a	went	were	(have been)
b	went	were	have been
c	were learning	learned	have learned
d	a lot	lot of	a lot of
e	have visited	visited	were visiting
f	some	any	much
g	watched	were watching	have watched
h	a lot	some	much
i	a few	a little	not much
j	did you	did you do	have you done

2 80 Listen and check your answers.

LISTENING

1 81 Listen to Melissa talking about her trip and tick the things she still needs to do.

- ☐ book her flight
- ☐ pay for her ticket
- ☐ collect her ticket
- ☐ arrange travel insurance
- ☐ get her vaccinations
- ☐ decide which clothes to take
- ☐ buy a sunhat
- ☐ buy a new backpack
- ☐ pack her backpack
- ☐ order pesos and US dollars
- ☐ collect her money from the bank
- ☐ buy a mosquito net

2 81 Listen again and answer the questions.

a What does Melissa have to get on Monday?

______

b What did she buy when she paid for her ticket?

______

c What did she do the day before yesterday?

______

d What does she need to buy before she starts packing?

______

e What has she ordered from the bank?

______

f What cities is she staying in, in Mexico?

______

g What isn't she going to buy for space reasons?

______

EXTENSION

Circle the correct words to complete the text.

Karl Bushby **a started / was starting** walking around the world on November 1, 1998, and he is still **b walk / walking**. He **c has already walked / already walked** through South, Central and North America. He is the first person who has **d ever / never** crossed the Bering Strait from Alaska to Russia on foot. Around the Bering Strait, he **e has become / became** terrified of polar bears. They **f attack often / often attack** humans when they are hungry. Luckily, they didn't **g tried / try** to get into his tent at night when he was camping there.

However, according to Bushby, the Bering Strait wasn't **h more / as** terrifying as the Darien Gap, the tropical jungle between Colombia and Panama. He says the Darien Gap was **i more frightening / the most frightening** than any other place. While he was **j walked / walking** through the jungle there, he became very frightened. At one point, he was **k more / too** frightened to walk, so he swam down a river full of alligators for **l a few / a little** days.

Bushby **m gets / has gotten** fitter since he started his walk. And he says walking has made him **n more ambitious / most ambitious** and more responsible. He loves **o spend / spending** time in the world's wildest places. But he has been lonely **p many / some** of the time. So walking has taught him **q a lot / some** of things about his most important friendships and relationships.

Bushby **r isn't / doesn't** walking for a special reason. He doesn't **s want / wants** to get rich from it or make money for charity. Apparently, every day people in cars offer him lifts, and every day he **t says / is saying** 'No, thank you.'

VOCABULARY PLUS

Health Problems and Cures

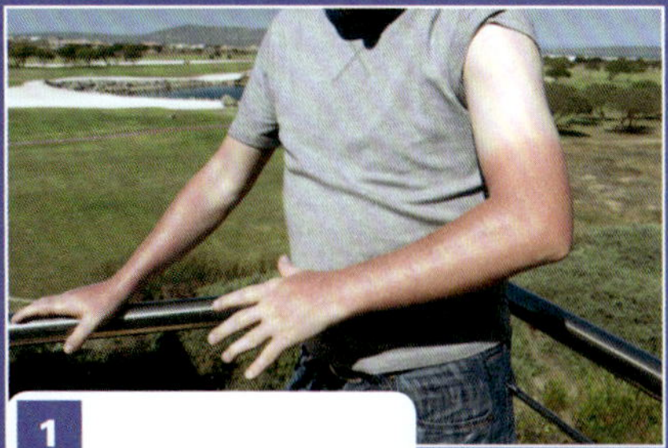

1 ______________

2 ______________

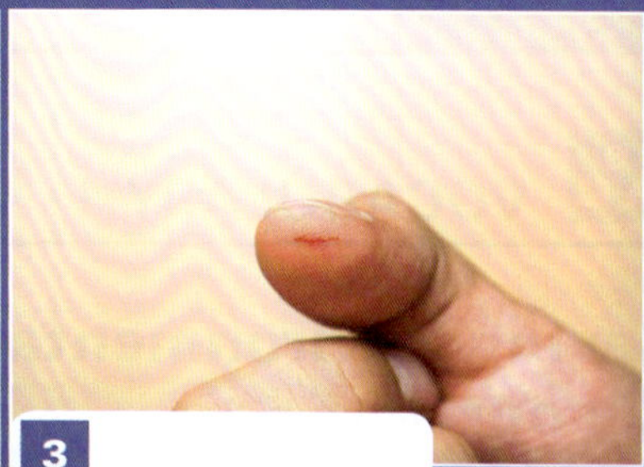

3 ______________

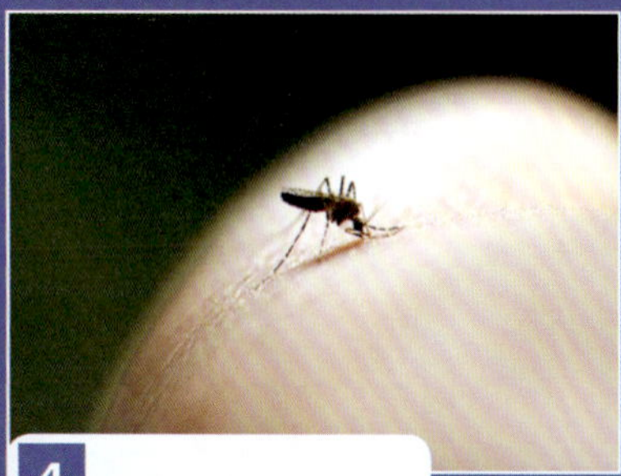

4 ______________

5 ______________

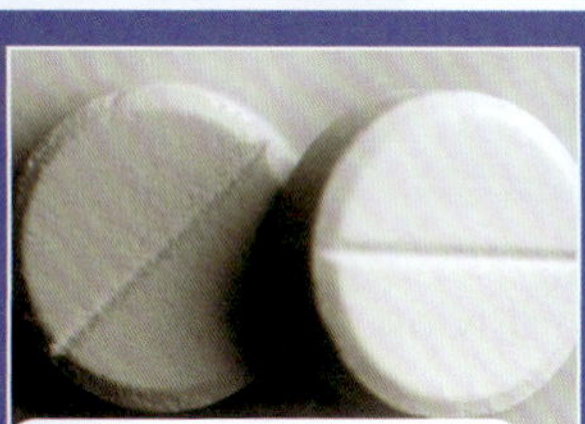

6 ______________

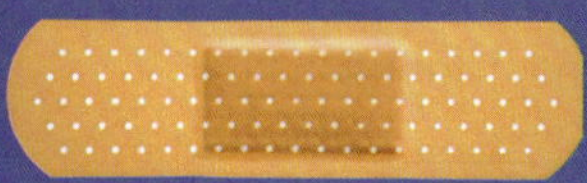

7 ______________

8 ______________

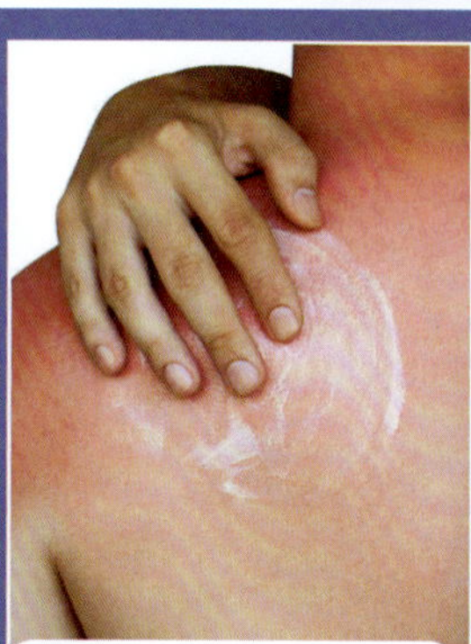

9 ______________

10 ______________

1 🔊 82 Listen to the words in the box. Then label the pictures with them.

a bandage	a cut	a migraine
a motion sickness pill	after sun lotion	
aspirin	an insect bite	antiseptic cream
sunburn	motion sickness	

2 Match the treatments a-d with the health problems in activity 1.

[4] antiseptic cream

a [ ] a motion sickness pill

b [ ] after sun lotion

c [ ] a bandage

d [ ] aspirin

3 Circle the correct words.

Turn the music down! I've got a terrible **insect bite** / **(migraine)**.

a If you spend a long time in the sun, you'll get a **cut** / **sunburn**.

b I take a **motion sickness pill** / **aspirin** because I always feel sick on planes.

c He woke up and he had four **insect bites** / **motion sickness** on his face.

d Take some **antiseptic cream** / **aspirin** and you'll feel better!

e Do you have any **after sun lotion** / **bandages**? I have a cut on my finger.

3 The World around Us

VOCABULARY 1

Saving Environmental Resources

1 Find five environment phrases in the word snake.

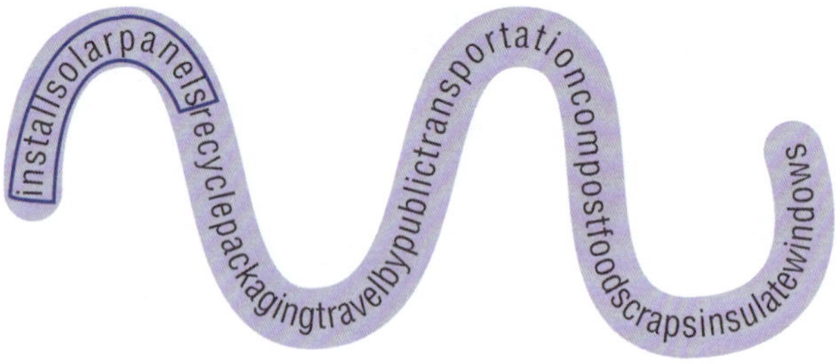

2 Match the columns to make phrases.

a	mend	a bike
b	ride	car journeys
c	save	old clothes
d	share	lights
e	turn off	rechargeable batteries
f	use	water

3 Match the sentences a-f with the instructions 1-6.

a Don't throw them away.
b It's good for your health and for the planet.
c It's very good for the garden.
d We need to save electricity.
e We need to save water.
f You'll save on central heating.

1 [*d*] Turn off the lights.
2 [ ] Compost your food scraps.
3 [ ] Mend your old clothes.
4 [ ] Insulate windows.
5 [ ] Turn off the faucet.
6 [ ] Ride a bike.

4 Complete the text with the phrases in the box.

install solar panels · rechargeable batteries · recycle packaging · share car journeys · ~~travel by public transportation~~

People should stop driving their own cars everywhere and start to *travel by public transportation*. It will reduce carbon emissions. And if they don't want to do that, they should at least **a** ________________ with people who work in the same area. We should all use **b** ________________ in our cameras and phones. And in houses which get a lot of sun on the roof, it's a good idea to **c** ________________. Finally, we shouldn't throw away so much paper, plastic and glass. The answer to that is to **d** ________________.

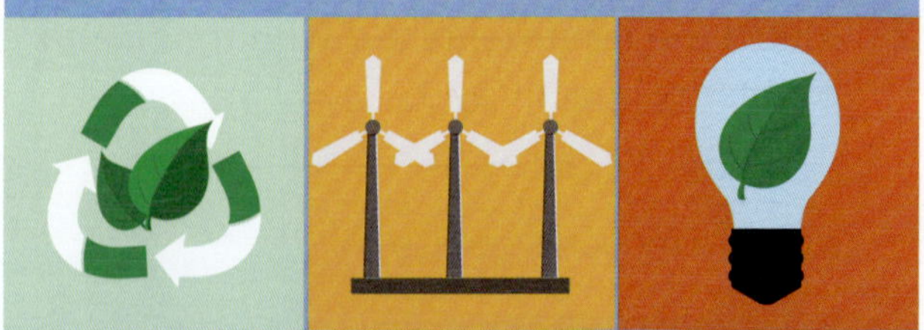

GRAMMAR 1

Review: Present Perfect + *for*, *since*, *how long*

1 Match the sentence beginnings with the endings. Then write sentences in the present perfect using *for* or *since*.

a [2] I (not see) a good movie
b [ ] We (know) each other
c [ ] The European Union (exist)
d [ ] Kate (have) a driving license
e [ ] There (be) life on earth
f [ ] You (be) sick with that cough
g [ ] Michael (work) in environmental projects

1 1993.
2 I saw *The Descendants 2*.
3 millions of years.
4 she was 17.
5 three days now.
6 two years.
7 we were in primary school.

a *I haven't seen a good film since I saw* The *Descendants 2.*
b ______________________
c ______________________
d ______________________
e ______________________
f ______________________
g ______________________

2 Write questions with *how long* and answers with *for* or *since*.

Q: you / have / a compost bin?
A: six months
Q: *How long have you had a compost bin?*
A: *I've had a compost bin for six months.*

a
Q: she / know / how to make her own clothes?
A: 2014
Q: ______________________
A: ______________________

b
Q: you / be / interested in environmental issues
A: I was 11
Q: ______________________
A: ______________________

c
Q: he / work / at the recycling center?
A: the past few months
Q: ______________________
A: ______________________

d
Q: they / had / solar panels?
A: last month
Q: ______________________
A: ______________________

3 Complete the text using the present perfect form of the verbs in parentheses.

From: Amy
To: Rob
Subject: Life in the country

Dear Rob,
I'm sorry I *haven't written* (not write) for a few months. I **a** ____________ (be) very busy since our move to the country. Since we arrived, we **b** ____________ (install) solar panels on our roof ourselves, and we **c** ____________ (insulate) all our windows. For the past few weeks, I **d** ____________ (spend) a lot of time working in the garden. I **e** ____________ (plant) a lot of vegetable seeds since the weather got warmer. We **f** ____________ (have) a compost heap for a year now, which is really useful (that's me working on it in the picture!). But life on our little farm is very hard work. I **g** ____________ (not see) a good movie for over six months and I **h** ____________ (not be) on vacation for a year. **i** ____________ (you / see) Peter since Thanksgiving? I **j** ____________ (not hear) from him for a very long time. If you see him, say hi from me. Write soon!
Amy

4 Underline the correct words.

I **have made** / **made** pancakes for breakfast yesterday.

a **Have you found** / **Did you find** your glasses yet?

b **You've never met** / **You never met** my cousin from Canada.

c When **have you got** / **did you get** back from your vacation?

d We **have already bought** / **already bought** food for the picnic.

e Who **have you danced** / **did you dance** with at the party?

f Oh no! Somebody **has stolen** / **stole** my cell phone.

5 Write sentences using the present perfect and *for* or *since*.

a this school / be / at / three years / I
I've been at this school for three years.

b work / at / Gavin / the recycling center / 2017
___

c your grandparents / not / you / two months / see
___

d on vacation / go / Geraldine / ten days
___

e have / I / three years / my computer / have
___

f emails / not / I / two weeks
___

g live / 2005 / Ontario / Susie
___

h play / Alice / electric bass / eight years
___

i country / work / Ronan / 2010
___

j eat / Fran / she was twelve / meat /not
___

6 Complete the texts using the present perfect or simple past form of the verbs in parentheses.

Joey lives in Sweden now. He *has lived* (live) there for a year. Before that he **a** ___ (live) in Norway. He **b** ___ (work) there for two years but he **c** ___ (not / like) it very much. He **d** ___ (think) the weather was too cold.

Martin Do you know Carmen's sister?
Rob I **e** ___ (see) her at the gym a few times but I **f** ___ (never / speak) to her. What about you? **g** ___ (you / ever / speak) to her?
Martin Yes. I **h** ___ (meet) her at a party two weeks ago. We **i** ___ (dance) together. It **j** ___ (be) fun.
Rob That's cool! I think Carmen **k** ___ (invited) me to this party, but I **l** ___ (not go) because it **m** ___ (be) my brother's birthday.

Emily **n** ___ (you / ever / be) to Rome?
Nick Yes, I **o** ___ (go) there on vacation last year.
Emily **p** ___ (you / have) fun?
Nick Yes, we **q** ___ (have) a great time. I **r** ___ (not be) to Florence, though. I'd like to go there this year.

VOCABULARY 2

Prefixes

1 Find seven verbs with prefixes in the word search beside.

M	I	S	P	L	A	C	E	T	R	M
Z	H	G	L	X	E	M	R	K	D	L
S	I	E	K	J	E	W	I	T	O	G
I	R	E	C	Y	C	L	E	W	V	P
B	B	Y	O	V	M	E	E	S	E	R
K	F	F	K	F	O	G	F	X	R	U
U	N	D	E	R	C	O	O	K	C	J
N	Z	W	G	X	J	C	T	N	R	D
U	N	D	E	R	P	A	Y	A	O	Z
O	V	E	R	E	A	T	E	A	W	K
R	E	P	L	A	C	E	P	G	D	B

2 Order the letters and write the words with prefixes.

mis + f r o m i n *misinform*

a over + l e t a p o u p ____________

b re + y a l p ____________

c under + e u s ____________

d re + a g r i z o n e ____________

e mis + d u n e r d a n t s ____________

f under + a m i s e t t e ____________

3 Complete the crossword using the clues and the words in the box.

misinform misplace ~~misunderstand~~
overcrowded overeat overpopulated
recycle reorganize replace replay
undercooked underestimate
underpay underused

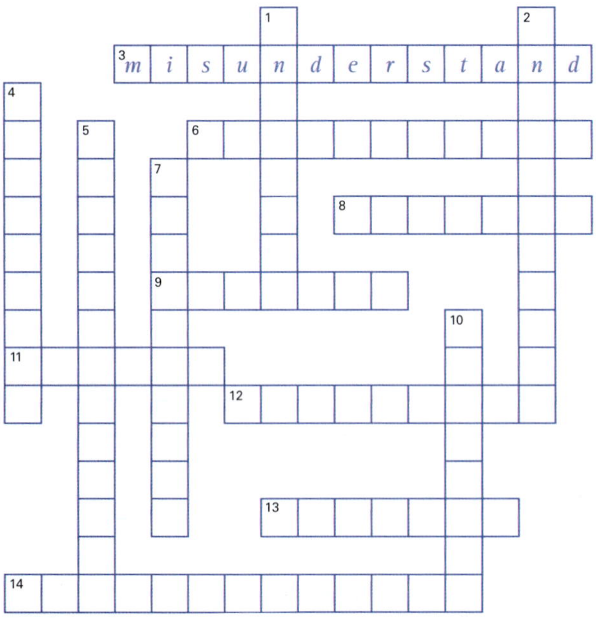

Across

3 I explained very clearly. Why did they *misunderstand* me?

6 Twelve of them live in a very small apartment. It's terribly ____________.

8 I broke my mother's favorite vase. I want to ____________ it with something similar.

9 Don't throw those bottles away. ____________ them.

11 The game was a draw. They are going to ____________ it next week.

12 They are going to shut down that gym. Nobody goes there. It is very ____________.

13 Try not to ____________. That is really harmful for your health.

14 Don't ____________ him. He's very clever but he pretends to be stupid.

Down

1 The money is bad at that job. They always ____________ their staff.

2 This meat is ____________. Could you do it a little longer, please?

4 Check the facts on the internet. I don't want to ____________ you.

5 There are too many people in this country. It's ____________.

7 I need to ____________ my cabinets. I can't find anything.

10 I don't often lose things so I hate it when I ____________ something.

GRAMMAR 2

Review: Present Perfect + *still, yet, already, just*

1 Underline the correct words.

I haven't done the activity **yet** / **still**.

a She has **just** / **still** put the leaves in the compost.

b Have you recharged those batteries **still** / **yet**?

c They haven't been to the recycling center **already** / **yet**.

d You **still** / **already** haven't given me the tickets.

e No more cake, thanks, I've **just** / **still** overeaten!

f You've **still** / **already** told me that twice!

2 Write sentences in the present perfect using *still, yet, already* and *just.*

already / Tim / leave ?
Has Tim already left?

a find / not / Peter / his keys / yet

______

b already / they / meet / Luke

______

c not / me / she / write / still / to / has

______

d make / you / dinner / yet / ?

______

e sort out / he / the garbage / just

______

f the game / they / not / still / replay

______

3 The Jackson family want to be more environmentally friendly. Write sentences about their progress using *still* and *already.*

plant a vegetable garden (✓)
They've already planted a vegetable garden.

install solar panels (✗)
They still haven't installed solar panels.

a insulate the windows (✓)

______

b buy bikes (✓)

______

c sell their car (✗)

______

d read an organic gardening book (✓)

______

e make a compost heap (✗)

______

f get a container to catch rain water (✗)

______

g start mending their old clothes (✓)

______

h stop buying new clothes (✗)

______

4 Rewrite the *still* sentences in activity 3 using *yet.*

They still haven't installed solar panels.
They haven't installed solar panels yet.

a ______

b ______

c ______

d ______

5 You and a friend are planning a biking vacation. Write your questions using *yet* and your friend's answers using *still, yet, already* and *just.*

Biking trip – things to do

buy the maps (already)
Have you bought the maps yet?
Yes, I've already bought them.

buy a tent (yet)
Have you bought a tent yet?
No, I haven't bought one yet.

a plan the route (still)

______

______

b choose the campsites (yet)

______

______

c buy bike shorts (already)

______

______

d check the bike lights (just)

______

______

e practice changing a tire (still)

______

______

GRAMMAR CHECK

1 Read the text and circle the correct answers.

Two years ago my family **a** ______ to do something for the environment. First, we **b** ______ taking our own shopping bags to the supermarket so we **c** ______ to use the supermarket's plastic bags. Then we **d** ______ a compost heap in the garden for all our food waste. My parents **e** ______ their bikes to work for years. But to be even greener, they **f** ______ their car. We **g** ______ put solar panels on our roof, but we will soon. I haven't bought any new clothes **h** ______ a year but last week I **i** ______ half my clothes with a friend who's the same size as me. And since the beginning of the year my sister and I **j** ______ an environmental group raise money.

A	B	C
a (decided)	has decided	were deciding
b start	started	have started
c aren't needing	haven't needed	didn't need
d were building	built	have built
e were riding	have ridden	rode
f have just sold	were just selling	did just sell
g yet haven't	still haven't	just didn't
h since	for	yet
i was swapping	have swapped	swapped
j were helping	helped	have helped

2 83 Listen and check your answers.

LISTENING

1 84 Listen to four teenagers discussing environmental issues. Check (✓) the things you hear about.

- ☐ improving insulation
- ☐ nuclear accidents
- ☐ people wasting electricity
- ☐ rainfall
- ☐ rechargeable batteries
- ☐ reducing our garbage
- ☐ saving water
- ☐ solar energy
- ☐ the weather
- ☐ taking action
- ☐ the climate in the US
- ☐ the need for better public transportation
- ☐ the need to recycle
- ☐ riding a bike

2 84 Listen again and complete the sentences with the correct names: Rawan, Jack, Anna or Caleb.

a ________ isn't sure if using nuclear energy is a good idea.

b ________ says floods are caused by climate change.

c ________ says it's easy to cut our electricity use.

d ________ says nuclear power plants don't emit carbon.

e ________ thinks it's too late to do anything about climate change.

f ________ thinks nuclear energy is too dangerous to use.

g ________ thinks people should use their cars less.

h ________ thinks the government should invest in solar and wind energy.

EXTENSION

Underline the correct words to complete the text.

The United Nations Environment Programme **a has calculated / calculated** that there are 3,000 pieces of plastic waste per square kilometer of the world's oceans. And all this garbage **b was killing / is killing** birds and sea creatures. Plastic waste **c has caused / caused** the death of a million seabirds and 100,000 sea mammals last year. **d For / Since** the past ten years, scientists have found more and more cigarette lighters and toothbrushes inside the stomachs of dead seabirds. Seabirds **e had eaten / eat** these things because they think they are food and then they **f can't / couldn't** get rid of them.
Charles Moore, an American oceanographer, **g believes / is believing** there are now 100 million tonnes of plastic waste in the Pacific Ocean. Mr. Moore **h used to be / has been** a sailor and in 1997, while he **i sailed / was sailing** from Los Angeles to Hawaii in a yacht race, he found himself in a huge area of garbage. 'I **j was moving / have moved** through garbage for a week,' he said. **k Since / For** that time, he has become an environmental activist.
The problem is that modern plastics **l are / were** not biodegradable. Plastic that got into the ocean 50 years ago **m still / yet** has not degraded.
The problem in the Mediterranean is very serious, too. In a recent study of dead loggerhead turtles off the coast of Spain, 75% of them **n had swallowed / were swallowing** plastic bags. Why? Plastic bags **o are looking / look** like jellyfish, the favorite food of these endangered animals.
So what plastic things **p do people throw / throw people** away? Plastic bags, bottles, containers, golf balls, plates, knives, forks, toothbrushes, helmets, beach toys, syringes and fishing lines is the short answer. And who **q does throw / throws** all this stuff away? We **r don't have / didn't have** any names. But please make sure it's not you.

VOCABULARY PLUS

Trees and Plants

1  ______

2  ______

3  ______

4  ______

5  ______

6  ______

7  ______

8  ______

9  ______

10  ______

1 85 Label the pictures with the words in the box. Then listen and repeat.

bark branch bud leaf petal root soil stalk trunk twig

2 Underline the correct words.

In fall, the **leaves** / **stalks** fall off the trees.

- **a** The **trunks** / **buds** on a plant will grow into flowers.
- **b** Several **roots** / **branches** fell off the tree during the storm.
- **c** You'll need to keep the **soil** / **twigs** wet if you want the plant to grow.
- **d** This flower has bright pink **petals** / **bark**.
- **e** To make the fire, we need to collect some dry **buds** / **twigs**.

3 Read the definitions and write the correct words.

A small round thing on a plant that grows into a flower.
bud

- **a** The hard brown material that covers a tree. ______
- **b** A flat green thing that grows on a twig. ______
- **c** The part of a tree or plant that grows under the ground. ______
- **d** The main brown part of a tree. ______
- **e** The long green part of a flower. ______
- **f** A twig grows from this part of a tree. ______
- **g** Both trees and plants have roots that grow in this. ______
- **h** This is the part of a flower that is colorful to attract insects. ______

4 Good Friends

VOCABULARY 1

Making Friends

1 Complete the phrases with the vowels.

interrupt a c *o* nv *e* rs *a* t *i* *o* n

a jump a l ___ n ___

b arrive ___ ___ rly

c be l ___ t ___

d be r ___ d ___

e be p ___ l ___ t ___

2 Match the phrases with the pictures.

[*f*] bring a present
[ ] snap your fingers
[ ] point at someone
[ ] shake hands
[ ] take off your shoes
[ ] tell jokes

3 Complete the phrases with the words in the box.

jump ~~polite~~ rude shake snap take off

It's *polite* to write a thank-you letter after a meal at someone's house.

a It's ________ to interrupt someone's conversation.

b Everybody is waiting their turn. Go to the back and don't try to ________ the line.

c After a tennis match, we always ________ hands to show we are still friends!

d Your house is very clean. Would you like us to ________ our shoes in the hall?

e It's rude in Britain to ________ your fingers to get the waiter's attention.

4 Match the phrases with the sentences.

arrive early be late bring a present ~~interrupt a conversation~~ point at someone tell jokes

Cam and I were talking and suddenly a guy came up and started talking about his phone.
interrupt a conversation

a Do you like chocolates? These are for you.

____

b Have you heard the one about two cats who had a swimming race?

____

c 'Look at that man, Mommy. He's walking in a funny way.' 'Don't point, Emma. It's rude.'

____

d 'I've been waiting an hour.' 'I'm really sorry. The traffic was terrible.'

____

e My watch was wrong and we arrived at seven. The invitation was for eight. It was embarrassing.

____

GRAMMAR 1

Obligation, No Obligation, Prohibition, Advice

1 Write pairs of sentences with *must* and *must not.*

Be here by six. Don't be late.
You must be here by six. You must not be late.

a Go to bed early. Don't stay up late.
______

b Be polite. Don't be rude.
______

c Don't wear jeans. Wear nice clothes.
______

d Put your cell phone on silent. Don't disturb people on the train.
______

e Take off your shoes. Don't get the carpet dirty.
______

f Don't jump the line. Wait for your turn.
______

2 Complete the sentences with *has to / have to* or *doesn't have to / don't have to.*

a 1 He *has to* be fit.
2 He *doesn't have to* wear a suit and tie.
3 He ______ train a lot.
4 He ______ use a computer in his job.

b 1 She ______ be calm and reliable.
2 She ______ wear a uniform.
3 She ______ like children.
4 She ______ travel for her job.

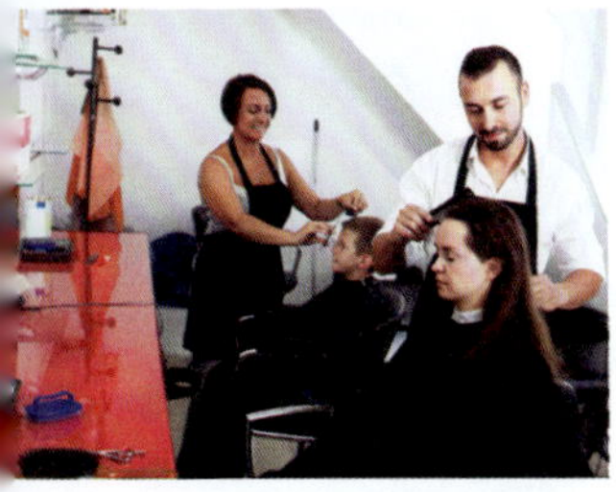

c 1 They ______ stand a lot.
2 They ______ have a driver's license.
3 They ______ be creative and good with their hands.
4 They ______ sit at a desk.

3 Write questions with *have to.* Then write answers for you.

In your country ...

How old / you / be / to drive a scooter ?
How old do you have to be to drive a scooter?
You have to be 17 to drive a scooter.

a you / pay / to see a dentist ?
______
______

b young people / do / military service ?
______
______

c how old / you / be / to get a job ?
______
______

At your school ...

d students / wear / a uniform ?
______
______

e How much homework / you / do ?
______
______

f students / go home / for lunch ?
______
______

4 Complete the sentences with *must not* or *don't / doesn't have to.*

You *must not* tell anyone. It's our secret. OK?

a Great! I ______ get up early. I can stay in bed until eleven!

b It's a pajama party, but you ______ wear pajamas if you don't want to.

c The bus leaves at seven. He ______ be late.

d My grandfather ______ pay on the bus. He has a free pass.

e We have lots of time. We ______ run to the bus stop.

f Your brother ______ park there. The police will tow his car away.

5 What things do you have to do at home? What about your friend? Complete the sentences.

I have to ___make my bed___. ✓
I don't have to ___cook___. ✗

- **a** I ________________. ✓
- **b** But I ________________. ✗
- **c** My friend ________________. ✓
- **d** He / She ________________. ✗

6 Give advice for each situation. Use *should / shouldn't* and the verbs in the box.

do drink eat ~~go~~ have put on sit sleep smoke ~~start~~

GET HEALTHY NOW!

My top tips for teenagers by Dr. Suzanne Golden

You ___should start___ the day with a healthy breakfast.
You ___shouldn't go___ to school with an empty stomach.

- ***a*** You ________ three meals a day.
- ***b*** You ________ plenty of water.
- ***c*** You ________ eight hours every night.
- ***d*** You ________ some exercise every day.
- ***e*** You ________ ever. It's the worst possible thing for your health.
- ***f*** You ________ in the sun in the middle of the day. It's bad for your skin.
- ***g*** You ________ sunscreen and a hat if you are out in the sun.
- ***h*** You ________ a lot of soft drinks, sweets, chocolate or junk food.

7 Write four tips for a happy life using *should* and *shouldn't*.

You ___should be friendly and helpful___.
You ___shouldn't worry too much___.

- **a** You should ________________.
- **b** You shouldn't ________________.
- **c** You should ________________.
- **d** You shouldn't ________________.

8 Underline the correct words.

Go back and take a shower, please. At this pool, you **must** / **should** have a shower before you go in the pool.

- **a** I have a headache. Perhaps I **must** / **should** take an aspirin.
- **b** The sign says NO SMOKING. That means you **must not** / **should not** smoke here.
- **c** I don't have to do my homework today, but I think I **must** / **should**. Then I'll be free all weekend.
- **d** People **must not** / **shouldn't** drive if it isn't necessary. It's bad for the environment.
- **e** You **must not** / **shouldn't** touch things in the museum. If you do, you will get into trouble.

9 Complete the summer camp rules with *have to, has to, should, don't have to* or *must not*.

Camp Rules

You can play music, but you ___must not___ make noise after eleven at night.

You a ________ light fires. It's very dangerous here in the forest.

You can swim in the lake but you b ________ dive. The water isn't deep enough.

Every child c ________ pass a water safety test. If you can't swim, you d ________ go out in the canoes.

You can do exercises before breakfast with Ms. Mortimer, if you like. You e ________ do them but it's a great way to start the day.

Group activities start at ten every morning. You f ________ be late. If you are late, we all g ________ wait for you and it is a waste of everyone's time.

You h ________ help with the cooking, but it's great if you do.

There are no cleaners so every camper i ________ help with the cleaning. If you don't clean your room, you will be in serious trouble!

We do a concert at the end of your stay. You j ________ be in it if you don't want to. But you k ________ because it's a lot of fun!

VOCABULARY 2

Verb and Noun Collocations

1 Find these nouns in the word search.

advice argument fun lies money ~~presents~~ time truth

P	R	E	S	E	N	T	S	O	A
E	I	F	B	I	X	C	Y	J	G
A	R	G	U	M	E	N	T	O	Q
B	N	A	F	R	X	Y	N	Q	P
A	D	V	I	C	E	Y	T	P	A
Q	S	E	U	Z	R	O	I	S	T
W	N	T	Q	V	T	I	M	Z	R
A	H	N	A	T	F	U	E	F	U
V	W	E	E	L	I	E	S	U	T
O	J	K	M	O	N	E	Y	N	H

2 Complete the phrases with the nouns from the word search.

a give / receive *presents*, ______.
b spend ______, ______.
c have an ______.
d tell ______.
e tell the ______.
f have ______.

3 Match the sentence beginnings with the endings.

a [3] On weekends I usually spend
b [ ] Let's go now. You don't need to spend
c [ ] She wanted my honest opinion so I had to tell
d [ ] She had health problems but she didn't receive any
e [ ] There's a page in this magazine where they give

1 advice about teenagers' problems.
2 her the truth.
3 money on eating out or going to the movies.
4 time changing your clothes.
5 useful advice from her doctor.

4 Complete the sentences with the words in the box.

argument fun ~~lies~~ presents receive

I never believe her stories. She always tells *lies*.

a I didn't want to have an ______, so I just agreed with her.
b We usually have ______ when we go to the beach.
c The best thing about birthdays is that you ______ presents from all your friends.
d How many people do you give ______ to at Christmas?

5 Answer the questions for you.

a What's the best thing you did for fun?
______

b Do you always tell the truth?
______

c What do you love spending money on?
______

d What's the best advice you have given to a friend?
______

GRAMMAR 2

Second Conditional

1 Match the sentence beginnings with the endings.

a [3] If I had enough money,
b [ ] If we had a cell phone with us,
c [ ] It would be fantastic
d [ ] I would tell you the answer
e [ ] If she didn't talk so much,
f [ ] I wouldn't ask her for advice

1 if I had wings and could fly!
2 she would be less annoying.
3 I'd buy an electric guitar.
4 if I were you.
5 we could call for help.
6 if I knew it.

2 Write sentences using the second conditional. Don't forget the comma where necessary.

If I (be) the prime minister / I (build) more hospitals
If I were the prime minister, I would build more hospitals.

a I (not ask) Bob for help / if I (be) you
______

b He (have) more money / if he (not spend) all his time dreaming
______

c If people (not drive) so much / this town (be) cleaner
______

d If you (wear) a coat / you (not feel) cold
______

e I (not have to) do the dishes / if we (have) a dishwasher
______

3 Complete the questions. Then choose your answers and write sentences with *I'd ...* .

The #InstaEnglish Personality Quiz

Are you a lion or a mouse? Find out with this quiz!

What would you do if you *saw* (see) a shark swimming towards you in the sea?
1 scream and prepare to die
2 stick your fingers in its eyes
3 swim away fast
I'd scream and prepare to die.

a What would you do if the principal ______ (ask) you to sing in front of the whole school?
1 pretend to be ill
2 agree to do it in a month
3 jump up and start singing
______

b What would you do if you ______ (break) your father's computer?
1 go and stay at a friend's house for a week
2 tell him and say sorry
3 start saving my allowance
______

c What would you do if you ______ (can) choose a vacation anywhere in the world?
1 choose a beach vacation in Europe
2 fly to New York and San Francisco
3 go walking in the Andes
______

d What would you do if you ______ (find) a snake in your tent when you were camping?
1 die of fright
2 get out of the tent fast
3 take a picture of it
______

e What would you do if you ______ (go) to a restaurant with a very unusual menu?
1 leave immediately
2 pretend to feel ill
3 order the snails and frogs' legs
______

GRAMMAR CHECK

1 Read the text and circle the correct answers.

WELCOME TO OAKWOOD SUMMER SCHOOL

We a _____ it if we didn't need to have rules! That's why we don't have very many. Please take the time to read them.

ROOMS

Students b _____ pay a $20 deposit for their room key. If you lose your key, you will lose your deposit. For security reasons, you c _____ lock your room when you go out. It's OK to make hot drinks in your rooms, but you d _____ cook in them.

CLASSES

Every student e _____ sign the register before morning classes. No student f _____ ever sign in for another student. It is strictly forbidden. Classes start at 9:30 in the morning. You g _____ be late.

EXCURSIONS

Life wouldn't be much fun for our students if we h _____ offer a wide range of excursions. We really recommend them. Of course, you i _____ go on them, but we think you j _____ try them.

	1	2	3
a	(would prefer)	preferred	prefer
b	should	must	don't have to
c	must not	should	shouldn't
d	must	have to	must not
e	doesn't have to	has to	must not
f	has to	must not	must
g	must not	must	don't have to
h	don't	wouldn't	didn't
i	don't have to	shouldn't	must not
j	must	have to	should

2 86 Listen and check your answers.

LISTENING

1 87 Listen and complete.

a All Francesca's friends are __________.

b Eugenie can keep a __________.

c Eugenie and Francesca both wanted the main __________ in a __________ at school.

d Francesca often sees Bryony on the __________.

e Francesca goes to a __________ after school.

2 87 Listen again and circle the correct answers.

a Francesca …
1 met Bryony at a sports club.
2 doesn't have a brother.
3 goes to a school for boys and girls.

b Her friend Eugenie …
1 doesn't like the other girls in the group.
2 is not at Francesca's school.
3 is in a group of six friends.

c Francesca …
1 sometimes asks Eugenie for advice.
2 doesn't like telling Eugenie her secrets.
3 usually tells the whole group her problems.

d Eugenie …
1 wasn't jealous of Francesca's role in the play.
2 didn't get a part in the play.
3 and Francesca think the same things are funny.

e Bryony …
1 has never met Francesca's new friends.
2 and Francesca are at different schools.
3 and Francesca usually meet during the week.

f Hannah …
1 and Francesca are going to their sports club this weekend.
2 is at Francesca's school.
3 and Francesca are doing something together this weekend.

EXTENSION

Underline the correct words to complete the text.

Amanda and I have known each other **a since** / **for** nearly ten years. We **b met** / **have met** at primary school, so we **c were** / **have been** friends since we were six years old. We are both very keen **d for** / **on** acting, dancing and music. Amanda is a better musician **e than** / **by** me. In fact, she's the **f best** / **better** singer I know. She **g must** / **should** be a professional singer right now, really. Anyway, I know she'll be famous one day. At the moment, we both **h playing** / **play** in a band called Infinity and she also **i is singing** / **sings**. I play the drums, but I've **j never sung** / **never sang** in public. Last summer, we **k played** / **were playing** at a school concert when there was a power cut. The lights went out and the microphone didn't **l work** / **worked**. Amanda was as **m cooler** / **cool** as a professional singer. She said **n a little** / **a few** words and apologized about the problem. She said something like, 'If it's light enough for you to **o see** / **saw** me, **p I would** / **I'll** sing.' And everybody clapped and she sang **q some** / **much** songs without a microphone and without her electric guitar. I wouldn't sing in public if you **r pay** / **paid** me a million dollars! Luckily, I **s don't have to** / **must not** sing because I'm just the drummer. But next year, **t I'll** / **I'm** going to learn to play the guitar as well.

VOCABULARY PLUS

Friendship

1 to arrange to meet someone

2 to become friends with someone

3 to fall out with someone

4 to fight with someone

5 to finish with someone

6 to get on with someone

7 to get to know someone

8 to be done with someone

9 to make friends with someone

10 to make up with someone

11 to meet a new person

1 🔊 88 Write the phrasal verbs in the correct box. Then listen and repeat.

☺	☹
to arrange to meet someone	

2 Match the verbs and the definitions.

a make friends with
b to get to know
c to be done with
d to make up
e to arrange to meet someone
f to fall out with

to invite someone to a place
to stop liking someone
to have an argument with
to learn more about a person
enjoy someone's company
to become friends again after an argument

3 Complete the sentences with the correct preposition.

~~with~~ in off with on up with

Have you heard? Emma and Jane fought with each other and now Emma is done *with* Jane.

a We're good friends. We really get ________ with each other.

b I don't want to be Paul's friend anymore. I'm going to finish ________ him.

c Lydia and Caroline are friends again. They made ________ with each other last night.

d 'Have you ever been ________ a fight with anyone?' 'No, never!'

e I'm done ________ Martin. I won't be friends with him anymore.

4 Answer the questions for you. Write in full sentences. Use phrasal verbs from activity 1.

a Do you sometimes fall out with your family?

____

b Do you always make up with your friends after arguing?

____

c Have you ever been done with someone?

____

5 Followers of Fashion

VOCABULARY 1

Style Adjectives

1 Complete adjectives a-f with vowels. Then match them with pictures 1-6.

- **a** [6] t _i_ g h t
- **b** [ ] s p ___ r t y
- **c** [ ] l ___ ___ s e
- **d** [ ] ___ l d - f a s h ___ ___ n ___ d
- **e** [ ] g l ___ m ___ r ___ ___ s
- **f** [ ] f ___ r m ___ l

2 Match the columns to make adjectives.

a	cas	[ ]	ventional
b	col	[ ]	practical
c	com	[ ]	dy
d	con	[ ]	fortable
e	fash	[ ]	ual
f	im	[ ]	ionable
g	tren	[ ]	orful

3 Complete the sentences with the style adjectives in the box.

colorful comfortable ~~fashionable~~
formal loose old-fashioned tight

She's very interested in fashion. All her clothes are very _fashionable_.

- **a** Those jeans are too ___________. She needs a bigger size.
- **b** He's very ___________. He even wears a tie on weekends.
- **c** You can walk all day in these shoes. They are really ___________.
- **d** His shirt was covered in big blue, red, green and yellow flowers. It was very ___________.
- **e** These shoes are one size too big. They are too ___________ for me.
- **f** At the costume party he wore one of those ___________ striped swimsuits from the 1920s that cover the top part of the body as well.

4 Match the descriptions with the style adjectives in the box.

casual conventional glamorous
impractical ~~sporty~~ trendy

He works at a gym so he often wears a track suit and sneakers. _sporty_

- **a** She was wearing a long silk dress and diamond earrings. She looked like a movie star. ___________
- **b** That's my father in the suit and white shirt with a blue tie. He works in a bank. ___________
- **c** She was wearing a long skirt and high heels on her bike. And she didn't have a helmet on. ___________
- **d** She's always very fashionable. Today she's wearing denim shorts with suede ankle boots. ___________
- **e** Adam is the guy in jeans and a pale blue sweater. ___________

GRAMMAR 1

Relative Pronouns

1 Underline the correct words.

Mary Quant was a fashion designer **which** / **who** became famous in London in the sixties.

- a The 1960s was the time **where** / **when** miniskirts first became fashionable.
- b The store **which** / **where** I bought this jacket is on Maple Street.
- c I know a girl **which** / **who** is a successful fashion model.
- d Why don't you wear those shoes **that** / **who** you bought last week?
- e I didn't like those people **which** / **that** we met in the park.
- f Let's go to that museum **who** / **which** has antique clothes on display.

2 Match the sentence beginnings with the endings.

- a [*3*] My friend has a cat
- b [ ] That's the girl
- c [ ] Do you remember that day
- d [ ] Are you the person
- e [ ] Can I see the dress
- f [ ] Let's go to that store
- g [ ] I don't like people

1. when we both wore the same clothes?
2. who smiled at you in the park.
3. that loves watching TV.
4. where you got your jacket.
5. who always show off.
6. that you wore to the party?
7. that I spoke to on the phone?

3 Complete the text using *which, who, where* or *when.*

A friend of mine ___*who*___ is studying fashion design recently had to create clothes from unusual materials. One material **a** ________ she used was plastic trash bags. She made clothes with them **b** ________ looked really expensive. There were other students in her course **c** ________ made amazing skirts and dresses out of newspaper **d** ________ they folded into pleats. My friend asked me to wear one of her creations on the day **e** ________ her teachers were coming to see her work. I agreed but I didn't realize it was a really big deal. I went to the college **f** ________ there was a room full of photographers. I found my friend and she took me to the back **g** ________ there was a changing room. I put on the black plastic dress **h** ________ she had made and **i** ________ looked amazing on me. Then I had to walk down the catwalk **j** ________ there were lots of other models and loads of photographers who took pictures of me. I enjoyed it, especially at the end **k** ________ a woman from a modeling agency offered me some paid work. But the best bit was **l** ________ I took off the plastic dress. It looked great but it was very hot under those bright lights!

4 Join the sentences using *who, which, where* or *when.*

I have some fashion magazines. They're from the sixties.

I have some fashion magazines which are from the sixties.

- a There's a man outside. He wants to see you.
  ____
  ____
- b There's a store on Santee Street. You can get two pairs of shoes for $30.
  ____
  ____
- c I can't wait for the summer. We can wear shorts and sandals.
  ____
  ____
- d I have a friend. She always makes her own clothes.
  ____
  ____
- e There's a bookstore on my street. You can look at books and have a coffee.
  ____
  ____
- f I have a dress of my grandmother's. It looks great on me.
  ____
  ____

5 Choose the correct alternative.

a Is that the store ______ you got your boots?

1 who **2** where **3** that

b There was a famous boutique in London in the 1960s ______ a minidress cost only £5.

1 that **2** where **3** who

c The baby ______ is crying is my sister.

1 who **2** which **3** when

d The book ______ won the Pulitzer prize is getting an illustrated edition.

1 which **2** where **3** when

e He does yoga in the same studio ______ I do Tai Chi.

1 which **2** where **3** who

f Nicki met the singer ______ performed last week at the Opera House!

1 which **2** where **3** who

g Bertrand finished college on the day ______ his daughter was born.

1 when **2** where **3** who

h In a year ______ platform heels are back in fashion, nothing can surprise me anymore!

1 who **2** which **3** when

6 Check the sentences in which the relative pronoun *which*, *who* or *that* can be omitted.

a ☐ This is the money **that** I will use to pay the electrician.

b ☐ My father is the man **who** always wears blue jeans.

c ☐ What's the fashion model **who** you saw at the store wearing?

d ☐ She is holding the umbrella **which** I found in her house.

e ☐ He mentioned the article **that** his professor wrote on the issue.

7 Underline the correct words to complete the text.

My two friends Maxine and Leonie have very different styles. I don't see Leonie during the week anymore because now she's at the school **a when / where** my cousins study. But we still hang out on weekends. And that's **b where / when** I notice their different styles.

Maxine's style is a little bit aggressive. She often wears blue jeans, a T-shirt and a red leather jacket. And she has a pair of red cowboy boots **c which / who** look great with her jeans. If we're going dancing or to a party, she still wears jeans, but she sometimes puts on a glamorous top, for example one **d which / who** is made of silk with gold and silver touches. School is the only place **e when / where** Maxine usually has her long blond hair in a pony tail, because everywhere else she wears it loose.

While Maxine nearly always wears jeans or pants, Leonie loves skirts and dresses. She is that friend **f which / that** was wearing that stunning blue dress at my birthday party last year. And her clothes are always unusual. She loves vintage clothes so she spends a lot of time mending old clothes **g which / where** she buys in thrift stores. She has one amazing coat **h where / that** belonged to her grandmother in the early sixties.

While Maxine looks very confident, Leonie always looks gentle, artistic and dreamy. But one thing is for certain, both Maxine and Leonie are really stylish in different ways!

VOCABULARY 2

Phrasal Verbs: Clothes

1 Order the letters and write the phrasal verbs. Then match them with the pictures.

a [5] k a t e f o f ___take off___
b [ ] e v i g y a w a ________
c [ ] t u p n o ________
d [ ] u p t w a y a ________
e [ ] t e g t o n i ________
f [ ] w o r t h y a a w ________

1

2

3

4

5
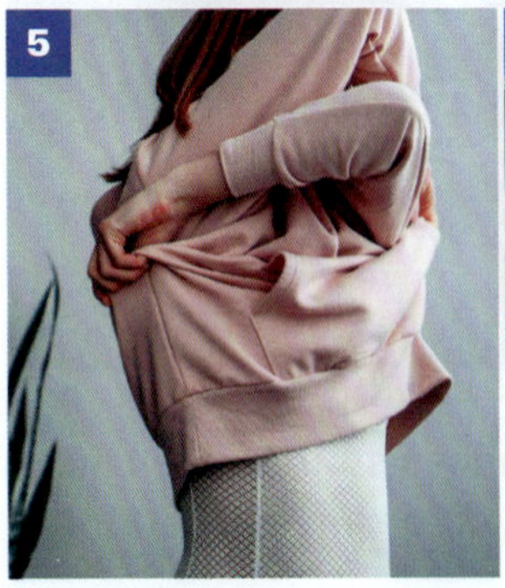
6

2 Underline the correct words.

I need to **go with** / **<u>look for</u>** a new top to wear to Jodie's party.

a I think these jeans will fit you. Why don't you **try them on** / **wear them out**?

b At the summer sales she managed to **look for** / **pick up** a designer handbag for half price.

c These boots are so strong and well made that it takes years to **wear them out** / **try them on**.

d I'm not sure if the blue shoes **go with** / **look for** your black jacket.

e When you don't know what to buy, you can ask the sales clerk to **pick up something** / **pick something out** for you.

3 Match the sentences a-f with the responses 1-6.

a [3] It's cold.
b [ ] Do you think this sweater will fit me?
c [ ] It's hot in here.
d [ ] Do you like my sweater?
e [ ] This sweater has holes in it.
f [ ] I want a cashmere sweater.

1 Take your sweater off.
2 Throw it away.
3 Put your sweater on.
4 Try it on.
5 Try to pick one up during the sales.
6 Yes, it goes well with your jeans.

4 Complete the sentences with the phrasal verbs in the box.

get into	give away	~~look for~~
pick out	put away	wear out

Let's go shopping. I need to ___look for___ a new jacket.

a If you don't like those clothes any more, ________ them ________ or take them to a thrift store.

b Can I ________ some earrings for you to wear with that dress?

c Do you get rid of your clothes when you're bored with them or do you keep them until you ________ them ________?

d I will have to buy some bigger clothes. I can't ________ this dress any more.

e There are clothes all over the floor. Can you ________ them ________?

GRAMMAR 2

some, any, no Compounds

1 Match the questions with the answers.

a [3] What would you like for your birthday?
b [ ] Where's Krasnodar?
c [ ] What kind of hotel would you like to stay at?
d [ ] What's your town like?
e [ ] Who's your best friend?
f [ ] What should I wear in Moscow in winter?

1 Someone from my primary school.
2 Something very warm.
3 Something expensive.
4 Somewhere with a pool.
5 Somewhere in Russia.
6 It's OK, but there's nowhere to go in the evenings.

2 Underline the correct words.

I've grown taller. **Something** / **Nothing** fits me now.

a I'm bored. There's **anything** / **nothing** to do in this town and **anywhere** / **nowhere** to go.
b 'Where should we eat?' '**Anywhere** / **Nowhere** – you choose!'
c Let's find **anywhere** / **somewhere** nice for a picnic.
d You're annoyed about **anything** / **something**. Please tell me the problem.
e **No one** / **Someone** liked the movie. We all left early.
f I don't have **anything** / **nothing** to wear to the party.
g There's **anyone** / **someone** at the door. Please can you go and open it?
h There isn't **someone** / **anyone** outside. I think it was a cat.

3 Complete the dialogue with the correct *some*, *no* or *any* compounds.

Eva Is there *anywhere* to buy a present for my parents?
Kate What kind of thing do you want?
Eva **a** ________ nice for the house, I think.
Kate You can't get **b** ________ nice in this area.
Eva I don't mind going downtown.
Kate There's **c** ________ really good for kitchen things on Katy Freeway, it's not too far from where we are. I bought **d** ________ there last week.
Eva Really? What was it?
Kate **e** ________ very exciting. It was just something cheap and useful.
Eva What?
Kate It was **f** ________ to keep food in, in the fridge.
Eva You mean a plastic container?
Kate Yes. My mom asked me to buy her one.
Eva Oh. Do they have **g** ________ more interesting than plastic food containers in this appliance store?
Kate Yes. They have lovely plates and bowls and really expensive glasses.

4 Complete the sentences so they are true for you. Use *some*, *no* or *any* compounds.

My best friend is *someone who lives on my street*.

a I grew up ________________.
b If I could meet ________ in the world, I would love to meet ________.
c ________ that I love to eat is ________.
d If I could travel ________ in Europe, I would choose ________.

GRAMMAR CHECK

1 Read the text and circle the correct answers.

Ding dong. The front doorbell rings.

Luke There's someone at the door.

Dan Don't answer it. It **a** ______ someone annoying **b** ______ wants to sell us something.

Luke OK, **c** ______ a look out of the window.

Dan Don't let them see you looking.

Luke looks out of the window.

Luke **d** ______ . I can't see **e** ______ .

Dan Are you sure?

Luke Quite sure. There's **f** ______ there.

Dan Perhaps they're **g** ______ in the garden. Or perhaps they've gone around the back of the house and they **h** ______ at the back door.

Knock knock. There's a knock at the back door.

Luke Yes. There's **i** ______ at the back door. It's a tall girl carrying a guitar case **j** ______ too big for her.

Dan Oh, that's Marianne.

Luke Why does she have such an enormous guitar?

Dan She **k** ______ in the school band, and that's a double bass, not a guitar!

	A	B	C
a	is	(might be)	is being
b	who	which	he
c	I'm taking	I'm going to take	I'll take
d	I'm not	I won't	I don't
e	no one	someone	anyone
f	someone	anyone	no one
g	anywhere	somewhere	nowhere
h	knocked	're going to knock	're knocking
i	someone	no one	anyone
j	when it's	it's	that's
k	's going to play	'll play	's playing

2 89 Listen and check your answers.

LISTENING

1 90 Listen to a radio show where four teenagers talk about clothes and fashion. Circle T (*true*), F (*false*) or DS (*doesn't say*).

a Georgia wears the same style of clothes every day. **T / F / DS**

b Georgia always feels aggressive. **T / F / DS**

c Daniel never wears sneakers. **T / F / DS**

d Daniel works after school to pay for his clothes. **T / F / DS**

e Serena often wears cheap clothes. **T / F / DS**

f Serena doesn't have any designer clothes. **T / F / DS**

g Serena's blue velvet pants cost her $200. **T / F / DS**

h Tim has a few different clothing styles. **T / F / DS**

i Tim has expensive jeans. **T / F / DS**

j He never wears natural materials like wool and cotton. **T / F / DS**

2 90 Listen again and write Georgia, Daniel, Serena or Tim next to each statement.

a Fashion's great because there are no rules.

____

b I can't afford new designer clothes but I sometimes get them secondhand.

____

c I express my feelings through my clothes.

____

d I might look the same every day but I'm never a mess.

____

e I spend a lot more than most people on my clothes.

____

f If it's not practical and comfortable, it's not for me.

____

g Shopping is about picking up bargains.

____

h I would never wear cheap shoes!

____

EXTENSION

Underline the correct words to complete the text.

a **Anyone / Someone** who thinks our interest in fashion and beauty is b **somewhere / something** new is mistaken. Beauty treatments and make up have been around c **since / for** thousands of years. The ancient Egyptians d **used / were using** ground minerals to make colored eye shadows and powders. And Queen Cleopatra e **was taking / used to take** baths in milk and honey.

f **Everywhere / Anywhere** in the world people decorate their bodies and faces in order to look more beautiful. But there are quite a lot of beauty practices g **where / which** seem strange to us in the west. For example, in Kenya, Masai girls h **think / are thinking** long ears are beautiful. So they i **are stretching / stretch** their ears with heavy weights.

A lot of beauty practices are painful. In China they j **have stopped / stopped** binding girls' feet now. Until the middle of the 20th century, older women k **were putting / used to put** tight cloth around the feet of three-year-old girls and break the bones in their feet so that they would have small feet. It l **hurt / was hurting** a lot and the girls m **have grown / grew** up with deformed feet, unable to walk normally.

And what painful things n **do we do / we do** in the West in the name of beauty? Well, o **I'm standing / I stand** outside a tattoo parlor at the moment and a few men and women p **go / are going** into it. That's one painful beauty practice q **when / that** people are happy to pay for in the west.

r **Will there be / Is there being** a time when people won't suffer to be beautiful? I don't think so!

VOCABULARY PLUS

Clothes and Accessories

1 ________ 2 ________ 3 ___tie___ 4 ________ 5 ________

6 ________ 7 ________ 8 ________ 9 ________ 10 ________

1 🔊 91 Label the pictures with the words in the box. Then listen and repeat.

belt button collar laces necklace pocket sleeve slippers ~~tie~~ zipper

2 Underline the correct words.

You look very stylish today. I like your **<u>tie</u>** / **slippers**.

a These jeans are too loose. I need a **belt** / **collar**.

b Hang on! I need to tie the **laces** / **sleeve** on my sneakers.

c I lost my keys because there was a hole in my **zipper** / **pocket**.

d Don't do up the top **button** / **necklace** on your shirt.

e Oh no! The **collar** / **zipper** is broken and I can't close my pants.

3 Complete the definitions with the correct words.

A ___pocket___ is a small bag in your clothes that holds small objects.

a Things you put on your feet to keep warm: ________ .

b Men often wear a ________ under their collar.

c The ________ is the part of a coat, jacket or shirt that goes round your neck.

d A ________ is a piece of jewelry you wear around your neck.

e The ________ is the part of a shirt, jacket or dress that covers your arm.

4 Answer the questions for you. Write full sentences.

a What do you keep in your pockets?

____

b Do you prefer jeans with buttons or a zipper?

____

c How often do you wear a belt?

____

d Do you wear slippers at home?

____

6 Work and Money

VOCABULARY 1

The World of Work

1 Complete the words with the vowels.

b _o_ n _u_ s

a c o n d ___ t ___ ___ n s

b ___ p p l ___ c ___ t ___ ___ n f ___ r m

c j ___ b ___ d v ___ r t ___ s ___ m ___ n t

d p ___ y r ___ ___ s ___

e ___ x p ___ n s ___ s

f p r ___ m ___ t ___ ___ n

g w ___ r k ___ x p ___ r ___ ___ n c ___

2 Find seven work and money words in the wordsnake.

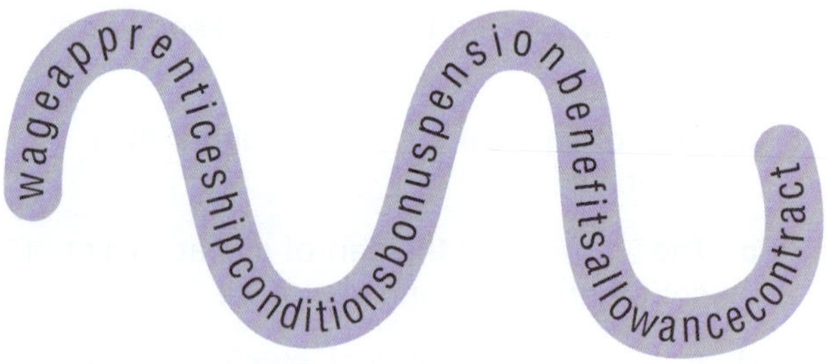

3 Imagine you are looking for a new job. Put these events in the correct order.

a ☐ application form

b ☐ contract

c ☐ interview

d [1] job advertisement

e ☐ promotion

f ☐ wage

4 <u>Underline</u> the correct words.

My older sister has to fill in her qualifications and experience on the **job advertisement** / <u>**application form**</u>.

a I want to train to be a plumber so when I am older I will have to do an **apprenticeship** / **application form**.

b As a waiter, his **pay raise** / **wage** isn't great but he gets tips from some customers.

c Let's go out for a meal to celebrate. My Dad's boss has given him a **pay raise** / **benefits** of $3,000 a year.

d When my mother goes abroad for her job, she gets a daily **apprenticeship** / **allowance** to cover her food, transportation and hotel.

e The salary is OK but the **expenses** / **conditions** aren't great at my uncle's job. He only gets ten days vacation a year and he has to work on Saturdays.

5 Complete the sentences with the words in the box.

allowance benefits bonus ~~contract~~ pension promotion wage work experience

I have a new job. They've sent me the _contract_ so now I must sign it and send it back.

a My father has to use his own car at his job but he gets an ___________ for gasoline.

b My grandfather retired a few years ago but he has plenty of money for vacations because he gets a good ___________.

c Her starting ___________ at the travel company is $1,500 a month but she gets a ___________ if she sells lots of vacation packages.

d My cousin got a ___________ last week. He's going to be Senior Sales Manager now.

e The salary isn't very good at that company but the ___________ are excellent. There are long vacations and free flights all around the world.

f I want to be a journalist, so I'm getting ___________ at a local newspaper.

GRAMMAR 1

First and Second Conditionals

1 Underline the correct words.

If you **will apply** / **apply** for this job, I'm sure you will get it.

a My father **wears** / **will wear** a suit if they call him for an interview.

b If my sister gets an application form, **will you help** / **do you help** her fill it out?

c He will lose his job if he **won't stop** / **doesn't stop** being late for work.

d If they **will offer** / **offer** her a job, will she take it?

e You **don't regret** / **won't regret** it if you go and work for them.

f If she **doesn't get** / **won't get** that job, she will be very disappointed.

2 Complete the sentences using the first conditional.

If you *don't work* (not work) harder, you *won't pass* (not pass) your exams.

a If you ___________ (not pass) your exams, you ___________ (not get) a job.

b If you ___________ (not get) a job, you ___________ (not earn) any money.

c If you ___________ (not earn) any money, you ___________ (not have) enough money for a vacation.

d If you ___________ (not have) enough money for a vacation, we ___________ (not be able) to go away together.

3 Complete the advertisements using *if* and the first conditional.

Workwise Employment Agency

We can find you your dream job!

If you need a job, we'll find you one today!

____

you (need) a job, we (find) you one today!

a **The Knocky 221 Smartphone Makes life easier!**

____

____

you (buy) one today / we (give) you $20 of free talk time!

b **Akiko XL Laptop**

Light, easy and fun to use!

____

____

you (want) to work on the move, you (love) this!

c **Student Supersaver Account**

The best bank account for young people

____

____

you (open) an account with us today, we (give) a free cell phone!

d **Traveler Watches**

Smart, stylish, accurate

____

____

you (like) good design, you (want) one of these!

4 Order the words to make second conditional sentences.

$5000, / had / how / If / it / spend / would / you / you ?

If you had $5000, how would you spend it?

a do / If / president, / the / were / what / would / you / you ?

____

b a / buy / house / I / I'd / if / lottery / my / new / parents / the / won

____

c a rock star / any / choose / could / I / I'd be / If / in the world, / job

____

d buy / cost / didn't / I / If / one / so much, / those laptops / would !

____

e a job, / didn't / father / bored / have / he / If / very / my / be / would

____

5 Complete the sentences using the second conditional.

If she (know) the answer, she (tell) us.
If she knew the answer, she would tell us.

a He (not be) so poor if he (not waste) all his money on expensive restaurants.

____

b If I (be) you, I (not lend) him any money.

____

c He (not work) for that company if he (can) get a job somewhere else.

____

d If I (have) enough money, I (start) my own design company.

____

e You (not like) it if you (lose) your job.

____

6 Match the sentence beginnings with the endings to make first or second conditional sentences.

a [6] If your sister doesn't apply for the job,
b [ ] If they offered him more money,
c [ ] What would your father say
d [ ] If I forget,
e [ ] Will you ask for help
f [ ] If he left his job tomorrow,

1 how would he pay for his apartment?
2 if I offered you a job?
3 if you have a problem?
4 will you please remind me?
5 would he stay at the job?
6 she won't get it.

7 Complete the dialogue using the first or second conditional.

Rose Let's do the quiz in this magazine.
Lila No, I'm busy.
Rose Please. If you *do* (do) it with me, I **a** __________ (help) you with your math homework.
Lila Fine. It's a deal.
Rose Here's the first question. What **b** __________ (you do) if you **c** __________ (see) a ghost?
Lila That's ridiculous. I don't believe in ghosts.
Rose Wait. **d** __________ (you scream)? **e** __________ (you call) the police? Or **f** __________ (you faint)?
Lila I can't choose any of those answers. What's the next question in this silly quiz?
Rose What **g** __________ (you do) if you **h** __________ (find) $500 in the street? **i** __________ (you keep) it, **j** __________ (you take) it to the police, or **k** __________ (you give) it to charity?
Lila I'm pretty honest so I **l** __________ (not keep) it. I **m** __________ (take) it to the police, probably.
Rose Me, too. Next question. If you **n** __________ (have) to parachute from a plane, swim with sharks or lie on a bed of hot coals, which **o** __________ (you do)?
Lila I don't know and I don't care.
Rose If you **p** __________ (not answer), I **q** __________ (not help) you with your homework. Remember the deal?
Lila I don't care. I'll do my homework without your help, thanks.

8 Complete the sentences for you. Use the first or second conditional.

If I had a magic carpet,
I would fly to India to see the Taj Mahal.

a If I do well on the exams this summer,
______________________.

b If I went to the fancy dress party,
______________________.

c If the weather is nice this weekend,
______________________.

d If I won the lottery,
______________________.

VOCABULARY 2

Work Verbs

1 Complete the phrases with the verbs in the box.

apply be earn fill out ~~have~~ have

have an interview

a ________ a salary

b ________ unemployed

c ________ a full-time job

d ________ an application form

e ________ for a job

2 Order the letters to make phrases.

m a l i c p e n s e x e s *claim expenses*

a k r o w t r a p - m i e t ________

b t e g a b o j ________

c e g t a n o s i n e p ________

d s o l e a o b j ________

e n i g s a c a n c r o t t ________

3 Match the sentence beginnings with the endings.

a [2] He should get a haircut before he has

b [ ] She decided to work

c [ ] It took her three hours to fill out

d [ ] If your cousin is late for work every day, he'll

e [ ] Make sure your uncle understands everything before

f [ ] They are accountants so they both

1 earn a good salary.

2 an interview.

3 lose his job.

4 part-time after having her second baby.

5 this application form.

6 he signs the contract.

4 Complete the sentences with the words in the box.

apply claim earn fill out ~~full-time~~ get get have lose sign unemployed work

He was only working 12 hours a week but now he has a *full-time* job and works a 40-hour week.

a There's an advertisement for a store assistant at the Surf Shack. Why doesn't your sister ________ for it? Look, I picked up the application form for her to ________.

b It isn't easy to ________ a job at the moment – more than two million people are ________.

c When my aunt retires from the police force, she will ________ good pension.

d She had to buy a train ticket for a work trip with her own money so now she needs to ________ expenses.

e I'm free on Tuesday and Thursday afternoons because I only ________ part-time now.

f Here's a pen. Can you ________ the contract, please?

g She loves being a cook but she doesn't ________ a very good salary.

h When they close the car factory, my brother will ________ his job.

i Your cousin looks really smart. Is he about to ________ an interview?

GRAMMAR 2

Gerunds and Infinitives

1 **Complete the sentences using the gerund form of the verbs in the box.**

clean get up learn read
~~see~~ sleep surf swim

Are you looking forward to *seeing* your American cousins again?

a Have you finished __________ *War and Peace* yet?

b What time did you finish __________ your bedroom?

c I don't enjoy __________ in cold water.

d __________ the internet is fun but you can waste a lot of time.

e I'm not looking forward to __________ at 5am on Monday.

f My sister really enjoys __________ languages.

g __________ takes up about one third of our lives!

2 **Match the sentence beginnings with the endings. Then change the verbs in parentheses to gerunds.**

a [4] I am looking forward to

b [ ] I'm always hungry and I enjoy

c [ ] When will you finish

d [ ] All children look forward to

e [ ] I haven't finished

f [ ] My sister spends a lot of time

1 __________ (eat) more than cooking.

2 __________ (look) in her mirror.

3 __________ (read) this wonderful book yet.

4 *starting* (start) my new job next week.

5 __________ (write) that essay?

6 __________ (open) their Christmas presents.

3 **Complete the sentences using the infinitive form of the verbs in parentheses.**

I can't afford *to buy* (buy) another pair of shoes.

a They've decided __________ (go) camping together.

b Would you like __________ (see) my application form?

c When did you learn __________ (speak) Russian?

d She doesn't want __________ (move) to a new house.

e We've arranged __________ (meet) at 7pm.

f I'm applying __________ (join) the police force.

4 **Complete the text using the infinitive or gerund form of the verbs in parentheses.**

Dear Felicity,

I'm really looking forward to *seeing* (see) you next week. I've decided **a** __________ (come) by bus because I can't afford **b** __________ (get) the train.

Have you finished **c** __________ (make) the costumes for your school play? How much time have you spent so far **d** __________ (work) on them? I'd like **e** __________ (help) with our school play, too. I really enjoy **f** __________ (paint) and I'm also learning **g** __________ (make) things out of wood, so maybe I can apply **h** __________ (be) one of the set builders. Do you want **i** __________ (come) and stay with us in August? Mom says she's going to be near your house in Hereford and she can arrange **j** __________ (pick) you up.

Bye for now,

Angie

5 **Complete the sentences for you, your friends or your family.**

My brother really enjoys *writing songs*.

a One day I would like __________.

b I am looking forward to __________.

c At the moment I am learning __________.

d My friend has decided __________.

e I can't afford __________.

f __________ spends a lot of time __________.

g I've arranged __________.

GRAMMAR CHECK

1 Read the text and circle the correct answers.

I am looking forward to **a** _____ high school. I've applied **b** _____ to college in Canada. If I got a scholarship, my parents **c** _____ have to pay the fees. But they still couldn't afford **d** _____ all my living costs there. So if they **e** _____ me a place, I'll need to get a vacation job in the summer before I go. I would like **f** _____ a job as a lifeguard at the beach. I've learned **g** _____ people in the water and I've spent a lot of time **h** _____ a training course on artificial respiration. So I **i** _____ what to do if somebody **j** _____ into trouble while I was on duty.

	A	B	C
a	leave	leaving	I leave
b	for go	for going	to go
c	won't	wouldn't	don't
d	to pay	paying	pay
e	are offering	will offer	offer
f	to get	getting	if getting
g	saving	to save	my saving
h	doing	to doing	to do
i	would know	knew	have known
j	will get	got	gets

2 92 Listen and check your answers.

LISTENING

1 93 Listen and circle T (*true*), F (*false*) or DK (*don't know*).

a Children under 14 can legally get a job doing 'light work.' T / F / DK

b Most employers don't give work to people younger than 15. T / F / DK

c More boys than girls get paid to deliver newspapers. T / F / DK

d The rules about working hours change when you are 16. T / F / DK

e Employers have to pay the minimum wage to people younger than 16. T / F / DK

f Fruit picking is better paid than store work. T / F / DK

2 93 Listen again and answer the questions.

a Name three of the jobs the speaker says someone under 15 might realistically get.

____

b How many hours a week can schoolchildren under 16 work during the school term?

____

c What's the latest time they can stop working?

____

d What's the maximum time people under 16 can work per week during the holidays?

____

e Is the maximum time 16- and 17-year olds can work per week limited by law?

____

EXTENSION

Underline the correct words.

Do you know **a somebody which / anybody who** chose their career when he or she was very young? Melissa Thornton **b has decided / decided** to become a vet when she was 7. 'I **c have grown up / grew up** on a farm and I **d used to help / was helping** my parents to look after the animals. I remember the day **e when / where** I thought, "I'm **f being / going to be** a vet when I grow up." I was seven years old and we had a horse which had **g something / anything** wrong with its leg. While the vet **h has checked / was checking** its leg, I watched her very carefully. This incident **i made up / makes up** my mind about my future career.'

When she was 16, Melissa **j was spending / spent** two weeks during her summer vacation helping in a veterinary office. 'It was very helpful and I **k learned / have learned** a lot about a vet's life and work.' She is now in her last year of secondary school and **l has applied / was applying** for a place at Edinburgh University to study veterinary medicine. 'They **m were offering / have offered** me a place but I won't be able to go there if I **n don't / won't** get three As in my exams. **o I work / I'm working** really hard at the moment. It would be terrible if **p I'll get / I got** two As and a B instead of three As. If I **q got / get** my grades, I'm going to spend a month in Ghana as a volunteer with local vets. Apparently, **r we're visiting / we'll visit** farms and **s I'm learning / I'll learn** about vaccinations. What an amazing experience before I start college!'

VOCABULARY PLUS

In the Office

1 
______

2 
______

3 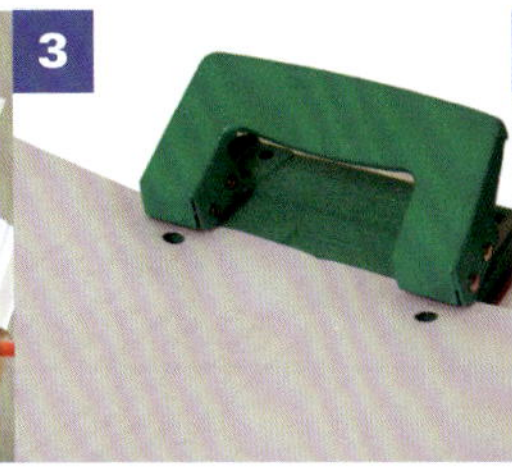
______

4 

______

5 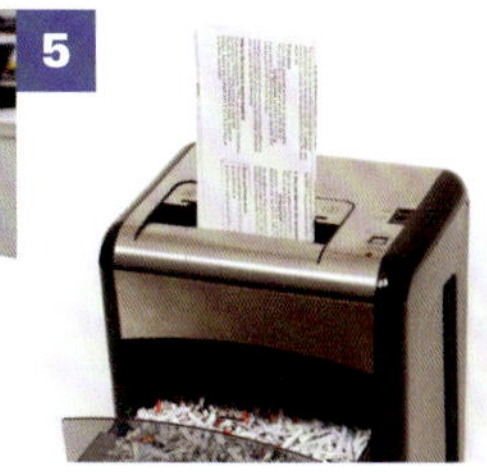
______

6 
______

7 
______

8 
______

9 
______

10 
______

1 🔊 94 Label the pictures with the words in the box. Then listen and repeat.

calendar	desk diary	drawers	file	filing cabinet	guillotine	hole punch	paper shredder	photocopier	safe

2 Read the definitions and write the correct words.

The part of your desk where you can keep small objects and papers.
drawers

a A secure place where you can keep money and important documents.
______

b An object that makes holes in paper.
______

c A machine that makes copies.
______

d A piece of office furniture where you can file away papers.
______

e A machine with a sharp blade to cut paper.
______

3 Circle the correct words.

My mom keeps all the information about her clients in a ______ .

1 (filing cabinet) **2** paper shredder **3** guillotine

a I have a ______ on my wall so I don't forget my friends' birthdays.

1 file **2** safe **3** calendar

b I'm not sure if I'm free on that date. I'll look in my ______ .

1 hole punch **2** desk diary **3** safe

c The information in that letter is confidential. Please destroy it after reading with the ______.

1 hole punch **2** photocopier **3** paper shredder

d I have some ______ under my desk for my pens, pencils, etc.

1 drawers **2** calendars **3** desk diaries

e We have a different ______ for all our school subjects.

1 guillotine **2** file **3** hole punch

f My aunt keeps her jewelry in a ______.

1 drawers **2** guillotine **3** safe

7 Crime Doesn't Pay

VOCABULARY 1

Crime Verbs

1 Match the beginnings and endings to make crime-related phrases.

a	catch	☐	a crime
b	commit	☐	clues
c	go to	☐	a fine
d	go on	*a*	a thief
e	do	☐	prison
f	look for	☐	trial
g	pay	☐	community service

2 Order the underlined letters to complete the crime-related phrases.

investigate a *crime*		m e r i c
a	be ________	o n c e n i n t
b	be ________	u g l i t y
c	________ a suspect	s t a r e r
d	________ a crime	l o v e s
e	________ a suspect	s t o n i q u e
f	________ someone	c e s s p u t

3 Match the definitions with the words in the box.

clues community service crime fine guilty innocent ~~prison~~ suspect thief trial

place where criminals are locked up: *prison*

a illegal action: ________

b adjective for a person who has done nothing wrong: ________

c money paid by someone who breaks the law: ________

d someone who steals: ________

e the legal process which finds out if someone is guilty or innocent: ________

f things that give the police information about a criminal: ________

g adjective for a person who has broken the law: ________

h useful work that a criminal does as a punishment: ________

i person that the police think is a criminal: ________

4 Complete the sentences with the words in the box.

arrest catch commit go to prison ~~investigate~~ pay a fine question solve suspect

She is the detective and it is her job to *investigate* this crime.

a The police want to ________ him about his activities on the night of April 23.

b Why did the murderer ________ these terrible crimes?

c The bank robbers will ________ for a long time.

d There were no clues, so the police couldn't ________ the crime.

e When the police ________ someone of a crime, they ________ him and take him to the police station for questioning.

f She drove away very fast and the police couldn't ________ her.

g If you park your car illegally, you might have to ________.

GRAMMAR 1

Modals of Deduction and Possibility

1 Order the words to make sentences.

after / be / journey / long / must / tired / You / your
You must be tired after your long journey.

a after / be / big bowls / can't / cereal / hungry / of / She / three / eating
____
____

b be / email / fraud / internet / might / of / some kind / This
____
____

c a / be / girl / could / model / over there / That
____
____

d problem / be / to / a solution / might not / this / There
____
____

e after / be / can't / hours of / sleep / tired / 12 / You
____

f have / the / must / thief / through / window / The / open / climbed
____
____

g our class / I / in / may / Russian / somebody / speak / think
____
____

2 Complete the sentences using *must be* or *can't be*.

He has an unusual accent. He *must be* foreign.

a He's had three car accidents this year so he ________ a good driver.

b He's just broken that car window. He ________ a thief.

c She always says horrible things about her friends so she ________ a nice person.

d Somebody has just stolen his passport so he ________ at the police station now.

e They started playing tennis in the hot sun two hours ago. They ________ thirsty.

f This dictionary has my name in it so it ________ yours.

g We've only walked 200 meters. You ________ tired already.

3 Underline the correct words.

The living room window is broken. There **can't** / **might** be a thief in there.

a They found the money and jewelry in her pockets. She **can't** / **must** be the thief.

b Her face is very red. She **could** / **can't** be guilty or she **could** / **must** just be hot!

c Don't try to catch the man because he **might** / **might not** have a knife and he **may** / **can't** be dangerous.

d The house is dark. They **must** / **can't** be out.

e Ask Andrew because he **can't** / **might** know the answer.

f He has a private plane so he **must** / **could** be a smuggler.

g The cat hasn't eaten for two days so I think it **can't** / **could** be sick.

4 Match statements a-h with responses 1-8. Then complete the responses with *must* or *can't*.

a [3] He hasn't slept for three days.

b [ ] It's freezing in this house.

c [ ] I don't have any money.

d [ ] Alex is in Australia at the moment.

e [ ] I haven't had anything to eat all day.

f [ ] Let's try the new restaurant on Second Avenue.

g [ ] It's illegal to park there.

h [ ] There's nothing to eat in this house.

1 He ________ be. I saw him in the mall an hour ago.

2 There ________ be some bread in the cabinet.

3 He *must* be exhausted, poor man.

4 It ________ be good. There's never anybody eating there.

5 The heating ________ be broken again.

6 It ________ be. Everybody always parks there.

7 That ________ be right. I gave you $30 yesterday.

8 You ________ be very hungry.

5 **Rewrite the sentences using the words in parentheses.**

He speaks English without an accent so he's almost certainly American. (must)

He speaks English without an accent so he must be American.

a She never smiles so I'm sure she isn't happy. (can't)

b He lives on the same road as Jill so perhaps he knows her. (might)

c I don't recognize this music but it's possibly Beethoven. (could)

d The police have arrested our neighbor. He is almost certainly a suspect. (must)

e Don't walk up those old stairs because they are possibly not strong enough. (might not)

f Don't go near that dog because it's possibly aggressive. (may)

6 **Rewrite the sentences using *must, can't, might* or *might not*.**

This thing isn't moving – it's almost certainly dead.

This thing isn't moving – it must be dead.

a It's definitely not a spider – it only has six legs.

b Well in that case it's definitely an insect.

c It's definitely not an insect because it doesn't have any wings.

d Not all insects have wings so it is possibly an insect.

e Maybe it's some kind of beetle.

f Let's ask Alan – he will possibly know.

g But Alan is possibly not in at the moment.

h I have a wildlife book and it possibly has a picture of a creature like this.

7 **Look at the pictures and write sentences. Use *must be, might be* and *can't be*.**

acting in a movie ~~cold~~
hot lost thirsty

It can't be cold.

a

b

c

d

asleep and dreaming real
somebody playing a trick

e

f

g

VOCABULARY 2

Crimes and Criminals

1 Complete the words with the vowels.

th _e_ ft

a m ___ rd ___ r

b p ___ ckp ___ ck ___ t ___ ng

c k ___ dn ___ pp ___ ng

d v ___ nd ___ l ___ sm

e r ___ bb ___ ry

2 Write the missing words for crimes or criminals.

crime	criminal
murder	*murderer*
a kidnapping	
b	robber
c pickpocketing	
d theft	
e	vandal

3 Find five criminals in the wordsnake.

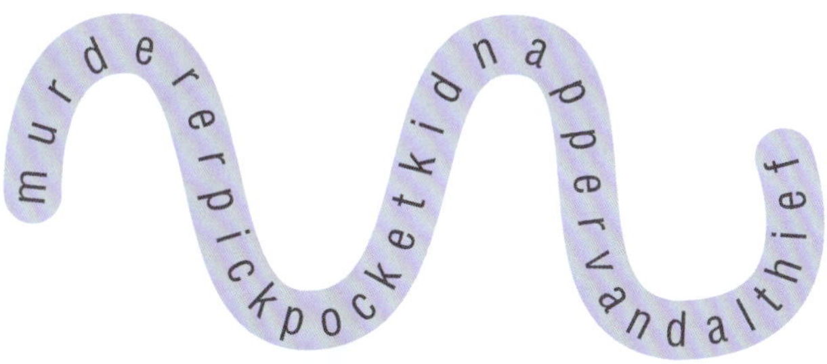

4 Match the news stories with the words in the box.

kidnapping murder ~~pickpocketing~~
robbery theft vandalism

The man stole a boy's mp3 player from his pocket.
pickpocketing

a They drove the boy away in a car and then asked his parents for money.

____

b A group of men stole $50,000 from the bank on 45th Street this morning.

____

c Teachers are concerned about the amount of graffiti at the school.

____

d The woman stole a laptop computer from the office.

____

5 Complete the sentences with the words in the box.

kidnapping pickpocketing
~~robbery~~ theft vandalism

There was a bank ___*robbery*___ here last week. The robbers stole $5 million.

a Keep your bag shut. It's very crowded here and that's when a lot of ___________ happens.

b She got arrested for ___________. She stole clothes from a department store.

c There's a lot of ___________ in this town. Last week some people spray-painted the swings in the park.

d He went to prison for ___________ last year after taking a child from its parents.

GRAMMAR 2

Review: *must / must not*

1 Match the sentence beginnings with the endings.

- **a** [2] In case you witness a crime
- **b** [ ] To have access to this email account,
- **c** [ ] In order to board the aircraft
- **d** [ ] To enter the country,
- **e** [ ] If you want to do research in the rain forest
- **f** [ ] To win the game *Risk*,

1. you must go through customs first.
2. you must inform the authorities.
3. you must accomplish your strategy.
4. you must get the yellow fever vaccine.
5. you must add two-factor verification of passwords.
6. you must not be carrying any flammable items.

2 Complete the sentences below with *must* or *must not*.

- **a** You ________ leave all electronic items at the door to enter this bank.
- **b** You ________ learn English if you want to survive in today's globalized world.
- **c** You ________ speak other languages in English class.
- **d** You ________ wear your seatbelt if you're a passenger in a car.
- **e** You ________ enter the classroom after the class has started.
- **f** You ________ smile when you get your picture taken.
- **g** You ________ copy off your friend's test.
- **h** You ________ use a baby car seat to carry toddlers in the car.
- **i** You ________ play your music loud after 10 pm.
- **j** You ________ use your cell phone during the test.

3 Choose the correct alternative.

a We ________ turn off our cell phones in the classroom.

1 must **2** must not **3** don't have to

b We ________ act like robots in class, but we sure have to behave well.

1 must **2** must not **3** don't have to

c We ________ wear a uniform at our school, so I can wear dresses if I want to.

1 must **2** must not **3** don't have to

d However, we ________ follow a dress code, so I can't wear a very short dress.

1 must **2** must not **3** don't have to

e If we are too sick to remain in school, we ________ officially sign out at the main office.

1 must **2** must not **3** don't have to

4 Complete the rules for card game *Uno* with *must*, *must not* or *don't have to*.

- **a** To be the winner, you __________ be the first player to score 500 points. [obligation]
- **b** You __________ trade cards with another player. [prohibition]
- **c** If the previous player plays the skip card, you __________ skip your turn. [obligation]
- **d** You __________ play your Wild card if you have other cards in hand. [not an obligation]
- **e** A player who plays their next-to-last-card __________ call "Uno" as a warning to the other players. [obligation]
- **f** If you draw a card from the deck, you __________ discard it. [prohibition]
- **g** When drawing from the deck, you __________ either play or keep that card. [obligation]

GRAMMAR CHECK

1 Read the text and circle the correct answers.

'Well one thing is for sure,' Detective Mactaggart said slowly, 'the thief **a** ________ be a woman.' 'How can you be so sure of that?' Morgan, his assistant, asked. 'Because he's left a footprint outside the window and it's very big,' Mactaggart answered. 'The criminal **b** ________ be a woman with very large feet,' his assistant suggested. 'I suppose that's possible,' Mactaggart agreed. 'Anyway this man or woman with big feet must **c** ________ red hair,' he said suddenly. 'Really? What tells you that?' Morgan asked. 'Well, there's a red hair here on the carpet,' said Mactaggart. 'That **d** ________ be a human hair,' Morgan said. 'The criminal **e** ________ have a dog with red hair.' 'No. It's definitely a human hair,' the detective said putting down his magnifying glass. 'And what about that open locker there?' said Detective Mactaggart, 'it **f** ________ someone with really good burglar skills.' 'Well, the proprietors **g** ________ a bit forgetful and left it just like that,' said the assistant. 'All right, all right, let's call it a day. It's too dusty in here anyway,' said Detective Mactaggart.

	A	B	C
a	mustn't	(can't)	shouldn't
b	can	must	could
c	have	to have	having
d	could not	might not	must not
e	might	must	can't
f	can't be	might be	must be
g	must be	may be	can't be

2 🔊 95 Listen and check your answers.

LISTENING

1 🔊 96 Listen and order 1-7. Be careful! Two events did not happen.

- **a** ☐ Anti-trafficking officers started watching the man secretly.
- **b** ☐ Anti-trafficking officers stopped the man and opened his suitcase.
- **c** ☐ One of the animals bit an officer's hand.
- **d** ☐ Someone drugged baby mammals and put them in flat cages.
- **e** ☐ The baby mammals yawned.
- **f** ☐ The man bought endangered baby mammals on the black market.
- **g** ☐ The man tried to smuggle snakes and turtles to China and Vietnam.
- **h** ☐ The man went to Bangkok airport.
- **i** ☐ They found endangered animals.

2 🔊 96 Listen again and circle T (*true*), F (*false*) or DK (*don't know*).

- **a** The man had just one suitcase full of animals. **T / F / DK**
- **b** Some of the animals were dead. **T / F / DK**
- **c** The man was on a plane when the officers arrested him. **T / F / DK**
- **d** The man has never smuggled snakes or lizards to China. **T / F / DK**
- **e** Leopards and panthers go for almost the same price on the black market in Bangkok and Dubai. **T / F / DK**
- **f** There is a lot of wildlife trafficking in Thailand. **T / F / DK**
- **g** The authorities in Thailand don't often catch people smuggling a large number of mammals. **T / F / DK**

EXTENSION

Underline the correct words to complete the text.

Someone's toy tiger **a has started / started** a big police operation in Hampshire, England, last week and stopped play at a nearby cricket ground and golf club. The police **b received / have received** calls from members of the public on Saturday about a white tiger **c who / which** was 'hiding in a field' near Hedge End. Armed police **d stood / stand** near the field while a helicopter prepared to take thermal images of it from above. Animal experts from nearby Marwell Zoo **e were also standing / have also stood** ready to provide help.

Golfers at a nearby golf club were told to stay indoors and cricket players at the Rose Bowl **f were stopping / stopped** their game for 20 minutes while the police **g were investigating / have investigated**.

The police officers **h saw / have seen** that the 'wild animal' was not moving and the helicopter didn't **i detected / detect** body heat. Then the tiger **j was falling / fell** onto its side as a rush of air from the helicopter knocked it over. At that stage, the team realized the tiger was a life-size toy. Here are some comments from people who read about the incident.

'It was very realistic. If you **k see / saw** it, you **l 'd be / were** scared.'

'When I saw the tiger I said "it **m mustn't / can't** be real."'

'It **n would / will** be funny if the police closed the road for a toy tiger.'

'I'm never **o forgetting / going to forget** this story.'

'I haven't laughed this much **p for / since** a very long time. It's the funniest news story **q I'm ever hearing / I've ever heard**.'

VOCABULARY PLUS

Breaking the Law

1

______

2

______

3

______

4
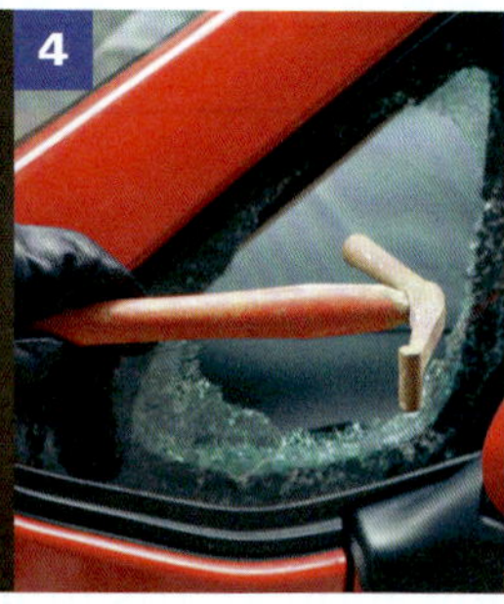
______

5

______

6
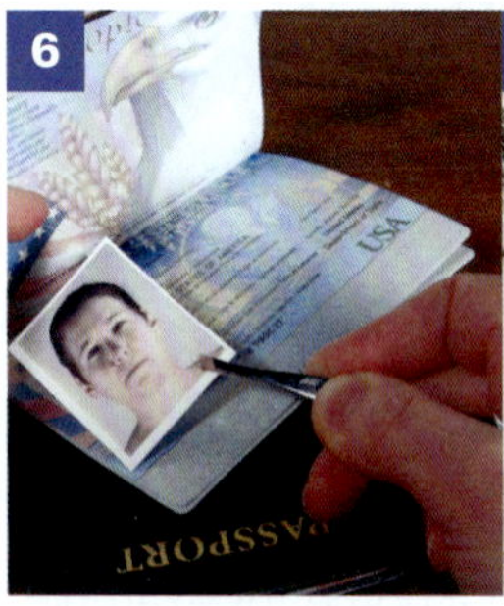
______

7

______

8

______

9

______

10

______

1 🔊 97 Label the picture with the words in the box. Then listen and repeat.

animal smuggling break into
file a police report fraud
get away indictment
hack press charges
smash a window witness a crime

2 Complete the definitions with the correct words.

If you *hack* something, you illegally access someone's computer, system or online accounts.

a If you ______, you officially register the crime you've suffered or witnessed.

b If you receive an ______, you are accused of a crime.

c If you ______, you see a crime taking place.

d If you ______, you break the glass into small pieces.

e If you ______ a building, you enter a place by force in order to steal.

3 The verbs in bold are wrong. Write the correct verbs using their correct form.

The burglars stole my mom's jewelry when they **got away** our house.
broke into

a The thieves ran out of the bank and **pressed charges** in a fast car.
______

b He was indicted for **animal smuggling** when he pretended to be someone else.
______

c Vandals **broke into** the windows and stole the furniture.
______

d The bank robbers **smashed** the bank's security network before breaking in.
______

4 Answer the questions for you. Write full sentences.

a Have you ever witnessed a crime?
______

b What would you do if you saw someone breaking into a building?
______

8 Communicate

VOCABULARY 1

The Written Word

1 Find six communication words in the word snake. Use the left-over letters in the boxes to make another communication word.

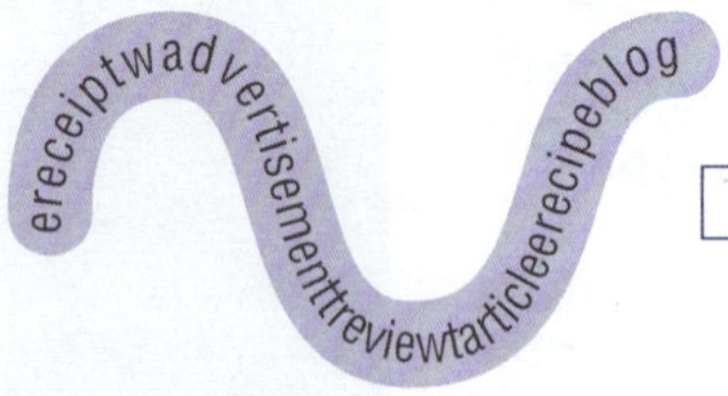

☐☐☐☐☐

2 Complete the communication words with the vowels.

b l _o_ g

a t r ___ v ___ l g ___ ___ d ___

b c ___ r t ___ ___ n

c d ___ c t ___ ___ n ___ r y ___ n t r y

d ___ n s t r ___ c t ___ ___ n m ___ n ___ l

e l ___ b ___ l

f q ___ ___ t ___

3 Underline the correct words.

I read a **travel guide** / **review** of the new Javier Bardem movie.

a I'm keeping the **recipe** / **receipt** for my new bag because I might take it back to the store and exchange it.

b I saw a funny **advertisement** / **article** for a new kind of lemonade. I'm going to try it soon.

c There's a really funny **quote** / **cartoon** in the paper. It's a picture of a cat saying to its human owner, 'I'm going out. Do you need any mice?'

d I read an interesting **dictionary entry** / **article** about global warming.

e I have a **blog** / **recipe** about food. I write new posts every week.

4 Match the definitions with the words in the box.

article dictionary entry label quote recipe travel guide ~~tweet~~

information posted online in very few words; the maximum number of letters or characters is 280 _tweet_

a piece of writing in a newspaper or magazine ______

b a book providing information about a place ______

c small piece of paper, on a bottle for example, or small piece of material on clothes, that gives information ______

d information given to explain the meaning of a word or phrase ______

e explains a way to prepare a particular food, for example apple pie or carrot soup ______

f exact words which someone said ______

5 Complete the sentences with the words in the box.

advertisement article ~~blog~~ instruction manual receipt recipe travel guide

Let's go online and read her _blog_ so we can see what she's up to at the moment.

a There are hardly any ______s or interesting ______s about food in Let's Cook magazine. It's full of ______s for fridges, cooktops and kitchen equipment.

b Here's your change. Your ______ for the shirt is in the bag.

c I want to see all the best things in Seville when I go there in the summer. I've already bought a ______.

d Can you help me install my new printer? The ______ is incomprehensible!

GRAMMAR 1

Tense Review

1 Complete the sentences with the time expressions in the box.

~~always~~ at the moment just last year next week since tomorrow two weeks ago while

My sister *always* sends me postcards from France.

a I spent three months in California ________.

b I got a text message from Fran ________.

c Dave hasn't called ________ Friday.

d We're going to meet one day ________.

e Joey is lying in bed ________.

f I was working ________ you were lying in bed.

g You've ________ sat on my glasses!

h I'm playing soccer at two o'clock ________.

2 Match the sentence beginnings with the endings.

a I don't [*5*]

b He used to be a designer but now [ ]

c She read the article while she [ ]

d At the moment Ellie is [ ]

e He didn't find [ ]

f You've never [ ]

g I'll send you [ ]

h She's going to [ ]

i We're meeting at Stacey's house [ ]

1 a text message later today.

2 at four o'clock tomorrow.

3 he writes movie reviews.

4 was waiting for the train.

5 read the cartoons in newspapers.

6 reply to the job advertisement.

7 that recipe on a website.

8 writing a letter to her cousin.

9 written an instruction manual.

3 Underline the correct form of the verbs.

Hello readers and welcome to my travel blog.

a I write / I'm writing this from a youth hostel in Sweden. It's a lovely day and the sun **b is shining / shines**. It **c doesn't shine / isn't shining** every day, though. In fact, it **d is raining / rains** quite often. I can see the beach from my window. It's only eight o'clock in the morning so people **e aren't swimming / don't swim** yet. **f I'm having / I have** a great time here. I have a great routine. Every day **g I'm getting up / I get up** at seven. Then I **h go / am going** for a run and I **i watch / am watching** the birds on the seashore. **j I begin / I'm beginning** to know the names of quite a lot of these birds.
After my run, I **k am sitting / sit down** with my Swedish books. Yes, guys, **l I'm learning / I learn** Swedish. I **m don't know / am not knowing** many words yet. 'Tack' is a very useful word, though. It **n is meaning / means** thank you. I **o am loving / love** the food here. Swedish people **p eat / are eating** a lot of raw and pickled fish. In fact, **q I'm eating / I eat** raw fish right now for my breakfast!

4 Complete the sentences with the correct form of the verbs in parentheses. Use the simple past, past progressive or present perfect.

She *hasn't answered* (not answer) my email yet.

a I got a text message from Jan while I ________ (talk) to my mom.

b Where is Tom? We ________ (not hear) from him in months.

c They ________ (have) their own computers since they were 12.

d I ________ (not read) her blog yesterday but I ________ (listen) to her podcast last week.

e My mom ________ (just join) Facebook. She ________ (spend) an hour doing her profile page yesterday.

f She ________ (call) me at 9am yesterday.

5 Complete the text with the correct form of the verbs in parentheses.

Maggie Wright is a cartoonist. She *has worked* (work) for Laugh Magazine for two years. She **a** ________ (start) drawing funny pictures when she was 14. 'I **b** ________ (go) to all my classes but often I couldn't concentrate on the lessons so I **c** ________ (begin) to draw penguins. While I **d** ________ (draw), I **e** ________ (start) to invent characters for them. I **f** ________ (stop) drawing penguins now but I **g** ________ (keep) all my first drawings.'
At 18, Maggie **h** ________ (go) to art college where she **i** ________ (learn) a lot about illustration. 'I **j** ________ (work) very hard there and I **k** ________ (develop) my own personal style.'

6 Underline the correct words.

Laura Do you want to come to Hyde Park with me and Izzie? The forecast says it's **a going to be / being** lovely and sunny tomorrow. **b We'll have / We're having** a picnic by the lake at two o'clock.

Claire I can't. **c I'll play / I'm playing** tennis in the club tournament all day. It's crazy because I know **d I won't win / I'm not winning**.

Laura Why do you say that?

Claire Because I'm sure Yasmin **e is winning / will win** again.

Laura Do you feel like coming to the movies on Sunday afternoon? There's a movie with Penelope Cruz. I'm sure **f you'll / you're** going to like it.

Claire No, thanks. **g I'm going to / I'll stay** at home. I need to work on my new blog. **h I'll / I'm going to** put some new pictures on it.

Laura New pictures? What are they of?

Claire **i You'll / You're going to** see when you log on! Hey! Is that a new camera?

Laura Yes. I'm **j going to take / taking** lots of pictures in the park. I think **k I'll email / I'm emailing** some of them to you if they're nice.

7 Complete the sentences about you and your friends.

I always *check my emails before I go to bed* ________.

a My friend usually ________.

b At the moment, I'm ________.

c Last year my friend ________.

d While I was ________.

e While my friend ________.

f Tomorrow I'm ________.

g One day ________.

h I've never ________.

VOCABULARY 2

Adjectives with *-able* and *-ible*

1 Complete the adjectives with the vowels. Then write their opposites.

r _e_ _a_ s _o_ n _a_ b l _e_

unreasonable

a r ___ s p ___ n s ___ b l ___
____

b v ___ s ___ b l ___
____

c r ___ l ___ ___ b l ___
____

d ___ c c ___ p t ___ b l ___
____

e f l ___ x ___ b l ___
____

f b ___ ___ r ___ b l ___
____

2 Underline the correct words.

People say the Great Wall of China is **reasonable** / **visible** from space.

a He is very **bearable** / **reliable**. If he says he'll do something, he does it.

b She didn't have any problems moving to New York. She is very **acceptable** / **flexible**.

c My tooth hurts but it's **bearable** / **responsible**. I can wait until tomorrow to see the dentist.

d He is very mature and **responsible** / **acceptable**. He works hard at school and has a part-time job.

e Jenny wouldn't help her brother with his homework because she was watching TV – she's so **responsible** / **unreasonable**!

f Will it be **bearable** / **acceptable** to wear jeans to their dinner party or will I have to wear something more formal?

3 Complete the sentences with the negative form of the correct adjectives.

He doesn't like traveling and he doesn't like foreign food. He is totally _inflexible_.
(responsible / reliable / flexible)

a I'm going to go crazy if that noise doesn't stop. It really is ___________.
(reasonable / bearable / reliable)

b You can see the trees moving but the wind itself is ___________.
(responsible / acceptable / visible)

c He adopted a dog but he doesn't look after it or take it for walks. He is completely ___________.
(flexible / responsible / bearable).

d She was supposed to bring food to the party but she forgot. She really is ___________.
(reasonable / responsible / reliable)

4 Complete the sentences with one of the adjectives or opposites from activity 1.

She'll be here on time. She's never late. She's very _reliable_.

a You can't go for a walk in the forest in those high heels. Don't be so ___________.

b When Superkid puts on his magic coat, you can't see him. He's ___________.

c Take me to the hospital now. This pain is ___________.

d Here are your tickets and passport. You are ___________ for them now, not me.

e A ___________ person like you will have no problems when you go and live in Australia.

f It's ___________ to play computer games during a family dinner.

GRAMMAR 2

Tense Review: Question Forms

1 Order the words to make questions. Then match the tenses of the verbs with tenses a-h.

a about / is / she / talking / What ? [1]
What is she talking about?

b Amanda, / have / how / I / known / long / you ? [ ]
______

c in / Do / go / vacation / on / they / usually / July ? [ ]
______

d back / did / from / get / he / Russia / When ? [ ]
______

e Are / going / jeans / party / to / to Tonya's / you / those / wear ? [ ]
______

f keys / leave / the / they / will / Where ? [ ]
______

g an / artist / become / her / made / What ? [ ]
______

h airport / drove / Scott / the / to / Who ? [ ]
______

1 present progressive
2 future
3 simple past
4 present perfect
5 *going to* for future
6 simple present

2 Match the question beginnings with the endings.

a What were you doing [3]
b Have you [ ]
c When will [ ]
d Are you [ ]
e What are [ ]

1 ever lost your cell phone?
2 going to get in touch with her?
3 when he walked into the room?
4 you give me an answer?
5 you writing on that postcard?

3 Read each sentence. Then write questions in the simple past or past progressive.

Liza fell off her bike yesterday.
(go / fast?) *Was she going fast*?
(hurt herself?) *Did she hurt herself*?

a (Where / it / happen?)
______

b I saw Kate and Andy at the beach.
(When exactly / see them?)
______

c (they swim / or lie in the sun?)
______

d (speak / to them?)
______

e A man stole my cell phone on the bus.
(he / sit / next to you?)
______

f (what / he / look like?)
______

g (go / to the police?)
______

4 Complete the dialogue with the correct form of the verbs in parentheses.

James Where *did you meet* (you meet) Ed?
Thomas In a movie.
James Really? **a** ______ (he act) in it?
Thomas Yes, and so was I.
James Wow! **b** ______ (you be) in a lot of movies?
Thomas Three so far. That was my first.
James **c** ______ (it be) his first, too?
Thomas Yes, it was. **d** ______ (he work) in TV and movies since he was eight.
James **e** ______ (you be) in any more productions together?
Thomas I hope so. We've both just done auditions for a movie called *Midnight*.
James When **f** ______ (you know) if you've got parts?
Thomas Tomorrow at 10am!
James **g** ______ (you celebrate) if you get the part?
Thomas Definitely!

GRAMMAR CHECK

1 Read the text and circle the correct answers.

Communication **a** ______ very easy. We **b** ______ in touch with people thousands of miles away. We **c** ______ to be in our homes near a telephone to do this. At the moment, 18-year-old Dave Roberts **d** ______ around Asia on his gap year. Mostly he **e** ______ in touch with friends and family by email. But last week he **f** ______ Skype to call his family on his grandmother's birthday. 'My granddaughter Tess **g** ______ her laptop to me and there was Dave on the screen. He **h** ______ on a beautiful white beach. He **i** ______ to me for about five minutes, and **j** ______ again at six tomorrow evening. Tess and Dave's father **k** ______ me a laptop. **l** ______ speaking to my friends in Australia and sending them emails.'

	A	B	C
a	became	becomes	(has become)
b	are staying	stay	have stayed
c	don't need	aren't needing	didn't need
d	was traveling	travels	is traveling
e	stayed	is staying	stays
f	was using	used	has used
g	brought	was bringing	has brought
h	sat	has sat	was sitting
i	spoke	was speaking	has spoken
j	will call	is calling	calls
k	will get	are going to get	gets
l	I'll enjoy	I'm enjoying	I enjoyed

2 🔊 98 Listen and check your answers.

LISTENING

1 🔊 99 Listen and answer the questions.

a How long does Mark spend online?

____

b How long does Angie spend online?

____

c How long does Dan spend online?

____

d Who uses the internet mainly for entertainment?

____

e Who uses it for research?

____

f Who uses it for communication?

____

2 🔊 99 Listen again and answer the questions.

a How long did Mark use to spend online?

____

b Why did he read about the nuclear disaster in Fukushima?

____

c When did he decide to reduce his internet use?

____

d What does Angie use Facebook for? (three things)

____

____

e What does she write a blog about?

____

f Why does Dan like virtual reality games?

____

____

g What was the video of that he put on YouTube?

____

EXTENSION

Underline the correct words to complete the text.

CELL PHONE NEWS

A cell phone expert **a is asking / was asked** why **b sales are / are sales** still increasing.
He said that sales **c have increased / is increasing** by 19% last year because people **d have bought / were buying** smartphones to send emails and surf the internet. He added that now people **e didn't just want / hasn't just wanted** extras like games and cameras on their phones.
Young people **f which / who** are good with technology **g are encouraged / are encouraging** by some cell phone companies to invent 'apps' or programs for smartphones. Fourteen-year-old Luke Firth from New York said: 'At the moment **h I develop / I'm developing** a game about an alien. It's fun but it's tiring and my mom **i isn't liking / doesn't like** me working on it. But if I **j sell / will sell** it to a cell phone company, **k I'll make / I made** a lot of money. I **l would have / have** perfected it by now if I didn't have to spend so much time at school.'
So what **m is being next big thing / will be the next big thing** in cell phone technology? Experts **n already developed / have already developed** technology **o which / who** turns your hand into a touchscreen. A user's hand **p is filmed / is filming** by a tiny camera and the information **q has sent / is sent** by computer to their phone. So in the future, phones **r will be left / are left** in a pocket or bag and a user **s is making / will make** calls from the palm of their hand. But who would buy this technology if it **t became / will become** available? Drivers? Cyclists? Who **u knows / does know**?

VOCABULARY PLUS

The Newspaper

1

2

3

4

5

6

7
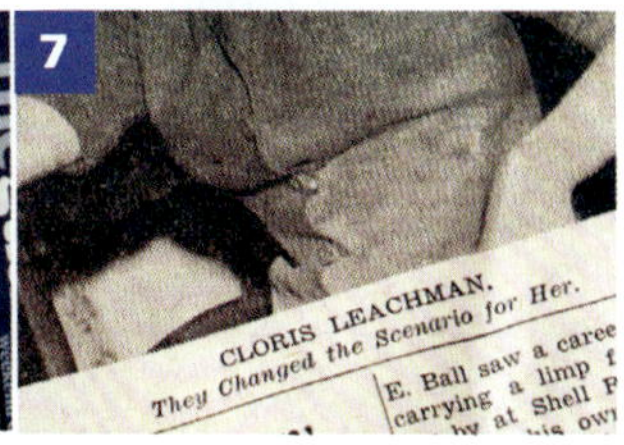

8

9

10
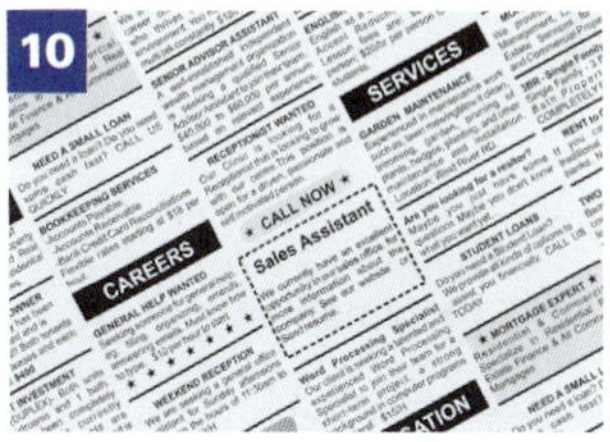

1 🔊 100 Label the pictures with the words in the box. Then listen and repeat.

caption cartoon classified ads crossword gossip columns headline horoscope letters page sports pages weather report

2 Underline the correct words.

The drawings in these **cartoons** / **crosswords** are really good.

a I always read the **headlines** / **gossip** first to see what the most important news is.

b My dad often reads out the clues to the **weather report** / **crossword** while we're having breakfast.

c If you want to know who won the game, read the **letters page** / **sports pages**.

d When my sister wanted to buy a laptop, she looked at the **captions** / **classified ads**.

e I like reading the **gossip columns** / **horoscope** to find out what famous people are doing.

3 Match extracts a-f with the newspaper sections in activity 1.

FIRE HITS THE CITY [1]

a Dear editor, I think the new mall ... [ ]

b TV star George Smith has just gotten divorced again. [ ]

c Matt Baker scored the winning goal. [ ]

d Gemini: money will come your way today. [ ]

e Tomorrow will be cloudy with rain in the east. [ ]

f 5 across: a female horse. [ ]

4 Complete the sentences for you. Try to use words from activity 1.

a My favorite part of the newspaper is ______________________.

b I never read the ______________________.

c My parents usually read the ______________________, but I prefer the ______________________.

Wordlist

PHONETIC CHART

VOWELS AND DIPHTHONGS 101

/ɪ/ p**i**g	/e/ br**ea**d	/u/ l**o**se	/aɪ/ **I**
/i/ sh**e**	/ɜr/ c**ur**ly	/ə/ act**o**r	/ɔɪ/ t**oy**
/æ/ c**a**t	/ɔ/ b**a**ll	/ʌ/ s**u**nny	/aʊ/ m**ou**ntain
/ɑ/ **a**rm	/ʊ/ g**oo**d	/eɪ/ US**A**	/oʊ/ b**oa**t

CONSONANTS 102

/p/ **p**otato	/ʧ/ **ch**air	/s/ **S**pain	/n/ **n**ewsstand
/b/ **b**lue	/ʤ/ fri**dg**e	/z/ ea**s**y	/ŋ/ spri**ng**
/t/ **t**axi	/f/ **f**inish	/ʃ/ **sh**ower	/l/ **l**ake
/d/ **d**rama	/v/ **v**erb	/ʒ/ televi**s**ion	/r/ **r**ead
/k/ **c**arrot	/θ/ ba**th**room	/h/ **h**i	/j/ **y**esterday
/g/ **g**randpa	/ð/ **th**ere	/m/ **m**outh	/w/ **w**ater

A 103

a few /ə fju/

a lot of /ə lɑt əv/

acceptable (adj) /ək'septəb(ə)l/

adaptable (adj) /ə'dæptəb(ə)l/

after sun lotion (n) /'æftər sʌn 'loʊʃ(ə)n/

agree about /ə'gri ə'baʊt/

agree with /ə'gri wɪð/

allowance (n) /ə'laʊəns/

amazing (adj) /ə'meɪzɪŋ/

American Sign Language /ə'merɪkən saɪn 'læŋgwɪdʒ/

animal migration (n) /'ænɪm(ə)l maɪ'greɪʃ(ə)n/

animal smuggler (n) /'ænɪm(ə)l 'smʌg(ə)lər/

animal smuggling (n) /'ænɪm(ə)l 'smʌg(ə)lɪŋ/

antiseptic cream (n) /ˌæntɪ'septɪk krim/

any (adv) /'eni/

application form (n) /ˌæplɪ'keɪʃ(ə)n fɔrm/

apply for a job /ə'plaɪ fɔr ə dʒɑb/

apprenticeship (n) /ə'prentɪsˌʃɪp/

architecture (n) /'ɑrkɪˌtektʃər/

argue about /'ɑrˌgju ə'baʊt/

argue with /'ɑrˌgju wɪð/

arrest a suspect /ə'rest ə sə'spekt/

arrive early /ə'raɪv 'ɜrli/

article (n) /'ɑrtɪk(ə)l/

aspirin (n) /'æsprɪn/

awful (adj) /'ɔf(ə)l/

B 104

bad (adj) /bæd/

bandage (n) /'bændɪdʒ/

bark (n) /bɑrk/

be charged with /bi tʃɑː(r)dʒd wɪð/

be guilty /bi 'gɪlti/

be innocent /bi 'ɪnəs(ə)nt/

be late /bi leɪt/

be polite /bi pə'laɪt/

be rude /bi rud/

be unemployed /bi ˌʌnɪm'plɔɪd/

bearable (adj) /'berəb(ə)l/

become rich /bɪ'kʌm rɪtʃ/

being friendly /'biɪŋ 'fren(d)li/

belt (n) /belt/

benefits (n) /'benəfɪts/

big (adj) /bɪg/

blog (n) /blɔg/

boiling (adj) /'bɔɪlɪŋ/

bonus (n) /'boʊnəs/

branch (n) /bræntʃ/

break into /breɪk 'ɪntu/

bring a present /brɪŋ ə 'prezənt/

bud (n) /bʌd/

business (n) /ˈbɪznəs/

button (n) /ˈbʌt(ə)n/

buy a guidebook /baɪ ə ˈgaɪdˌbʊk/

Buy Nothing Day (n) /baɪ ˈnʌθɪŋ deɪ/

buy souvenirs /baɪ suvəˈnɪrz/

C 105

calendar (n) /ˈkæləndər/

can't /kænt/

caption (n) /ˈkæpʃ(ə)n/

cartoon (n) /kɑrˈtun/

casual (adj) /ˈkæʒuəl/

catch a thief /kætʃ ə θif/

change schools /tʃeɪndʒ skulz/

claim expenses /kleɪm ɪkˈspɛnsəz/

classified ads (n) /ˈklæsɪˌfaɪd ædz/

cold (adj) /koʊld/

collar (n) /ˈkɑlər/

colorful (adj) /ˈkʌlərf(ə)l/

come back home /kʌm bæk hoʊm/

comfortable (adj) /ˈkʌmfərtəb(ə)l/

commit a crime /kəˈmɪt ə kraɪm/

compost food scraps /ˈkɑmˌpoʊst fud skræps/

computer science (n) /kəmˈpjutər ˈsaɪəns/

conditions (n) /kənˈdɪʃ(ə)nz/

contract (n) /ˈkɑnˌtrækt/

conventional (adj) /kənˈvenʃ(ə)nəl/

crossword (n) /ˈkrɔsˌwɜrd/

cut (n) /kʌt/

D 106

delighted (adj) /dɪˈlaɪtəd/

depend on /dɪˈpend ɑn/

dependable (adj) /dɪˈpendəb(ə)l/

desk diary (n) /desk ˈdaɪəri/

dictionary entry (n) /ˈdɪkʃəˌneri ˈentri/

do community service /du kəˈmjunəti ˈsɜrvɪs/

do the washing up /du ði ˈwɑʃɪŋ ʌp/

drawers (n) /drɔrz/

dream about /drim əˈbaʊt/

drop out of college /drɑp aʊt əv ˈkɑlɪdʒ/

E 107

earn a wage /ɜrn ə weɪdʒ/

electric vehicle (n) /ɪˈlektrɪk ˈviɪk(ə)l/

engineering (n) /ˌendʒɪˈnirɪŋ/

enormous (adj) /ɪˈnɔrməs/

exhausted (adj) /ɪgˈzɔstəd/

expenses (n) / ɪkˈspɛnsəz/

F 108

fashionable (adj) /ˈfæʃ(ə)nəb(ə)l/

file (n) /faɪl/

file a police report /faɪl ə pəˈlis rɪˈpɔrt/

filing cabinet (n) /ˈfaɪlɪŋ ˈkæbɪnət/

fill out an application form /fɪl aʊt æn ˌæplɪˈkeɪʃ(ə)n fɔrm/

fine art (n) /faɪn ɑrt/

flexible (adj) /ˈfleksəb(ə)l/

folk music (n) /foʊk ˈmjuzɪk/

formal (adj) /ˈfɔrm(ə)l/

fraud (n) /frɔd/

freezing (adj) /ˈfrizɪŋ/

G 109

garbage (n) /ˈgɑrbɪdʒ/

get a pension /get ə ˈpenʃ(ə)n/

get away /get əˈweɪ/

get into /get ˈɪntu/

get into trouble /get ˈɪntu ˈtrʌb(ə)l/

get off a bus /get ɔf ə bʌs/

get on a train /get ɑn ə treɪn/

give advice /gɪv ədˈvaɪs/

give away /gɪv əˈweɪ/

give customers advice /gɪv ˈkʌstəmərz ədˈvaɪs/

give presents /gɪv ˈprezənts/

glamourous (adj) /ˈglæm(ə)rəs/

go abroad /goʊ əˈbrɔd/

go for a job interview /goʊ fɔr ə dʒɑb ˈɪntərˌvju/

go on trial /goʊ ɔn ˈtraɪəl/

go to prison /goʊ tu ˈprɪz(ə)n/

go with /goʊ wɪð/

good (adj) /gʊd/

gossip (n) /ˈgɑsɪp/

graffiti (n) /grəˈfiti/

guillotine (n) /ˈgɪləˌtin/ or /ˈgɪjəˌtin/

H 110

hack (v) /hæk/

happy (adj) /ˈhæpi/

have a full-time job /hæv ə fʊl taɪm dʒɑb/

have adventures /hæv ædˈventʃərz/

have an accident /hæv æn ˈæksɪdənt/

have an argument /hæv æn ˈɑrgjəmənt/

have an interview /hæv æn ˈɪntərˌvju/

have fun /hæv fʌn/

headline (n) /ˈhedˌlaɪn/

historical journey (n) /hɪˈstɔrɪk(ə)l ˈdʒɜrni/

hole punch (n) /hoʊl pʌntʃ/

horoscope (n) /ˈhɔrəˌskoʊp/

I 111

immigrant (n) /ˈɪmɪgrənt/

immigration (n) /ˌɪmɪˈgreɪʃ(ə)n/

impractical (adj) /ɪmˈpræktɪk(ə)l/

indictment (n) /ɪnˈdaɪtmənt/

inflexible (adj) /ɪnˈfleksəb(ə)l/

insect bite (n) /ˈɪnˌsekt baɪt/

install solar panels /ɪnˈstɔl ˈsoʊlər ˈpænəlz/

instruction manual (n) /ɪnˈstrʌkʃ(ə)n ˈmænjuəl/

insulate windows /ˈɪnsəˌleɪt ˈwɪndoʊz/

interrupt a conversation /ˌɪntəˈrʌpt ə ˌkɑnvərˈseɪʃ(ə)n/

investigate a crime /ɪnˈvestɪˌgeɪt ə kraɪm/

invisible (adj) /ɪnˈvɪzəb(ə)l/

irresponsible (adj) /ˌɪrɪˈspɑnsəb(ə)l/

isn't true /ˈɪz(ə)nt tru/

it is possible /ɪt ɪz ˈpɑsəb(ə)l/

J 112

job advertisement (n) /dʒɑb ædˈvɜrtɪsmənt/

jump a line /dʒʌmp eɪ laɪn/

K 113

kidnapper (n) /ˈkɪdˌnæpər/

kidnapping (v) /ˈkɪdˌnæpɪŋ/

L 114

label (n) /ˈleɪb(ə)l/

laces (n) /ˈleɪsəz/

law (n) /lɔ/

leaf (n) /lif/

leave faucet off /liv ˈfɔsɪt ɔf/

letters page (n) /ˈletərz peɪdʒ/

listen to /ˈlɪs(ə)n tu/

look for /lʊk fɔr/

look for clues /lʊk fɔr kluz/

look forward to /lʊk ˈfɔrwərd tu/

loose (adj) /lus/

lose a job /luz ə dʒɑb/

M 115

make a playlist /meɪk ə ˈpleɪˌlɪst/

make coffee /meɪk ˈkɑfi/

make new friends /meɪk nu frendz/

many (adv) /ˈmeni/

media studies (n) /ˈmidiə ˈstʌdiz/

medicine (n) /ˈmedɪsɪn/

meet people /mit ˈpip(ə)l/

mend old clothes /mend oʊld kloʊðz/

might /maɪt/

migraine (n) /ˈmaɪˌgreɪn/

misinform (v) /ˌmɪsɪnˈfɔrm/

misplace (v) /ˌmɪsˈpleɪs/

misunderstand (v) /ˌmɪsʌndərˈstænd/

motion sickness (n) /moʊʃ(ə)n ˈsɪknəs/

motion sickness pill (n) /moʊʃ(ə)n ˈsɪknəs pɪl/

move /muv/

much (adv) /mʌtʃ/

murder (n) /ˈmɜrdər/

murderer (n) /ˈmɜrdərər/

must /mʌst/

N 116

necklace (n) /ˈnekləs/

nursing (n) /ˈnɜrsɪŋ/

O 117

old-fashioned (adj) /oʊld ˈfæʃənd/

one by one /wʌn baɪ wʌn/

overcrowd (v) /ˌoʊvərˈkraʊd/

overeat (v) /ˌoʊvərˈit/

overpopulate (v) /ˌoʊvərˈpɑpjəleɪt/

P 118

pack a suitcase /pæk ə ˈsutˌkeɪs/

paper shredder (n) /ˈpeɪpər ˈʃredər/

participate in /pɑrˈtɪsɪˌpeɪt ɪn/

part-time job /pɑrt taɪm dʒɑb/

pay a fine /peɪ ə faɪn/

pay raise (n) /peɪ reɪz/

pension (n) /ˈpenʃ(ə)n/

petal (n) /ˈpet(ə)l/

photocopier (n) /ˈfoʊtoʊˌkɑpiər/

pick out /pɪk aʊt/

pick up /pɪk ʌp/

pickpocket (n) /ˈpɪkˌpɑkɪt/

pickpocketing (v) /ˈpɪkˌpɑkətɪŋ/

plan a journey /plæn ə ˈdʒɜrni/

play music at a party /pleɪ ˈmjuzɪk æt ə ˈpɑrti/

pocket (n) /ˈpɑkɪt/

poem (n) /ˈpoʊəm/

point at someone /pɔɪnt æt ˈsʌmwʌn/

press charges /pres ˈʧɑrʤəz/

prom night /prɑm naɪt/

promotion (n) /prəˈmoʊʃ(ə)n/

protest song (n) /ˈproʊˌtest sɔŋ/

punishment (n) /ˈpʌnɪʃmənt/

put away /pʊt əˈweɪ/

put on /pʊt ɔn/

Q 119

question a suspect /ˈkwestʃ(ə)n ə səˈspekt/

questionnaire (n) /ˌkwestʃəˈner/

quote (n) /kwoʊt/

R 120

reasonable (adj) /ˈriz(ə)nəb(ə)l/

receipt (n) /rɪˈsit/

receive advice /rɪˈsiv ədˈvaɪs/

receive presents /rɪˈsiv ˈprezənts/

recipe (n) /ˈresəpi/

recycle packaging /riˈsaɪk(ə)l ˈpækɪdʒɪŋ/

reliable (adj) /rɪˈlaɪəb(ə)l/

reorganize (v) /riˈɔrgəˌnaɪz/

replace (v) /rɪˈpleɪs/

replay (v) /ˈriˌpleɪ/

responsible (adj) /rɪˈspɑnsəb(ə)l/

retire (v) /rɪˈtaɪr/

review (n) /rɪˈvju/

ride a bike /raɪd ə baɪk/

robber (n) /ˈrɑbər/

robbery (n) /ˈrɑbəri/

root (n) /rut/

S 121

safe (n) /seɪf/

sailor (n) /ˈseɪlər/

save water /seɪv ˈwɔtər/

sell clothes /sel kloʊðz/

send postcards /send ˈpoʊstˌkɑrdz/

serve customers /sɜrv ˈkʌstəmərz/

set off /set ɔf/

settle down /ˈset(ə)l daʊn/

shake hands /ʃeɪk hændz/

share car journeys /ʃer kɑr ˈʤɜrniz/

sign a contract /saɪn ə ˈkɑnˌtrækt/

sleeve (n) /sliv/

slippers (n) /ˈslɪpə(r)z/

small (adj) /smɔl/

smash a window /smæʃ ə ˈwɪndoʊ/

snap your fingers /snæp jʊr ˈfɪŋgərz/

soil (n) /sɔɪl/

solve a crime /sɑlv ə kraɪm/

some (adv) /sʌm/

spend money /spend ˈmʌni/

spend time /spend taɪm/

sports pages (n) /spɔrts ‘peɪʤ(e)z/

sporty (adj) /ˈspɔrti/

stalk (n) /stɔk/

start your own business /stɑrt jʊr oʊn ˈbɪznəs/

still (adv) /stɪl/

sunburn (n) /ˈsʌnˌbɜrn/

suspect someone /səˈspekt ˈsʌmwʌn/

T 122

take a gap year /teɪk ə gæp jɪr/

take off /teɪk ɔf/

take off your shoes /teɪk ɔf jʊr ʃuz/

talk to /tɔk tu/

teacher training (n) /ˈtitʃər ˈtreɪnɪŋ/
tell jokes /tel dʒoʊks/
tell lies /tel laɪz/
tell the truth /tel ði truθ/
terrifying (adj) /ˈtɛrəˌfaɪɪŋ/
theft (n) /θeft/
thief (n) /θif/
throw away /θroʊ əˈweɪ/
tie (n) /taɪ/
tight (adj) /taɪt/
tiny (adj) /ˈtaɪni/
tired (adj) /ˈtaɪrd/
to arrange to meet someone /tu əˈreɪndʒ tu mit ˈsʌmwʌn/
to become friends with someone /tu bɪˈkʌm frendz wɪð ˈsʌmwʌn/
to be done with someone /tu bi dʌn wɪð ˈsʌmˌwʌn/
to fall out with someone /tu fɔːl aʊt wɪð ˈsʌmwʌn/
to fight with someone /tu faɪt wɪð ˈsʌmwʌn/
to finish with someone /tu ˈfɪnɪʃ wɪð ˈsʌmwʌn/
to get on with someone /tu get ɔn wɪð ˈsʌmwʌn/
to get to know someone /tu get tu nəʊ ˈsʌmwʌn/
to make friends with someone /tu meɪk frɛndz wɪð ˈsʌmwʌn/
to make up with someone /tu meɪk ʌp wɪð ˈsʌmwʌn/
to meet a new person /tu mit ə nu ˈpɜrs(ə)n/
trash-free /træʃ fri/
travel by public transport /ˈtræv(ə)l baɪ ˈpʌblɪk trænsˈpɔrt/
travel guide (n) /ˈtræv(ə)l gaɪd/
trendy (adj) /ˈtrendi/
trunk (n) /trʌŋk/
try on /traɪ ɔn/
turn off lights /tɜrn ɔf laɪts/
tweet (n) /twit/
twig (n) /twɪg/

U 123

unacceptable (adj) /ˌʌnəkˈseptəb(ə)l/
unadaptable (adj) /ʌnəˈdæptəbəl/
unbearable (adj) /ənˈbɛrəbəl/
undependable (adj) /ʌndɪˈpɛndəbəl/
undercook (v) /əndərˈkʊk/
underestimate (v) /ˌʌndərˈestɪˌmeɪt/
underpay (v) /ˌʌndərˈpeɪ/
underuse (v) /ˌʌndərˈjuz/
unreasonable (adj) /ənˈriznəbəl/
unreliable (adj) /ˌʌnrɪˈlaɪəb(ə)l/
use rechargeable batteries /juz riˈʧɑrʤəbəl ˈbætəriz/

V 124

vandal (n) /ˈvænd(ə)l/
vandalism (n) /ˈvænd(ə)lˌɪzəm/
visible (adj) /ˈvɪzəb(ə)l/

W 125

wage (n) /weɪdʒ/
wait for /weɪt fɔr/
wear out /wer aʊt/
weather report (n) /ˈweðər rɪˈpɔrt/
went /went/
wheels (n) /wilz/
witness a crime /ˈwɪtnəs ə kraɪm/
work experience (n) /wɜrk ɪkˈspɪriəns/
work part-time /wɜrk pɑrt taɪm/
worry about /ˈwʌri əˈbaʊt/
would /wʊd/

Z 126

zipper (n) /zɪpɜr/

Based on *Motivate!*
© Macmillan Publishers Limited 2013
Written by Patrick Howarth, Patricia Reilly and Olivia Johnston
Grammar, Speaking, Culture and *Life Skills* pages adapted by Gisele Marçon Bastos Périgo

Director of Languages Brazil: Patricia Souza De Luccia
Publishing Manager and Field Researcher: Patricia Muradas
Content Creation Coordinator: Cristina do Vale
Art Editor: Jean Aranha
Content Editors: Ana Beatriz da Costa Moreira, Tatiana Martins Santana
Assistant Editors: Daniela Gonçala da Costa, Roberto Homem de Mello, Larissa Vannucci
Digital Editor: Ana Paula Girardi
Editorial Assistants: Nádia Muniz, Roberta Somera, Sheila Folgueral
Graphic Production: Thais Mendes P. Galvão, Tatiane Romano
Academic Consultants: Alex Tamulis (Coordinator), Bruno Lancellotti, Pablo Matos, Rodrigo Marques, Sérgio Lins, Virgínia Galvão
Proofreaders: Larissa Vazquez, Paulo Winterstein, Márcia Leme, Danielle Costa
Design Concept: Martha Tadaieski
Page Make-Up: Figurattiva Editorial
Photo Research: Marcia Sato
Image Processing: Jean Aranha, Denis Araujo
Cover Concept: Jean Aranha
Audio: Argila Music

We would like to dedicate this book to teachers all over Brazil. We would also like to thank our clients and teachers who have helped us make this book better with their many rich contributions and feedback straight from the classroom along our long-lasting partnership!

Acknowledgments:
Adriana Dias, Adriana Leonzo, Aída Rocha de Almeida, Alessandra Andrade Nepomuceno Cirino, Alessandra Gavilan, Alessandra Marques, Alice Stela Ornelas Machado, Aline Bellarmino, Andrea Muner Paulavicius, Angela Burile Carvalho, Angela Melendez Conigliaro, Angela Segatti, Bianca Dewes, Bruno Andrade, Camila Ramalho, Cintia Galendi, Clice Pereira Salles, Clovis Viana Tavares, Cristiane Ramires, Daniela Murasaki, Danielle Pereira, Debora de Conti, Debora Thome, Eduardo Rodrigues Polidorio, Elaine Perrone, Erik Moreira, Euler França do Nascimento Júnior, Evila Rita Pinheiro Damaceno, Felipe Diesel, Fernanda Harrisberger, Fernanda Inácio, Fernanda Lucia Rocha de Sá Freire, Fernanda Maciel Machado Horta, Flavia Viana, Geraldo Vieira Júnior, Giovanna Meneguetti, Gisele Regina Dias da Silva, Glenda Rabitsch, Graciela Irene Turco, Grasiela Marques, Gustavo Rodarte Boechat, Isabella Villas-Boas, Itana Lins, Jacqueline Alves de Souza Carvalho, Juan Pablo Uribe, Juliana Gebra, Juliana Macedo Fiuza, Kelly Barboza da Silva, Kelly Cardoso, Lais Lara Maia Araújo, Leonardo Gomes de Souza, Ligia Araki, Luciana Melarato, Luciana Carnev, Malyina Kazuo, Marcela Cintra, Marcela Maria Vieira Thomazzi, Marcia Akemi, Maria Noeme de Magalhães Oliveira Monteiro, Mariani Barbosa, Michele Geledan, Milena Matos Carmona, Nair Domingues Guimarães, Patricia Salvo, Paula Bitondi, Paulo Rogério, Priscilla Rodrigues Lauro, Regina Lucia Fernandes, Renata Condi de Souza, Renata Perche, Renata Picasso Amarante, Renata Soares Cozzi Bahia, Roberta Silva, Roberta Tassinari Saraiva, Rodrigo Leão, Rôsangela Maria Silva, Samara Formagio, Sandra Magalhães, Sandra Regina Esteves Cardoso de Mello, Santo Tomaz Aquino, Sillas Paulino da Silva, Silvana Reis, Solange Ortencio, Solange Ulhoa Goulart Lucena, Soraya Bernardes da Silva, Ulysses Camargo Corrêa Diegues, Vagner Serafim, Vera Lacava.

The authors, adaptor and publishers would like to thank the following for permission to reproduce the photographic material:
p. 8: Monkey Business Images/iStockphoto/Getty Images, Anttohoho/iStockphoto/Getty Images, Rzdeb/iStockphoto/Getty Images; p. 10: Anagramm/iStockphoto/Getty Images; p. 12: Yearbook Library Partnership/Seth Poppel, Elizabeth Goodenough/Everett Collection/Fotoarena, Paramount Pictures/Everett Collection/Fotoarena, Jerod Harris/WireImage/Getty Images, Stefanie Keenan/Getty Images; p. 14: Dee Cercone/Everett Collection/Fotoarena; p. 15: Arthur Hidden/iStockphoto/Getty Images, Cecilie Arcurs/iStockphoto/Getty Images; p. 16: YinYang/iStockphoto/Getty Images; p. 17: Cement jungle/iStockphoto/Getty Images, Weim/iStockphoto/Getty Images, kate_sept2004/iStockphoto/Getty Images, Alexsl/iStockphoto/Getty Images; p. 19: Lhongfoto/iStockphoto/Getty Images, Valerie Barry/iStockphoto/Getty Images, Ddukang/iStockphoto/Getty Images, Lighthousebay/iStockphoto/Getty Images, Marian Vejcik/iStockphoto/Getty Images, Stígur Már Karlsson/Heimsmyndir/iStockphoto/Getty Images; p. 20: Baptiste Le Bouil/iStockphoto/Getty Images, Sekarb/iStockphoto/Getty Images, 25krunya/iStockphoto/Getty Images; p. 21: ljubaphoto/iStockphoto/Getty Images, Maya/iStockphoto/Getty Images, fstop123/iStockphoto/Getty Images, tommaso79/iStockphoto/Getty Images, fstop 123/iStockphoto/Getty Images, Chaay Tee/iStockphoto/Getty Images, vgajic/iStockphoto/Getty Images, kali9/iStockphoto/Getty Images, oneinchpunch/iStockphoto/Getty Images, Gustavo Frazao/iStockphoto/Getty Images, Monkey business images/iStockphoto/Getty Images, Rawpixel/iStockphoto/Getty Images, Joel Carillet/iStockphoto/Getty Images, Skynesher/iStockphoto/Getty Images, People Images/iStockphoto/Getty Images, Stock-eye/iStockphoto/Getty Images, Fat Camera/iStockphoto/Getty Images, Wavebreakmedia/iStockphoto/Getty Images, PeopleImages/iStockphoto/Getty Images, Natalia Deriabina/iStockphoto/Getty Images, andyparker72/iStockphoto/Getty Images, Pekic/iStockphoto/Getty Images, People Images/iStockphoto/Getty Images, fzant/iStockphoto/Getty Images; p. 24: Mihtiander/iStockphoto/Getty Images; p. 26: Seb Ra/iStockphoto/Getty Images, Poike/iStockphoto/Getty Images, Extreme Photographer/iStockphoto/Getty Images, Oleh Slobodeniuk/iStockphoto/Getty Images; p. 27: Acero/EFE; p. 29: Aluxum/iStockphoto/Getty Images, iStockphoto/Getty Images, Alamy/Fotoarena, Marina 113/iStockphoto/Getty Images, Davor Lovincic/iStockphoto/Getty Images; p. 30: Davidf/iStockphoto/Getty Images, 4FR/iStockphoto/Getty Images, Sean Pavone/iStockphoto/Getty Images; p. 31: Duncan 1890/iStockphoto/Getty Images, Untitled Images/iStockphoto/Getty Images; p. 32: Pkazmierczak/iStockphoto/Getty Images, Barcroft Media /Getty Images; p. 33: Lazareva/iStockphoto/Getty Images, MR1805/iStockphoto/Getty Images, Robert Mcgillivray/iStockphoto/Getty Images, Lakov Kalinin/iStockphoto/Getty Images, 4FR/iStockphoto/Getty Images, Traveling Freckles/iStockphoto/Getty Images, Don Kurto/iStockphoto/Getty Images, Leez snow/iStockphoto/Getty Images; p. 35: fstop123/iStockphoto/Getty Images, Btrenkel/iStockphoto/Getty Images, Visual Space/iStockphoto/Getty Images, Gligatron/iStockphoto/Getty Images, iStockphoto/Getty Images, Alvarez/iStockphoto/Getty Images, Vetkit/iStockphoto/Getty Images, Nullplus/iStockphoto/Getty Images, Filistiml Yanin/iStockphoto/Getty Images, Seb Ra/iStockphoto/Getty Images, Flair Images/iStockphoto/Getty Images, Mstudio Images/iStockphoto/Getty Images, Antagain/iStockphoto/Getty Images, Michael Ver Sprill/iStockphoto/Getty Images, Efired/iStockphoto/Getty Images, Leonid Eremeychuk/iStockphoto/Getty Images, Prasit Chansarekorn/iStockphoto/Getty Images, Nick Pandevonium/iStockphoto/Getty Images, Sturti/iStockphoto/Getty Images, South Agency/iStockphoto/Getty Images, Robert Breitpaul/iStockphoto/Getty Images, People Images/iStockphoto/Getty Images, People Images/iStockphoto/Getty Images, People Images/iStockphoto/Getty Images, fstop123/iStockphoto/Getty Images, Filipe Frazao/iStockphoto/Getty Images, Mbbirdy/iStockphoto/Getty Images Dzurag/iStockphoto/Getty Images, Ryerson Clark/iStockphoto/Getty Images, Grand River/iStockphoto/Getty Images; p. 38: Phototropic/iStockphoto/Getty Images, Golero/iStockphoto/Getty Images, Martin Dm/iStockphoto/Getty Images, People Images/iStockphoto/Getty Images, Mazartemka/iStockphoto/Getty Images, Vesnaandjic/iStockphoto/Getty Images, Elisha Donkin/iStockphoto/Getty Images, Anyaberkut/iStockphoto/Getty Images, Pablo Rodriguez Merkel/iStockphoto/Getty Images, Monkey Business Images/iStockphoto/Getty Images, Tatomm/iStockphoto/Getty Images, Sol Stock/iStockphoto/Getty Images, Golubovy/iStockphoto/Getty Images, People Images/iStockphoto/Getty Images, Mihailo Milovanovic/iStockphoto/Getty Images; p. 42: Kirillm/iStockphoto/Getty Images; p. 44: Peter Spiro/iStockphoto/Getty Images, Image Source/iStockphoto/Getty Images, Meinzahn/iStockphoto/Getty Images, Rawpixel/iStockphoto/Getty Images; p. 45: Cjp/iStockphoto/Getty Images; p. 47: Aris Su/iStockphoto/Getty Images, Panptys/iStockphoto/Getty Images; p. 48: Asiseeit/iStockphoto/Getty Images, Tassii/iStockphoto/Getty Images, VM/iStockphoto/Getty Images; p. 49: Shaunl/iStockphoto/Getty Images, Onfokus/iStockphoto/Getty Images, Alexsl/iStockphoto/Getty Images; p. 50: Denozy/iStockphoto/Getty Images, STEEX/iStockphoto/Getty Images, Patrick Heagney/iStockphoto/Getty Images, Sharonotai/iStockphoto/Getty Images; p. 51: Louis Hiemstra/iStockphoto/Getty Images; p. 52: Alamy/Fotoarena, Tony Russell/Redferns/Getty Images; p. 53: Lisaln Glasses/iStockphoto/Getty Images, Manfredxy/iStockphoto/Getty Images, Banks Photos/iStockphoto/Getty Images, Noi Pattanan/iStockphoto/Getty Images, Yin Yang/iStockphoto/Getty Images, Kate Sept 2004/iStockphoto/Getty Images, Dorin S/iStockphoto/Getty Images, Sol Stock/iStockphoto/Getty Images, krblokhin/iStockphoto/Getty Images, Tatomm/iStockphoto/Getty Images, Clubfoto/iStockphoto/Getty Images, Rober Thyrons/iStockphoto/Getty Images, Exipreess/iStockphoto/Getty Images, Photography/iStockphoto/Getty Images, Maxi Photo/iStockphoto/Getty Images, Stormcab/iStockphoto/Getty Images, Visual Space/iStockphoto/Getty Images, iStockphoto/Getty Images, Rawpixel/iStockphoto/Getty Images, Kate Sept2004/iStockphoto/Getty Images, Monkey business images/iStockphoto/Getty Images, Faysal Ahamed/iStockphoto/Getty Images, Pmmart/iStockphoto/Getty Images, Laflor/iStockphoto/Getty Images, Woolzian/iStockphoto/Getty Images, Katarzyna Bialasiewicz/iStockphoto/Getty Images; p. 56: Filipe Frazao/iStockphoto/Getty Images; p. 58: 1001nights/iStockphoto/Getty Images, Gold Faery/iStockphoto/Getty Images, Alamy/Fotoarena, Steve Debenport/iStockphoto/Getty Images, Dex Images/iStockphoto/Getty Images, Antonio Guillem/iStockphoto/Getty Images; p. 59: 1gmel/iStockphoto/Getty Images, Monkey Business Images/iStockphoto/Getty Images; p. 60: Vesmil/iStockphoto/Getty Images, Wunder Visuals/iStockphoto/Getty Images; p. 61: Monkey Business Images/iStockphoto/Getty Images; p. 62: Igor Kardasov/iStockphoto/Getty Images, Andrey Popov/iStockphoto/Getty Images, Rawpixel/iStockphoto/Getty Images; p. 63: Rawpixel/iStockphoto/Getty Images, Dragon Images/iStockphoto/Getty Images; p. 64: Serr Novik/iStockphoto/Getty Images, Milkos/iStockphoto/Getty Images, Juanmonino/iStockphoto/Getty Images, Jacob Ammentorp Lund/iStockphoto/Getty Images, Digital Skillet/iStockphoto/Getty Images, Paul Bradbury/iStockphoto/Getty Images, FatCamera/iStockphoto/Getty Images, Alex Potemkin/iStockphoto/Getty Images, kali9/iStockphoto/Getty Images, JackF/iStockphoto/Getty Images; p. 66: JackF/iStockphoto/Getty Images; p. 67: Chalabala/iStockphoto/Getty Images, Innovated Captures/iStockphoto/Getty Images, George Clerk/iStockphoto/Getty Images, Nyul/iStockphoto/Getty Images, People Images/iStockphoto/Getty Images, Central ITA lliance/iStockphoto/Getty Images, Sky Nesher/iStockphoto/Getty Images, Vm/iStockphoto/Getty Images, Liderina/iStockphoto/Getty Images, Fizkes/iStockphoto/Getty Images, Tsuyoshi Kinjyo/iStockphoto/Getty Images, People Images/iStockphoto/Getty Images, Images by barbara/iStockphoto/Getty Images, Fstop 123/iStockphoto/Getty Images, Rapid Eye/iStockphoto/Getty Images, Casarsa/iStockphoto/Getty Images, Sol Stock/iStockphoto/Getty Images, Digital Skillet/iStockphoto/Getty Images, Nicoleta Ionescu/iStockphoto/Getty Images, Rich Legg/iStockphoto/Getty Images; p. 70: Image Source/iStockphoto/Getty Images, Vchal/iStockphoto/Getty Images, Stafford Studios/iStockphoto/Getty Images, Wavebreakmedia/iStockphoto/Getty Images, Nicolas McComber/iStockphoto/Getty Images, ViewApart/iStockphoto/Getty Images, Echo1/iStockphoto/Getty Images, Ribeiro Rocha/iStockphoto/Getty Images; p. 71: Media Production/iStockphoto/Getty Images, JackF/iStockphoto/Getty Images, Wave break media/iStockphoto/Getty Images, Steve Debenport/iStockphoto/Getty Images, Steve Debenport/iStockphoto/Getty Images, Johnny Greig/iStockphoto/Getty Images, Martine Doucet/iStockphoto/Getty Images; p. 76: Mbbirdy/iStockphoto/Getty Images; p. 78: Web Photographeer/iStockphoto/Getty Images, Believe In Me/iStockphoto/Getty Images, Pearleye/iStockphoto/Getty Images, Serge-75/iStockphoto/Getty Images, Srdjan Pav/iStockphoto/Getty Images, Photominus/iStockphoto/Getty Images, Grinvalds/iStockphoto/Getty Images; p. 80: Alvarez/iStockphoto/Getty Images; p. 81: 01dalmatians/iStockphoto/Getty Images, Daniele Venturelli/Getty Images, Estrop/Getty Images; p. 82: kali9/iStockphoto/Getty Images, POMPIXs/iStockphoto/Getty Images, Dwphotos/iStockphoto/Getty Images, Chris Ryan/iStockphoto/Getty Images; p. 83: Yaromir M/iStockphoto/Getty Images, Igor Alecsander/iStockphoto/Getty Images, Michael Jung/iStockphoto/Getty Images; p. 84: Eva Katalin/iStockphoto/Getty Images; p. 85: VM Jones/iStockphoto/Getty Images; p. 86: Aivita/iStockphoto/Getty Images, PA Images via Getty Images; p. 87: izusek/iStockphoto/Getty Images, Urosh Petrovic/iStockphoto/Getty Images, no_limit_pictures/iStockphoto/Getty Images, Vrabel peter1/iStockphoto/Getty Images, Alija/iStockphoto/Getty Images, Global Stock/iStockphoto/Getty Images, Belchonock/iStockphoto/Getty Images, Konstantin Balezin/iStockphoto/Getty Images, Chagin/iStockphoto/Getty Images, Sdominick/iStockphoto/Getty Images, Roman Samokhin/iStockphoto/Getty Images, Lambada/iStockphoto/Getty Images, Tatiana1987/iStockphoto/Getty Images, Bobbieo/iStockphoto/Getty Images, STEEX/iStockphoto/Getty Images, Oleh photographer/iStockphoto/Getty Images, Krakozawr/iStockphoto/Getty Images, Creativa Images/iStockphoto/Getty Images, m-image photography/iStockphoto/Getty Images, Artranq/iStockphoto/Getty Images, People Images/iStockphoto/Getty Images, Pavlen/iStockphoto/Getty Images, Ljupco/iStockphoto/Getty Images, Maica/iStockphoto/Getty Images, Jarretera/iStockphoto/Getty Images; p. 89: Monkey Business Images/iStockphoto/Getty Images; p. 90: Monkey Business Images/iStockphoto/Getty Images; p. 92: Andrey Popov/iStockphoto/Getty Images, Brazzo/iStockphoto/Getty Images, People Images/iStockphoto/Getty Images, Monkey Business Images/iStockphoto/Getty Images; p. 93: Eddie Safarik/Tourism Australia/Getty Images,

Eddie Safarik/Tourism Australia/Getty Images; p. 94: Sergey Ryzhov/iStockphoto/Getty Images; p. 95: Shootdiem/iStockphoto/Getty Images, Johnny Greig/iStockphoto/Getty Images, John Fedele/Getty Images; p. 96: Steve Debenport/iStockphoto/Getty Images, Stock StudioX/iStockphoto/Getty Images, Kali9/iStockphoto/Getty Images; p. 97: Juan Monino/iStockphoto/Getty Images, Sturti/iStockphoto/Getty Images; p. 98: Eva Katalin/iStockphoto/Getty Images, Wavebreak Media/iStockphoto/Getty Images, Wavebreak Media/iStockphoto/Getty Images, Fstop 123/iStockphoto/Getty Images, Khosrork/iStockphoto/Getty Images; p. 99: IPG Gutenberg UK Ltd/iStockphoto/Getty Images; p. 100: Ranta Images/iStockphoto/Getty Images; p. 101: Chesiire Cat/iStockphoto/Getty Images, istockphoto/Getty Images , Monkey Business Images/iStockphoto/Getty Images, Cnythzl/iStockphoto/Getty Images, Magnetic Mcc/iStockphoto/Getty Images, Enotmaks/iStockphoto/Getty Images, Antonio Guillem/iStockphoto/Getty Images, Mango Star Studio/iStockphoto/Getty Images, Mp, Eternal Creative/iStockphoto/Getty Images, Creative Family/iStockphoto/Getty Images, Antonio Guillem/iStockphoto/Getty Images, Andrey opov/iStockphoto/Getty Images, Yuri Arcurs/iStockphoto/Getty Images, Fizkes/iStockphoto/Getty Images, Tommaso79/iStockphoto/Getty Images, Oddrose/iStockphoto/Getty Images, Zest Marina/iStockphoto/Getty Images, Milindri/iStockphoto/Getty Images, Nikada/iStockphoto/Getty Images, Monkey Business Images/iStockphoto/Getty Images, Portra/iStockphoto/Getty Images, Steve ebenport/iStockphoto/Getty Images, Vadim Guzhva/iStockphoto/Getty Images, People Images/iStockphoto/Getty Images, Maroke/iStockphoto/Getty Images; p. 103: Eugenio Marongiu/Getty Images; p. 104: sturti/iStockphoto/Getty Images, Golero/iStockphoto/Getty Images, People Images/iStockphoto/Getty Images, Mango Star Studio/iStockphoto/Getty Images, SI photography/iStockphoto/Getty Images, Ryan J Lane/iStockphoto/Getty Images, Monkey Business Images/iStockphoto/Getty Images, JackF/iStockphoto/Getty Images, Yagi Studio/iStockphoto/Getty Images, Light Field Studios/iStockphoto/Getty Images, Antonio Guillem/iStockphoto/Getty Images, Andrey Popov/iStockphoto/Getty Images, Vgajic/iStockphoto/Getty Images, MN Studio/iStockphoto/Getty Images, South Agency/iStockphoto/Getty Images; p. 108: Bjdlzx/iStockphoto/Getty Images; p. 110: Alex Raths/iStockphoto/Getty Images, D-Keine/iStockphoto/Getty Images, Raw Pixel/iStockphoto/Getty Images, Antonio Guillem/iStockphoto/Getty Images; p. 111: Rich Legg/iStockphoto/Getty Images Fly Dragonfly/iStockphoto/Getty Images; p. 112: Ivan Mollov/iStockphoto/Getty Images, Michael Burrell/iStockphoto/Getty Images, Kvsan/iStockphoto/Getty Images, Deep Blue4 You/iStockphoto/Getty Images, Urfinguss/iStockphoto/Getty Images, Pro Art Work/iStockphoto/Getty Images; p. 113: Hadi Altay/iStockphoto/Getty Images, Frank Vanden Bergh/iStockphoto/Getty Images, Katarzyna Bialasiewicz/iStockphoto/Getty Images; p. 114: Kali9/iStockphoto/Getty Images, p. 115: Domoyega/iStockphoto/Getty Images, Zmeel/iStockphoto/Getty Images; p. 116: Steve Cole Images/iStockphoto/Getty Images, Ferran Traite/iStockphoto/Getty Images; p. 117: Anna_leni/iStockphoto/Getty Images; p. 118: Andi Pantz/iStockphoto/Getty Images, Drima Film/iStockphoto/Getty Images, Hanohiki/iStockphoto/Getty Images; p. 119: Kzenon/iStockphoto/Getty Images, Wave Break Media/iStockphoto/Getty Images, IPG Gutenberg UK Ltd/iStockphoto/Getty Images, Bowie15/iStockphoto/Getty Images, Highwaystarz Photography/iStockphoto/Getty Images, Steve Debenport/iStockphoto/Getty Images, Rich Legg/iStockphoto/Getty Images, IPG Gutenberg UK Ltd/iStockphoto/Getty Images, South Agency/iStockphoto/Getty Images, Zoka74/iStockphoto/Getty Images, Alina555/iStockphoto/Getty Images, Katarzyna Bialasiewicz/iStockphoto/Getty Images, Wragg/iStockphoto/Getty Images, People Images/iStockphoto/Getty Images, Choja/iStockphoto/Getty Images, Image Depotpro/iStockphoto/Getty Images, Lampixels/iStockphoto/Getty Images, D-Keine/iStockphoto/Getty Images, D-Keine/iStockphoto/Getty Images, Pmc Donald/iStockphoto/Getty Images, Kittisak Jirasittichai/iStockphoto/Getty Images, Tommaso79/iStockphoto/Getty Images, Kosmos 111/iStockphoto/Getty Images, Tagstock1/iStockphoto/Getty Images, Power Offorever/iStockphoto/Getty Images, Image Source/iStockphoto/Getty Images, Jens Rother/iStockphoto/Getty Images, 2399/iStockphoto/Getty Images; p. 121: Light Field Studios/iStockphoto/Getty Images; p. 122: Badahos/iStockphoto/Getty Images; p. 124: Bubaone/iStockphoto/Getty Images, Doug Savage; p. 125: Martin Turzak/iStockphoto/Getty Images, Barry King/Alamy Stock Photo, Wenjie Dong/iStockphoto/Getty Images; p. 127: Margherita Lettina/iStockphoto/Getty Images, Albuquerque/iStockphoto/Getty Images, Mr Moda/iStockphoto/Getty Images; p. 128: Kali9/iStockphoto/Getty Images, Neustock Images/iStockphoto/Getty Images, Joshblake/iStockphoto/Getty Images; p. 129: Lpettet/iStockphoto/Getty Images, Phoenixns/iStockphoto/Getty Images; p. 130: Ondine32/iStockphoto/Getty Images, Doug Savage; p. 133: Milindri/iStockphoto/Getty Images, Alessio Slo/iStockphoto/Getty Images, Robas/iStockphoto/Getty Images, Ekaterina79/iStockphoto/Getty Images, Djmilic/iStockphoto/Getty Images, Peepo/iStockphoto/Getty Images, RT Images/iStockphoto/Getty Images, Luckyj1/iStockphoto/Getty Images, Triloks/iStockphoto/Getty Images, Javi M Bravo/iStockphoto/Getty Images, People Images/iStockphoto/Getty Images, Darren Mower/iStockphoto/Getty Images, Frances Coch/iStockphoto/Getty Images, Nycshooter/iStockphoto/Getty Images, Brian A Jackson/iStockphoto/Getty Images, Fertnig/iStockphoto/Getty Images, Epicurean/iStockphoto/Getty Images, Tim Halstenbach/iStockphoto/Getty Images, Triloks/iStockphoto/Getty Images, Catalin205/iStockphoto/Getty Images, Wild Pixel/iStockphoto/Getty Images, Ognianm/iStockphoto/Getty Images, Sunstock/iStockphoto/Getty Images, Pannonia/iStockphoto/Getty Images, Skynesher/iStockphoto/Getty Images, Wjarek/iStockphoto/Getty Images; p. 136: Yipengge/iStockphoto/Getty Images, Sestovic/iStockphoto/Getty Images, Carrie Captured/iStockphoto/Getty Images, People Images/iStockphoto/Getty Images, Katarzyna Bialasiewicz/iStockphoto/Getty Images, Rich Legg/iStockphoto/Getty Images, Abu/iStockphoto/Getty Images, Anthonysp/iStockphoto/Getty Images, Istimages/iStockphoto/Getty Images, Ekaterina79/iStockphoto/Getty Images, Guvendemir/iStockphoto/Getty Images, Keine/iStockphoto/Getty Images, Kittisa k Jirasittichai/iStockphoto/Getty Images, Michael Burrell/iStockphoto/Getty Images, Ian Langley/iStockphoto/Getty Images; p. 138: Arakawa Tomoko/iStockphoto/Getty Images Badahos/iStockphoto/Getty Images, Adekvat/iStockphoto/Getty Images; p. 140: Ismagilov/iStockphoto/Getty Images; p. 141: Ad Shooter/iStockphoto/Getty Images, Seewhatmitchsee/iStockphoto/Getty Images; p. 144: Marina Mays/iStockphoto/Getty Images; p. 146: Joel Carillet/iStockphoto/Getty Images; p. 148: Retro Atelier/iStockphoto/Getty Images; p. 151: Lise Gagne/iStockphoto/Getty Images, subman/iStockphoto/Getty Images; p. 152: Alamy/Fotoarena; p. 153: Yuri Arcurs/iStockphoto/Getty Images, Milan Virijevic/iStockphoto/Getty Images, Selimaksan/iStockphoto/Getty Images, Natee Meepian/iStockphoto/Getty Images, Hedgehog 94/iStockphoto/Getty Images, Nakic/iStockphoto/Getty Images, Franck Boston/iStockphoto/Getty Images, Ronstik/iStockphoto/Getty Images, Berezko/iStockphoto/Getty Images, Cesar Okada/iStockphoto/Getty Images; p. 154: Bibigon/iStockphoto/Getty Images; p. 155: Weekend Images/iStockphoto/Getty Images; p. 156: Shutter Worx/iStockphoto/Getty Images; p. 157: Bogdan Kosanovic/iStockphoto/Getty Images, Farinosa/iStockphoto/Getty Images; p. 159: Oleg66/iStockphoto/Getty Images, Elkor/iStockphoto/Getty Images; p. 160: Pop Jop/iStockphoto/Getty Images; p. 161: Johnny Greig/iStockphoto/Getty Images, Eye Joy/iStockphoto/Getty Images, Tonpick Nick/iStockphoto/Getty Images, Sakchai_R/iStockphoto/Getty Images, 9nong/iStockphoto/Getty Images, Mike Rogal/iStockphoto/Getty Images, Ljupco/iStockphoto/Getty Images, Mille Flore Images/iStockphoto/Getty Images, Dimid 86/iStockphoto/Getty Images, Traveler1116/iStockphoto/Getty Images; p. 163: Neyya/iStockphoto/Getty Images; p. 164: Mmac72/iStockphoto/Getty Images; p. 167: Monkey Business Images/iStockphoto/Getty Images, Jacoblund/iStockphoto/Getty Images; p. 168: Canaran/iStockphoto/Getty Images; p. 169: Sunny beach/iStockphoto/Getty Images, Jorge Villalba/iStockphoto/Getty Images, Stdemi/iStockphoto/Getty Images, Tortoon/iStockphoto/Getty Images, Kari Hoglund/iStockphoto/Getty Images, Borchee/iStockphoto/Getty Images, Achisatha Khamsuwan/iStockphoto/Getty Images, Don Nichols/iStockphoto/Getty Images, Ampols/iStockphoto/Getty Images, theJIPEN/iStockphoto/Getty Images; p. 170: Yin Yang/iStockphoto/Getty Images, 3bugsmom/iStockphoto/Getty Images, People Images/iStockphoto/Getty Images, Juan Monino/iStockphoto/Getty Images, Baona/iStockphoto/Getty Images, DG Limages/iStockphoto/Getty Images; p. 171: Ilbusca/iStockphoto/Getty Images, Grady Reese/iStockphoto/Getty Images, JackF/iStockphoto/Getty Images; p. 172: Simply Creative Photography/iStockphoto/Getty Images; p. 173: Creativa Images/iStockphoto/Getty Images; p. 175: champlifezy@gmail.com/iStockphoto/Getty Images; p. 176: Ryan JLane/iStockphoto/Getty Images; p. 177: Gam1983/iStockphoto/Getty Images, Milan Markovic/iStockphoto/Getty Images, Nicolas McComber/iStockphoto/Getty Images, Pixdeluxe/iStockphoto/Getty Images, PaolaV1/iStockphoto/Getty Images, Jacob Lund/iStockphoto/Getty Images, kali9/iStockphoto/Getty Images, Bojan89/iStockphoto/Getty Images, Wunder Visuals/iStockphoto/Getty Images, Marija Radovic/iStockphoto/Getty Images, Pixelfit/iStockphoto/Getty Images; p. 178: Alija/iStockphoto/Getty Images, Microgen/iStockphoto/Getty Images, Linda Yolanda/iStockphoto/Getty Images, Paul Bradbury/iStockphoto/Getty Images, Fotorince/iStockphoto/Getty Images, DigitalVision/Getty Images; p. 179: Anytka/iStockphoto/Getty Images; p. 180: Photology1971/iStockphoto/Getty Images, Amesy/iStockphoto/Getty Images, kasto80/iStockphoto/Getty Images; p. 181: Voyagerix/iStockphoto/Getty Images, Steve Debenport/iStockphoto/Getty Images, Esolla/iStockphoto/Getty Images, OSTILL/iStockphoto/Getty Images, Misuma/iStockphoto/Getty Images, Style Photographs/iStockphoto/Getty Images; p. 182: Fam Veld/iStockphoto/Getty Images, Martin Dm/iStockphoto/Getty Images; p. 183: Oatawa/iStockphoto/Getty Images; p. 184: Bartosz Hadyniak/iStockphoto/Getty Images; p. 185: Heinteh/iStockphoto/Getty Images, Leitmotif 425/iStockphoto/Getty Images, Bonetta/iStockphoto/Getty Images, Devin Pavel/iStockphoto/Getty Images, Bogdan Kosanovic/iStockphoto/Getty Images, Tarzhanova/iStockphoto/Getty Images, People Images/iStockphoto/Getty Images, Zocha K/iStockphoto/Getty Images, Makidotvn/iStockphoto/Getty Images, kirill4mula/iStockphoto/Getty Images; p. 186: Pixsooz/iStockphoto/Getty Images; p. 187: Fotostorm/iStockphoto/Getty Images; p. 189: People Images/iStockphoto/Getty Images; p. 191: Alizada Studios/iStockphoto/Getty Images, Pixelfit/iStockphoto/Getty Images; p. 192: Oscarhdez/iStockphoto/Getty Images; p. 193: Simonkr/iStockphoto/Getty Images, Andrey Popov/iStockphoto/Getty Images, Thiroil/iStockphoto/Getty Images, Jummie/iStockphoto/Getty Images, Brad Wynnyk/iStockphoto/Getty Images, Tiero/iStockphoto/Getty Images, AxPitel/iStockphoto/Getty Images, Stan Rohrer/iStockphoto/Getty Images, Limpido/iStockphoto/Getty Images, Henrik 5000/iStockphoto/Getty Images; p. 194: Photoservice/iStockphoto/Getty Images; p. 195: KenTannenbaum/iStockphoto/Getty Images; p. 196: Amygdala Imagery/iStockphoto/Getty Images, ArtMarie/iStockphoto/Getty Images; p. 197: Simonkr/iStockphoto/Getty Images; p. 198: Ekaterina79/iStockphoto/Getty Images; p. 199: Kutsuks/iStockphoto/Getty Images, Feryjory/iStockphoto/Getty Images; p. 200: Michael Burrell/iStockphoto/Getty Images; p. 201: Andrey Popov/iStockphoto/Getty Images, Katarzyna Bialasiewicz/iStockphoto/Getty Images, Slphotography/iStockphoto/Getty Images, KLH49/iStockphoto/Getty Images, Katarzyna Bialasiewicz/iStockphoto/Getty Images, Karenfoley Photography/iStockphoto/Getty Images, PeopleImages/iStockphoto/Getty Images, iggy1965/iStockphoto/Getty Images, Manuel Faba Ortega/iStockphoto/Getty Images, Pyrrpree/iStockphoto/Getty Images; p. 204: Scott Talent/iStockphoto/Getty Images; p. 205: Lucky Business/iStockphoto/Getty Images, Fat Camera/iStockphoto/Getty Images; p. 207: Anya Berkut/iStockphoto/Getty Images, Sturti/iStockphoto/Getty Images; p. 208: Bowden Images/iStockphoto/Getty Image; p. 209: Skhoward/iStockphoto/Getty Images, Andrew Genn/iStockphoto/Getty Images, Devonyu/iStockphoto/Getty Images, Robeo/iStockphoto/Getty Images, George Clerk/iStockphoto/Getty Images, iStockphoto/Getty Images, AnthiaCumming/iStockphoto/Getty Images, cyther5/iStockphoto/Getty Images, Lya Cattel/iStockphoto/Getty Images, Mattjeacock/iStockphoto/Getty Images.

Dados Internacionais de Catalogação na Publicação (CIP)

Bibliotecária responsável: Aline Graziele Benitez CRB-1/3129

R675i Reilly, Patricia

1.ed. Insta English 3 / Patricia Reilly ... [et al.]. – 1.ed. – São Paulo: Macmillan Education do Brasil, 2019.

216 p.; il.; 21 x 29,7 cm. – (Coleção Insta English, v.3)

ISBN: 978-85-511021-38 (aluno)
ISBN: 978-85-511021-45 (professor)

1. Inglês – ensino fundamental II. I. Howarth, Patrick. II. Johnston, Olivia. III. Mauchline, Fiona. IV. Myers, Cathy. V. Título. VI. Série. CDD 371.3

Índice para catálogo sistemático:

1. Inglês: ensino fundamental II

MACMILLAN EDUCATION DO BRASIL
Av. Brigadeiro Faria Lima, 1.309, 3° Andar –
Jd. Paulistano – São Paulo – SP – 01452-002
www.macmillan.com.br
Customer Service: [55] (11) 4613-2278
0800 16 88 77
Fax: [55] (11) 4612-6098

Printed in Brazil. Nov, 2023.